Ret.ᵒ de la Venerable Sierua de Dios, Doñ
María Vela, Religiosa Bernarda Murió en el
Conu.ᵗᵒ de Sᵗᵃ Annâ de Avila, Domingo 24 d Septbᵉ
año de 1617

The Third Mystic of Avila

*The self revelation of María Vela,
a sixteenth century Spanish nun*

Foreword and Translation by Frances Parkinson Keyes

FARRAR, STRAUS AND CUDAHY   NEW YORK

❧ Introduction

I consider most commendable the project of the well-known writer, Frances Parkinson Keyes, to bring out for the first time the autobiography of the Venerable María Vela.

The Cistercian nuns of the Convent of Santa Ana in this city, with a generosity which honors them, have had no hesitation in placing at the disposition of this author the invaluable original of the autobiography.

It seems strange that it has not yet been published in the Spanish language and that its first publication should be in English.

Gratitude is due Frances Parkinson Keyes, who has decided to make public this manuscript, which is not a mere curiosity, but a work of great intrinsic value and from the Catholic point of view, a veritable treasure.

I pray that this edition may have a great success, and I hope that the noble aspirations of the distinguished writer, who has brought it to the attention of her publishers, will meet with fulfillment, for she is undoubtedly interested not only in reaching a wide audience but in having her readers profit by the lessons of spirituality which permeate the pages of this unusual and unknown manuscript. Not unlike the works of Saint John of the Cross and Saint Treesa of Jesus, the other two contemporary glories of this ancient diocese, these autobiographical sketches are sayings of "light and love" which, we hope, will illumine the minds of such readers with rays of Increate Light, warming their hearts and lifting these up with a desire for higher things.

(*signed*) ✝ *Santos, Bishop of Avila*

Avila, September 18, 1957

⤙ Contents

⚜ Foreword

My discovery of the diary, written by the *Avilesa*, María Vela, a sixteenth-century Cistercian Nun, was accidental—at least I suppose it would generally be so regarded, for, at the time, I had never heard of María Vela, much less was I considering her the object of study and of presentation to the reading public. On the contrary, I was doing research about Isabel of Castile, and had found that much of this should be undertaken in Avila—a city with which a very important part of the great queen's history is connected, though this fact has been largely, and strangely, overlooked by many historians and stressed by almost none. However, I have long since ceased to feel that such experiences as the one which led to a further and wholly different preoccupation are accidental—I believe that each forms part of a pattern, which we are given an opportunity to weave if we choose to do so. Over and over again, in the course of my life, something which seemed trivial has proved important and something which seemed to happen quite by chance has actually proved providential. Both were true in this case.

It all came about in this way: I had been admitted, by special permission, to certain portions of the Convent of Santa Ana in Avila, in order that I might see the apartments occupied by Isabel when she took refuge there after the death, probably by poisoning, of her younger brother Alfonso, heir to the throne of Castile. This tragedy had occurred in the nearby village of Cardeñosa, and it was natural for Isabel, who had been summoned thither from Segovia, to pass the period of her mourning in the place where she had received a large part of her education. She was sympathetically welcomed by the kindly Cistercian Nuns who had been her teachers, and found solace in the peaceful and familiar surroundings they provided. It did not occur to her or to the Community that the Abbess would soon summon her to receive the nobles of Castile, led by Alonso Carrillo de Acuña, the powerful Archbishop of Toledo, who had rebelled against her elder half-brother, the evil King Enrique. They were awaiting her in the parlor, to offer her the crown.

Isabel had the sound sense, as well as the flawless integrity, to refuse it, and the nobles left in some confusion and embarrassment. She had even insisted on remaining behind the grille, with the Abbess at her side, so that the assembly of nobles was separated from her by iron bars, and not a man in it, not even the great Carrillo himself, could kneel close to her to do her homage and kiss her hand. Nevertheless, in spite of his disappointment, the Archbishop was not blinded to her remarkable personal qualities and extraordinary political potentialities. As he went down the narrow staircase leading from the *locutorio* to the courtyard, he said to the Marqués de Villena, on whose arm he was leaning, "*Acepta que la admitan como Princesa . . . esta muchacha es nuestra salvación . . .*"

("She is willing to be accepted as our Princess . . . this young girl is our salvation . . .")[1] He was right. Two months afterward, Enrique himself admitted that she was his rightful heiress, and signed the extraordinary treaty which proclaimed her as such at Toros de Guisando, in the presence of these same nobles. She then accepted as her due what she had declined to seize as a prize[2] and thus took the first step toward the dominion that made her a queen of queens. In the meanwhile, she remained quietly at the Convent of Santa Ana, occupied with her needlework, her thoughts, her reading and her prayers.

Though it is a matter of record that Isabel later visited the convent at least once with her husband Fernando, it was many years before she stayed in Avila for any length of time again, and then it was not at Santa Ana's, but in the summer palace which the Catholic Kings had built for themselves after the conquest of Granada, and where they spent some of the happiest periods of their lives surrounded by their young family, before death and disaster came to separate parents and children.[3] But it is not strange that, to this day, Isabel's connection with Santa Ana is regarded in Spain as extremely important. Together with other significant events so associated, it is officially commemorated by a tablet on the outer wall of the convent; and, throughout the centuries, Abbesses have been careful to tell their successors as Superiors, their archivists and, indeed, all the members of their Communities exactly what happened when the brave and beautiful young princess was their guest.

This story was still so vivid, when it was shared with me, that I seemed to see Isabel sitting by the window in her great raftered room, missal in hand, or treading slowly over the pavement of the long arcade in the cloister, her fair hair falling over her shoulders, her mourning robe of white wool trailing behind her, as she listened to the message that had summoned

her to the parlor. And perhaps it was because the present Abbess saw how I kindled to this moving tale that she decided
to tell me another. At all events, it was after I had sat with
her in Isabel's apartment and walked with her through the
cloister to the place behind the grille, where the princess had
stood so steadfast, that the Superior asked me if I had ever
heard of the Venerable María Vela, who was called the Strong
Woman of Santa Ana.

"No," I said. "Tell me about her. When did she live? What
did she do? Why is she called the Strong Woman of Santa
Ana?"

"She lived in the late sixteenth and early seventeenth century. Her home was in Cardeñosa, the same village where the
poor little 'King of Avila,' Isabel's brother Alfonso, met his
death. Her people were gentlefolk—indeed, the maternal grandmother for whom she was named was the sister of Peru's first
viceroy, Blasco Núñez Vela, another *Avilés,* and her paternal
grandfather, Diego de Alvarez de Cueto, accompanied this dig-
nitary to the New World as his admiral. She was educated
with the greatest thoroughness and care by her mother, who
was also a remarkable woman, and she might have made a
brilliant marriage and graced an exalted position in the world.
But, when she was only fifteen, she chose to come here as a
novice; and though she never made irrevocable decisions hastily, she at last decided, six years later, that she had a true vocation and took her final vows. Afterward, she became an
ornament to the Community in many ways. She had a thorough knowledge of the Scriptures, which her ready command
of Latin enabled her to read and quote in that language, and
she was also well versed in hagiology, which permitted her to
make comparisons between the saints and draw conclusions
regarding the lessons taught by their lives. She was very skill-
ful in the use of her hands, which were beautiful. She made
exquisite artificial flowers to adorn the altars and also em-

broidered frontals for these altars, in most delicate designs. And she was accomplished as a musician; she sang sweetly, played with ease any available instrument and became director of the choir. As Sacristan, she took the most meticulous and reverent care of the vestments and holy vessels. And, as Mistress of Novices, she showed rare tact and tenderness in dealing with those young girls who were placed in her charge. But she also had many tribulations. She was ill a great deal."

"And still she is called the Strong Woman?"

"Yes, *Doña* Francisca, because she was so strong in her faith that this enabled her to follow the Divine Will, as it was revealed to her, even though others about her questioned her judgment and even her veracity. Also, because she had great powers of self-control. For instance, when the news of her mother's death was brought to her, she was at the organ, and she continued playing, without any outward sign of grief, until the Office came to an end. With the same fortitude, she bore the death of her sisters—Jerónima, who entered the convent with her and was of great help to her in the choir, and a beloved younger one, Isabel, who had joined them there and who was her special charge. When she was told she must lose the confessor who had been her refuge and her guide for many years, she made no protest and no outcry—her calmness was a marvel to the others who were present when the Abbess gave her this stern order. And, despite her fragile health, she persevered and did all that was required of her and more, to fulfill her duties, though she suffered greatly. At times, her jaws were locked, so that she could not eat, or even receive Communion. It was a very strange thing—so strange, that some in the Community were offended by it."

"Surely, it wasn't her fault that her jaws were locked!"

"No, of course not. We know that now. But there were those who thought it was only pretense. For there were other strange things about her. Sometimes she would not eat, even when she could. She wished to return to the Primitive Rule and even to go beyond it, in fasting, in dress, in all sorts of ways; but when this caused disapproval among the unenlightened, she showed no resentment, but a spirit of true Christian humility. She had great devotion to Catherine of Siena and strove to emulate that saint.[4] Some of their experiences were not unlike; María Vela also heard voices and saw visions. She thought Our Lord spoke to her direct, just as He had spoken to St. Catherine and to the Great St. Teresa, who was still alive, though a very old woman, when María Vela was a young girl and whose works she read and pondered."

"Then she was a mystic, too?"

"Yes, she was a mystic, too. Not a great mystic like Teresa, but still one who enjoyed special favors and graces, many of them little understood at first, though, toward the end of her life, she was recognized by many as one apart. And, after her death, she was declared a Venerable by popular acclamation, which could be legally done in those days, with the sanction of the Church, though that is no longer possible, as you doubtless know, *Doña* Francisca. Furthermore, it was granted that her body should remain incorruptible. Her tomb has been opened several times, to verify this phenomenon, the last time only a few years ago. You may see where she is entombed, if you like, in a niche, placed high above the grille of our chapel."

"I should like very much to see it. But I should like even better to hear more about her, about the experiences that were not unlike those of the great St. Catherine, about the voices she heard and the visions she saw. I do not doubt that these occurred. But how is it possible to know so much about them?"

"Because she wrote everything down herself, upon order from her confessor."

"Because she wrote everything down herself! Then how does it happen that all this is not generally known?"

"Because, *Doña* Francisca, her book has never yet gone out of our archives."

"Her book! You mean she wrote a whole book about her mystical experiences and that this has never been published?"

"That is what I am telling you, *Doña* Francisca. The book she wrote herself is in our archives, beautifully preserved—that and two copies of it, which were made after her death, are also here in the convent. Her last and greatest confessor, Dr. Vaquero, wrote a biography of her that was published the year after her death. And, within the past fifty years, another biography has been written, anonymously, by a parish priest of Cardeñosa—the village where she was born and grew up. But it has never been widely circulated. And her own book, together with the two copies of which I told you—those are here in our archives. Would you care to see them?"

My first visit to the cloister of Santa Ana took place several years ago. So I cannot swear, after so much time, that I have recorded this conversation with the Abbess word for word, with complete exactitude, or that everything I have written down here was actually said in the course of a single conversation, rather than in two or three on the same subject, held close together. But I can swear that what I have recorded is substantially what was said on that first occasion and other occasions of about the same period and that, shortly thereafter, I was privileged to hear more of María Vela's story, to see her tomb, the bloodstained clothes she had worn when she died, and one of the altar frontals she had embroidered. Then came the greatest privilege of all. The books she had written were put into my hands, together with the two copies made in the convent, one, in all probability, shortly after her death, the other in 1747; also the first edition of Vaquero's

Biography, which was published in 1618 and which, therefore, must have been begun, at least, while she was still alive.

All of these books are in a state of perfect preservation. The original is in two parchment bound volumes, dissimilar in size and shape; the one with the smaller pages is almost twice as thick as the other and is square, rather than rectangular, in form; neither volume has a title page, but every page in each is initialed by María Vela. The title page of the first copy—also parchment bound, but in one volume—makes the contents unmistakable and no part of the text, which is written in a clear hand, on linen paper, is missing. The text of María Vela's Diary is divided into two parts, the first being a straight recital. (In the copies, this is divided into chapters and for the convenience of the average reader, I have followed this format.) The second is an undivided record of the "Mercies" received by María Vela. This has nothing to indicate the months when these "Mercies" occurred and only two references to years— 1598 and 1608—so other years are unaccounted for, and we have merely repeated notations of weekdays and saints' days to guide us. This omission seems especially strange because, in other ways, María Vela is so obviously conscious of time that she mentions it constantly: "I spent four hours in prayer at the shrine, two hours standing and two on my knees." . . . "The tautness continued until seven in the evening." . . . "Afterward, I spent an hour and a half at prayer, striving not to fall asleep and incapable of doing anything else." . . . "The Lord held me rapt for four hours." . . . "I was in this state for one hour, my heart aflame." . . . "I felt well and rested, though I had slept four hours on my knees." Detailed statements such as these are scattered throughout the "Mercies."

Both the Diary proper and the record of "Mercies" contain many marginal references to the source of the quotations, which are almost invariably given in Latin, thus revealing that María Vela was, to all intents and purposes, as much at home in this "dead language" as she was in her native Spanish.[5] The style is pleasantly flowing and, for the most part, couched in classical language, but every now and then a distinctly colloquial phrase, such as "give and take" or "up one's sleeve" is used.

In the second copy of the original, which is bound in tooled leather, there is a beautiful illuminated frontispiece, showing María Vela seated, an illuminated title page for the Diary proper, another for the "Mercies," and numerous illuminated capitals. The earlier copy contains no illustrations or illuminated capitals, and the "Mercies" are in a different handwriting from that of the Diary. The endpapers, like the binding, are of parchment, but these have been colored in alternating stripes of dark and light purple, and are quite obviously a later addition to the early seventeenth-century volume, as are also the faded and tattered blue ribbons which fasten the edges of the binding over the leaves and effectively prevent curling.

The first edition of Vaquero's Biography—several later editions are still extant and are still preserved at Santa Ana's—is an unusually beautiful book. Its title page is adorned with an engraving of María Vela, which shows her at prayer beside a crucifix that surmounts a skull. The words, *Mi amado para mi, y yo para mi amado* (My Beloved for me and I for my Beloved), are inscribed on a shaft of light beside her; and a book, fastened with the metal clasps typical of the times and lettered with the initials, IHS, lies on a table beside her. The capital letters with which the chapters begin show a great variety of design; some of them stand out against a background of cherubs, flowers and birds and some of them are interwoven with these figures. I cannot recall having seen any other work so outstanding, both as an example of an early printer's art and of the material on which this was based.[6]

After due consideration and some discussion, it was agreed

that the time had come when the Convent of Santa Ana should share its treasure with the world. There was, of course, no question that the original script should remain in the archives. But it was then decided that one of the two copies might be entrusted to the Prior of Santo Tomás, a man of exceptional culture and knowledge, and whose command of English is extraordinary; and that I might take the other to the United States, on condition that I would have it insured, and keep it under lock and key, with my jewelry. The Prior undertook to translate Vaquero's Biography and to make, or supervise, a literal translation of both the Diary and the "Mercies"; I undertook to revise these, to the degree which might appear necessary in order to make the phraseology more intelligible and, possibly, more pleasing to a modern public, though without in any way changing the sense, and to do such editing and abbreviating as might seem advisable in order to avoid repetition in places where this seemed superfluous. (And let me say here and now, parenthetically but no less emphatically, that I could not possibly have done this, either as quickly or as efficiently as it has been done, were it not for the invaluable assistance of my friend, Muna Lee, Chief of the North and West Coast Section of the Public Affairs Staff of the Bureau of Inter-American Affairs in the Department of State, whose knowledge of both Spanish idiom and Spanish literature far surpasses mine and whose reputation as a translator is based not only on her admirable presentation of Rafael Altamira's *History of Spain*, but on many other important works.) I also agreed to make known my discovery to an American publisher, and to show him both the original Spanish script and the Prior's translations, while retaining all these in my possession, with the understanding that, if they were favorably received, I should be free to negotiate for publication in the United States.

I must confess to many anxious moments while that very

precious volume—the first copy of María Vela's Diary and the "Mercies"—was in my charge. In the course of my travels, I could never bear to let out of my sight the briefcase which contained it; and as various pencil drafts, notes, typescripts and other documents were necessarily carried in the same briefcase, it became something of a problem to a person so lame that she could not carry it herself or easily keep in view any other person to whom it might temporarily be entrusted. Even at home, visions of fire, flood and theft constantly beset me. True, the book was amply insured, as I had promised it would be; nevertheless, if it were lost or damaged, this would be disastrous. It was with a sigh of infinite relief that I finally replaced it in the *torno* beside the grille in the parlor of Santa Ana's Convent, and watched this *torno* revolve until the book was safely back in the hands of the Abbess.

Aside from this natural anxiety created by a sense of responsibility, I had another problem: as I have said, I had promised that neither the Prior's translations nor the priceless seventeenth-century volume should go out of my personal possession; as a result of this promise, an understandable difficulty arose. Editors are apt to be skeptical, both by instinct and experience, about material which they have not had a chance to examine themselves and to discuss with their associates in the publishing business. It was one thing for me to feel that I had in my keeping—the Spanish expression for this is *en mi poder* (in my power) and I felt it all too true in this case!—a valuable contribution to Catholic literature and a proof that the remote and rocky Province of Avila, in Old Castile, had produced not only two great mystics—Teresa of Jesus and John of the Cross—but another who, though of lesser stature, was not unworthy of their company and of posterity's consideration. It was quite another thing to persuade one of those wary potentates who bring out books to accept my unsupported word that I had found a treasure. It is due to the confidence in my judgment, by which I feel greatly honored, shown by Sheila Cudahy and Roger Straus, and their realization that three and a half centuries is already too long a time for a work of great potential value to remain unheralded and, indeed, practically unknown, that María Vela's story, as she herself has told it, is now made available in English to the reading public, though it has never before been released in Spanish or any other language.

To a great extent, this story tells itself, and comment and explanation seem superfluous. However, as María Vela, very naturally, does not identify any of the persons about whom she writes, except by name, it will probably be helpful for the average reader to know a little more concerning them, in order to understand the part they played in her life. The same is true of the circumstances and events which she did not consider it important to record, or which occurred too late for her to record, but which are intimately associated with her.

The aunt of whom she makes such frequent mention was *Doña Isabel de Cueto*, the sister of her father, *Don* Diego Alvarez de Cueto, the cousin of the Archbishop of Burgos, of a general in command of His Catholic Majesty's artillery, and the close relative of various other distinguished persons, many of whom claimed royal descent.[7] *Doña* Isabel had already been a professed nun for some time when María Vela and her sister Jerónima entered the convent as novices; and, both on account of their aristocratic background and connections—which, at this period, it was regarded quite proper to consider, in the cloister as well as in the world—and of her relationship with the two young girls, she was permitted far more voice in their training than would generally be accorded to anyone but an Abbess. It was quite natural that she should make María the object of great concern; the girl had been so ill, just before coming to Santa Ana, that she was carried there in a chair;

and she so early revealed a penchant for austerities and for what seemed to be supernatural gifts, that *Doña* Isabel may be forgiven her feeling that this precious niece should be restrained from doing too much penance and spending too much time in practices which led to rapture. Viewed from the safe distance of centuries, she appears to have been unsympathetic, meddlesome and unreasonable. However, there can be no doubt that she was a practical woman who thought she was acting for the best. Her removal from the scene, by timely death, was probably one which the young nun, whom she had so persistently badgered, was able to accept with Christian resignation.

María Vela's father died when she was a small child; her mother, shortly before she made her profession; and her sisters, shortly after that; but two brothers, *Lorenzo* and *Diego*, reached maturity. Lorenzo became a Cistercian Monk; Diego married, advantageously, a wealthy lady by the name of Ana María de Zuñiga, and lived the pleasant and leisurely life of a well-to-do country gentleman in Cardeñosa. For a time, neither brother seems to have been greatly concerned about either the spiritual or physical welfare of their remarkable sister; but when the sincerity and the source of her supernatural experiences were questioned, both came valiantly and effectively to her defense. Indeed, Diego declared so openly and vehemently that "everyone knew his sister was a saint" that many persons, hitherto antagonistic, began to believe this; and his declaration marked an important turning point in the opinion about her, not only in the convent but in the countryside. Diego died before she did and, as a matter of course, she sent her own confessor to solace and support him during his last days; but before this, the two brothers and their sister had enjoyed a family reunion, Lorenzo coming from his isolated monastery and Diego from his comfortable country estate for a prolonged visit in Avila. This visit marked one of the calmest and happiest interludes in María Vela's troubled and agitated life.

Far closer to her heart than any of these blood relations, however, was *María de Avila*, the friend to whom María Vela usually refers merely as María in her Diary. This girl, who also came of a very aristocratic family, had been a novice at the same time as our María, but had not taken nearly as long to make up her mind about her vocation. She had an unusually sunny disposition, as well as a great deal of sound sense; so, by temperament, she was ideally suited to give her more hesitant and sensitive companion exactly the sort of support and encouragement which the latter required. María de Avila sustained María Vela in her difficulties with *Doña* Isabel; gave her confidence to believe in the guidance of God; adroitly contrived that omissions of standard fare in the refectory should go unperceived and that the ideal confessor should be found and kept; and, finally, during the last hard hours when the life of the "Strong Woman" was ebbing painfully away into blessed oblivion, encircled her with firm and loving arms until she no longer needed earthly succor.

Next to her aunt and her best friend—perhaps even more than *Doña* Isabel—the persons who had the greatest effect on María Vela's life were undoubtedly her confessors; and, as far as posterity is concerned, it is to a couple of them, Salcedo and Vaquero, that the greatest debt is owed. Her first confessor was *Gaspar de Avila*, a chaplain of the cathedral, who performed the same service for *Doña* Isabel—a fact which almost certainly influenced the young novice's choice. Although he did not suggest that she should write, either about her ordinary problems or her extraordinary experiences, he listened with a sympathetic ear when she confided these to him and gave her wise and understanding counsel. For fifteen years he supplied the spiritual support of which she stood in such obvious need; then a paralytic attack deprived him of his physical faculties to such an extent that he could no longer visit the convent, though the clarity of his mind remained unclouded. For a time, he and his outstanding penitent continued to communicate with each other through correspondence. She was extremely loath to lose touch with him, or to confide in anyone else as freely as she had in him, for she was well aware that it would be hard for her to find another confessor who would understand her so well. Fortunately, Gaspar de Avila himself selected his successor, showing the same sagacity in this respect that he had already revealed in many other ways: his choice fell upon *Francisco de Salcedo*, the nephew of St. Teresa's famous confessor, Baltasar de Alvarez, who, like his uncle, was an outstanding member of the newly-founded Society of Jesus.[8]

For a period, the supervision of María Vela was divided between Gaspar de Avila and Salcedo; but the time came when such division was recognized as unwise and Salcedo assumed complete charge of the penitent. I know of nothing to indicate that either the Abbess or María Vela herself felt that he was not in every way adequate to her needs; but he was only a little older than she was—thirty-four when he first assumed his important duties in her connection—and there was murmuring in the Community that he was not sufficiently mature or sufficiently enlightened to guide such a privileged soul as that of María Vela. Considering that this murmuring came largely from those who had looked askance at her every departure from the habitual, whether physical or spiritual, their attitude seems to us slightly inconsistent—but again, this is after the lapse of centuries! Be that as it may, Salcedo himself was quite aware of his responsibilities; he did not need to be goaded into action by complaints which had their source in small minds, jealous hearts and neurotic imaginations. He first took counsel with the chaplains of the convent and then set out for Salamanca where he consulted the learned Rector of the Jesuit College in that great university city, José de Acosta, a native of Medina del Campo, who was the author of numerous important works, mostly on the geography and peoples of the Indies, where he had labored for over twenty years. Among these books was one entitled *The Natural and Moral History of the Indies*, which was highly praised by the eminent German naturalist, Humboldt, and which was translated into French and German. But though primarily a cosmographer and historian, he was regarded by the Pope and the College of Cardinals as the most learned man in the Society of Jesus and Philip II conferred with him on many matters of great consequence. Salcedo had certainly aimed high, for he could hardly have chosen a more widely accepted source of information.

When he undertook his journey, he bore with him something besides the customary staff and script: some notes—they could hardly be called anything more finished than that—written by María Vela. For he had gone a step further than Gaspar de Avila: he had not only encouraged her to tell him, as her confessor, about her experiences, he had encouraged her to record these; and that she might do this with more confidence, he had also encouraged her to read the mystical works of Teresa de Ahumada, who was already very generally regarded as having been supernaturally inspired, though she was not formally recognized as a saint until some years later.

The report of José de Acosta and those whom he, in turn, consulted was extremely favorable. He "approved the spirit of the servant of God and did not find in her revelations and exercises anything suspicious or subject to condemnation. Her doctrine was sane and sound. Some of the revelations did not come, perhaps, directly from God, but were rather mental images of her own creation. However, those in this category were only a few among many and in no way contradictory to the others." [9]

But Salcedo did not rest there. He wrote to Valladolid, to consult the Jesuit, Luis de la Puente, a native of that city who was—and, indeed, still is—held in high esteem. After finishing his studies, he had taught Philosophy and Theology and, when ill health forced him to abandon such an active career, he continued to give spiritual direction to those who sought it of him and to write "esthetic books" which are in use to this day.[10] Again the report was favorable and again, despite this, Salcedo was not content to let the matter rest. He consulted, in turn, Father Juan de Torres, a fellow teacher in the Jesuit College of Avila, "a grave religious of much experience and ability"; Father Juan de Alarcón, Lector of Sacred Scripture at the Royal Convent of Santo Tomás; and Father Pedro Martínez, Professor of Theology at Santo Tomás; also, the confessor of the Cellarist at Santa Ana, who was also the prospective Abbess, for election time was drawing near.

It is in no way disparaging to any of these eminent churchmen to say that, in his zeal, Salcedo had, perhaps, sought too many opinions, which, inevitably, would not all be harmonious, and that he might have done well to rest content with the views expressed by José de Acosta and Luis de la Puente. At all events, it was at this stage that María Vela began to have the strange intermittent seizures resembling lockjaw, and a veritable furor ensued. Father Torres suggested that the seizures might well be the devil's own work; Father Pedro Martínez and Father Juan de Alarcón were inclined to doubt this, especially as Father Torres had made his report "without firm conviction." On the other hand, they did not know what else to believe, as all the reports which reached them were contradictory. The tumult had now spread far beyond the seemingly solid walls of Santa Ana and involved both Jesuits and Dominicans who, as groups, were at loggerheads with each other.

Fortunately, "in the midst of this confusion and bewilderment, Divine Providence ordained that there should drop into town Father Gonzalo de Avila, S.J., brother of the Abbess [this was the former Cellarist, now newly appointed] and of

Don Rodrigo de Aguila, Knight of Calatrava, chief steward of the empress and founder of the Convent of San Antonio of Discalced Franciscans in this city [Avila]. He was the Provincial of New Castile, a man of great authority in his Order, not only because of his nobility and amiability, but also because of his virtues and holiness. Father Salcedo hastened to inform him of what was going on at Santa Ana and asked him to speak to *Doña* María. She gave him a detailed account of her life, answering fully all the doubts and questions he put forth. He also listened to the arguments of her opponents and, after mature deliberation, voted decidedly in favor of the penitent. He convinced his sister, the Abbess, that she should give María Vela all necessary permission to carry out her penitential discipline. The Provincial was astonished to witness the sudden recovery of the sick nun with this change of treatment, and went on his journey, remaining a great admirer of his new friend." [11]

Unhappily, Father Gonzalo did not remain in Avila very long and hardly had he taken his departure when the tumult began to rage anew. Disastrous as were its consequences, we cannot blame Salcedo for feeling that he had reached the end of his rope; he had not only advised and supported his penitent, carefully and prayerfully himself; he had taken long journeys and engaged in voluminous correspondence in order to consult with master minds, and they had upheld his opinion regarding the mode of life best suited to her, the great supernatural gifts of which she was possessed and her saintly character. We may feel—indeed, the present chronicler does feel—that it would have been the better part of wisdom to give more consideration to her mystic qualities, and less to when and how much she should eat and drink and how far she should carry her austerities; but we cannot detach these persons from the place and the period to which they belong and, in those days, it was rare indeed to find anyone who did not believe that bodily sufferings and spiritual welfare were closely allied. The Great St. Teresa did say, at least once, that the practice of prayer could be more effectively pursued if the supplicant at the throne of grace were not physically ill at ease. But the only detailed instructions from a superior to a neophyte along these lines, at least among all those which I have come across, were those sent by Ignatius Loyola, then General of the new Society of Jesus, to the nobleman, Francisco Borgia, Duke of Gandía, who was impatiently awaiting a propitious moment to detach himself from the world and join the ranks of militant missionaries:

"1) 'As to the hours to be spent in interior and exterior exercises, spend just half the time . . . devote the remaining half to study, the governing of your estates, and spiritual conversations, always managing to keep the spirit quiet and peaceful and ready to receive God. . . . It is a far greater virtue to be able to enjoy God at various occupations and places than at one alone.'

"2) 'As for fasting and abstinence . . . do not weaken the body, for when it is feeble, the internal organs cannot function properly. . . . We should love and care for our body as long as it helps our soul . . .'

"3) 'As for scourging our body for Our Lord, it is better to leave it alone. . . . Instead of trying to achieve some benefit from drawing blood, look closer for God . . . in tears provoked by contemplation of our own or of others' sins, or of the mysteries of Christ in this life or the other, or of the love of the Divine Persons. . . . Any one of these sacred gifts should be chosen in preference to corporeal acts. . . . With a sound mind in a sound body, everything becomes more sound.' " [12]

Unfortunately, no such advice, which nowadays seems to us so sensible, was given to María Vela, for the simple reason that none of the worthy clerics who were counseling her would have subscribed to it themselves. Salcedo resigned his charge, to his distress no less than to that of his penitent; and the first confessor chosen to succeed him, *Julián de Avila,* was so obviously unfitted for the task, both from his point of view and from hers, that inside of a few months a definite, not to say violent, break took place between them. The next incumbent was *Father Jerónimo de San Eliseo,* a "Carmelite of highly virtuous life that merited him the title of Venerable." Though he had not been long in Avila, he already enjoyed an enviable reputation and was renowned as a preacher; some of his discourses found their way into more permanent form in a book which he called *Sermons of Our Lady.* He was evidently far more successful than his predecessor in dealing with his penitent; not only was María Vela much happier under his guidance than she had been under that of Julián de Avila; but her two brothers, whose concern for her welfare was by this time at its height, and the new Abbess, an aunt of her great friend, María de Avila, were also satisfied that, at last, the right man had been found. Unfortunately, at least from their point of view, his outstanding qualities had been recognized elsewhere; and again, after only a few months, a change was precipitated, not this time because of any friction, but because he was entrusted with an important mission which was to keep him indefinitely out of Spain.

Father Jerónimo did not divulge the nature of this mission, and from that day to this it has remained generally undisclosed in Avila. According to a private letter of María Vela's, he left the Carmelite Order and became a Dominican. What we do know is that María Vela was so utterly discouraged in regard to confessors by this time that she declined to take any active steps, on her own initiative, about securing another. Intermittently, she confessed to her brother Lorenzo, who came down to the city from his hillside monastery, as often as it was feasible for him to do so. They both knew that such an arrangement could not be lasting; but Lorenzo was evidently discouraged, too, and felt that, temporarily, she would be as well off in his care as in charge of someone more exalted in station, who would either make her miserable or be whisked away from her. Fortunately, at this stage, that cheery and sagacious friend, María de Avila, came to the rescue; she was a woman who kept her feet on the ground and her eyes and ears open; and she had heard good reports of a certain secular priest, *Miguel Gonzalez Vaquero,* the Chaplain either of the Convent of San José or of the Hospital of Mosen Rubi.[18] She had no fixed confessor herself at the time and, without difficulty, she persuaded Vaquero to come to Santa Ana in that capacity. Both had an ulterior purpose: she had in mind that he might be the answer to prayer, as far as her distraught friend was concerned; he had heard all kinds of reports, both true and false, about that remarkable but difficult nun, María Vela. His curiosity was piqued; he wanted to see her for himself, talk with her himself and form his own opinion. Once inside the convent, as María de Avila's confessor, it would be easy enough to acquire a second penitent.

Unquestionably, this seems to be another case where the hand of the Lord is visible. Vaquero had confessed María Vela only once when he wrote, "I have counseled some very superior souls, but none has impressed me as much for [her] humility and sincerity and [the] fullness of her love of God." [14] In this viewpoint, he remained steadfast and, very shortly, was recognized officially as her confessor, to the inestimable benefit of his important penitent, to the Community and to the world at large. She was quick to respond to the sympathetic understanding of which she had been deprived, to such a large degree, ever since the loss of Salcedo; and, at Vaquero's behest, she gladly resumed her long interrupted task of writing. With more self-confidence than she had at first been able to put down words on paper, she proceeded with her chronicle; she was no longer ashamed or afraid to record her supernatural experiences. She had done a great deal of thoughtful reading by this time, she had examples of great literary and spiritual value to guide her. What was more important still, she had been assured that her writings would be seen by no one except her confessor, and she was sure that he would never misinterpret anything she had set down or the spirit that prompted it.

He was in every way worthy of her trust—and of our grateful admiration. For the next fifteen years—that is, until she died—he watched over her with loving-kindness and shielded her revelations from the prying and unenlightened scrutiny of her would-be critics. But he himself had no doubt that the document she had produced was one of immense value in the annals of mysticism. Though this is undated, it is probable that he himself caused the first copy of it to be made—one of those to which I have previously referred. The second was made much later—to be exact, in 1747. Both, as I have said before, are preserved with the original in the archives of Santa Ana; and Vaquero himself wrote a Biography of María Vela which is a masterpiece of its kind, and which has the great advantage, unlike any that might subsequently be written, of being the work of a contemporary and, therefore, unobscured by those faults of omission and commission which, almost inevitably, creep into later chronicles, however meticulous their compilers.

This, as well as I can tell it, is the story of the "accidental" discovery I made, while doing research on Isabel of Castile at the Cistercian Convent of Santa Ana in Avila, together with the identification of the persons, and descriptions of the events, which seem indicated in order to make María Vela's Diary intelligible to the average modern reader. But I believe that still a little more needs to be said, in order to forestall certain questions which such a reader is very likely to ask. For instance: Can you tell us what sort of a place María Vela lived in? Can you tell us what she looked like? Can you tell us something about her last days, when she was no longer able to write? Can you tell us about her death and burial? Above all, can you tell us why, since she was so quickly acclaimed as a Venerable, she has not been beatified—even canonized—long before this?

The first question is comparatively easy to answer: the village of Cardeñosa, where María was born and spent her early youth, has no especially distinguishable characteristics now and I have found no mention of any that it may have had in the historic past, though traces have been found of a flourishing colony predating the Roman invasion of Spain. Its small houses, built of brick and roofed in tile, are mostly one-storied and line narrow, ill-paved streets. Its communal fountain is its most utilitarian feature, its church its dominant attraction. It contains few trees and little other greenery, though here and there a flowerpot brightens the deep embrasure of a window. Its coloring is such that it merges into the surrounding landscape so completely that it seems to be actually a part of this. Like other villages of Castile, it forms a striking contrast, in this respect, to the villages of Andalusia, where the Moorish influence is still prominent, where the houses are kept so freshly whitewashed that they gleam, and where an attached pergola, covered with abundant vines, provides welcome shade. On the outskirts of Cardeñosa some of the farmhouses are encircled with productive fields, each neatly separated from its neighbor by a low wall carefully constructed from the rough stones in which the region abounds; and though some of these farmhouses are very humble, others bear more resemblance to the *dehesas*, or country seats, of the Castilian gentry and nobility. Considering her family background, it is probable that the house in which María Vela grew up was one of this type, well ordered and comparatively spacious. Though, after her father's death, the family was for a time in straitened circumstances, her brother Diego was evidently able to repair the family fortunes, for we are led to believe that he lived the pleasant and prosperous life of a country squire, once his sisters were settled in a convent and he was married to a wealthy gentlewoman.

Regarding Avila, the capital of the Castilian province of the same name, a great deal more can be said. Few cities in Spain, if indeed any, have had a more intriguing history or are more arresting architecturally. According to most authorities, it was built by the Romans, though some ascribe to an even earlier civilization the origin of the stone animals—bulls, swine and other such creatures, which still abound there. From the beginning, Avila was a walled city, though the original Roman fortifications were destroyed and replaced, in the eleventh century, by those which are still standing, in a perfect state of preservation. They rise direct from the rocks of which they are built and, as in the case of the villages and their surrounding countryside, it is sometimes difficult to tell where the one begins and the other ends. More than eighty merlons tower above them and they are entered through four different gates, strategically placed. Their coloring is as extraordinary as their formation—a blend of soft rose, tawny yellow and pale gray. Seen either in the dazzling light of afternoon, when each turret casts its dark shadow on the one next to it, or under the radiance of moonlight, when these turrets stand out in a union of impregnability against the brilliant sky, the walls of Avila are, in themselves, one of the greatest sights in the world; and they enclose a collection of churches and convents, plazas and patios, palaces and *palacetes*—that is, noble houses which do not quite rank in size and importance with actual *palacios*— which are in every way worthy of their splendor.

In the fields of public service, both military and civil, and of arts and letters, Avila has made notable contributions to the world, many of which have gone too long unrecognized in connection with it. The most surprising of all these, perhaps, are the cases of Isabel of Castile, which I have already mentioned, and of George Santayana, one of the greatest modern figures in philosophy and literature. But the contribution of the city and the province to religion have, fortunately, been more generally acclaimed, though still not as universally as might be expected. In María Vela's time, Avila already had to its credit San Segundo—a disciple of St. James himself—who built the first Christian church in Castile, became the first bishop of the diocese and suffered martyrdom; the young Roman martyrs, San Vicente and his sisters, Santa Cristeta and Santa Sabina, who were given a superb sepulchre in the church which bears Vicente's name; San Pedro del Barco, the holy hermit who lived in a hillside cave and was also buried in San Vicente; and Santa Barbada, the young girl who came from María Vela's own village of Cardeñosa and who was saved from seduction by a disfiguring miracle. Teresa de Jesús was already hailed as a saint, though she was not formally canonized before María Vela died; and María Díaz, who was Teresa's humble fellow guest at the hospitable home of Doña Guiomar Ulloa and who afterward lived as a hermit, had been declared a Venerable by popular acclamation. The Carmelite, Juan de la Cruz, was widely recognized as a holy man; and the news that Philip II had refused to allow the Augustinian, Alonso Orozco, to retire to a monastery because "saints could not be spared at court" must certainly have penetrated to the walls of Santa Ana, even if his formal recognition as a *beatus* had not. So must the news that a Franciscan, Pedro Bautista, had gone as a missionary to Mexico and the Philippines and as ambassador to Japan, and that he had been crucified at Nagasaki with twenty-five companions—a record which, sooner or later, would almost inevitably lead to beatification at least. In other words, María Vela had as examples which seemed close and real to her, no less than eleven men and women of recognized holiness, some of them actually her contemporaries, all of them her fellow *Avileses,* whose saintly lives had found fulfillment in such various ways as living the isolated lives of hermits and going forth as missionaries and following the mystic way and suffering martyrdom. It is hardly a matter of wonder that, under these circumstances, a devout and emotional girl should grow up with the "yearning for perfection" which her Diary so movingly describes, and that, as time went on, she should actually aspire to sainthood and frequently voice and record this longing.

The Convent of Santa Ana, which María Vela chose as the place most suited, and most likely, to satisfy this yearning, as far as she was concerned, is situated just outside the walls in the southeast section of the city. (Directly across the street from it is the house which once belonged to the Santayana family and which its most famous member so feelingly describes in *People and Places,* the first volume of his great autobiography. It bears no inscription of any kind to set it apart from those which surround it, all of which have, unfortunately, seen better days.) The convent property covers a tremendous amount of ground, for, besides the cloistral patio—which is, in itself, immense—with its central fountain, it includes a walled orchard and kitchen garden, which, in turn, have enough supplementary space for the pasturage of cows. It also has a large chapel, to the greater part of which the public is admitted for regular services, though it is not kept open all the time; and this chapel, with its lofty arches, noble statues, inspiring inscriptions and gorgeous golden altars—all so typical of Spanish churches, both large and small—presents a beautiful sight, especially when lighted with hundreds of candles and adorned with hundreds of flowers, to celebrate the feast day of the convent's patroness, Santa Ana.

Except for this chapel, no part of the convent property is entered directly from the street, but by means of a rather bare courtyard, through whose great doors is admitted anyone, within reason, who chooses to come there; and these doors open wide enough to admit cattle and horse-drawn carts. This courtyard is flanked by quarters for lay workers, such as the portress, and their families. At its right, a much smaller door leads into a rather gloomy stone vestibule, also open to the public, which, in turn, contains three more doors: one, at the left, opens into two very small parlors, where expected visitors may be received by nuns—never less than two at a time—who sit behind the grille at the rear; a second door, at the top of a short stone staircase with an iron railing, leads to the principal parlor, called the *locutorio*, a very large room with a grille— flanked by a *torno*, or turnstile—that extends all the way across the rear. This grille divides the main part of the *locutorio* from the alcove, which is spacious enough to accommodate all the members of the Community at once; and, on special occasions, like the Feast Day of Santa Ana, a privileged visitor may be received by this assemblage, though more usually the number of nuns will be limited to those whom the guest has some good reason for seeing. This *locutorio* is the same where Carrillo and his band of rebellious noblemen foregathered to offer Isabel the crown; it was behind this grille that she stood beside the Abbess and refused their offer; and it was while descending this small stone staircase that Carrillo said to Villena, "This young girl is our salvation."

The third door of the gloomy little vestibule, which faces the entrance, is the one that leads into the cloister, and it is rare indeed that this is opened for any outsider except necessary workmen, doctors and dentists.[15] It is no secret, however, that the chapter house harbors artistic treasures of considerable merit and value, and that the cloister contains other spacious apartments, besides the one made famous by Isabel. Some of the so-called cells are divided into an anteroom and a sleeping alcove and could, in former times, be adorned at will by their occupants, like the similar ones at the Carmelite Convent of

La Encarnación. Privileged laywomen, who wished to live, at least temporarily, in seclusion not infrequently occupied these, though this is no longer permitted; and there is no doubt that María Vela could have had such an apartment, when the state of her health indicated the need for special treatment, if she had desired it. But she honestly preferred to live under conditions of great austerity in every respect, and she died in a small interior cell of unmitigated bareness. However, like all other members of the Community, both past and present, she was not required to share this with anyone, but was given the privilege of privacy which, from time immemorial, has seemed so essential to gentlewomen.

María Vela's greatest physical discomfort, aside from those she deliberately invited, was probably caused by cold. Nothing could be more erroneous than the general belief that if the weather is not actually torrid all over Spain, it is at least always pleasantly warm. This is true only in the southern provinces and, even there, except in summer, only in the sun; in winter, and often in the spring and fall, it can be cold after sunset and before sunrise; and as neither private houses nor public buildings are ever adequately heated, according to American standards, and the beneficent sun is carefully excluded from them, it can seem chilly indoors at midday. Avila is seldom really hot; not only is its situation northerly, this is high—about four thousand feet above sea level. Its designation as the "Spanish city nearest heaven" does not refer alone to its religious character, but also to its geographical elevation. Its summers are delightful, mellow and golden; but they are short. Snow has been known to fall there as late as June and as early as September; and though the city takes on almost celestial beauty when it is mantled with white, this loveliness is bought at a price of much human misery. Even the wealthy and well housed shiver as they huddle around their braziers, which can be moved at will from place to place, but which never satisfactorily heat a whole room, even a small one. The nuns, vowed to lives of poverty and living in convents, have no such meagre comfort; the great stone staircases, the interminable brick-paved corridors, the small stark cells—all these are permeated with such frigidity as most of us have never known. True, these women have known it all their lives; but it is the only aspect of their austere existence of which I have ever heard them speak as if it were difficult to endure. María Vela was, from childhood, subject to respiratory diseases and died of pleurisy, after having more than once been close to death from pneumonia. She would have been less than human if she had not watched the swirling of autumnal leaves in the walled orchard with apprehension, and gazed, with tempered joy, on the "new soft-fallen mask of snow" that surrounded the frozen fountain in the central courtyard.

"Although my main purpose is not to write about the dead stones of this convent, but about the living ones, I am forced to say something of its antiquity and magnificence, since it is one of the oldest and most distinguished in Spain." This is the way Vaquero felt and what he wrote, more than three centuries ago; and as I feel the same way, I, too, have been swerved from my purpose of writing about its "living stones" to write about its dead stones, also; as a matter of fact, they do not seem dead to me, but impregnated with life. The Convent of Santa Ana was founded in 1388 by *Don* Sancho Dávila, Bishop of Avila, First Notary of Castile and tutor of King Alfonso XI. His tomb, surmounted by his statue and inscribed with verses extolling his merits and accomplishments, remains one of the chapel's chief ornaments to this day. And he not only founded the convent; he saw to it that this was suitably endowed. At the time María Vela was a member of its Community, which then numbered seventy religious, including some of the "second habit" (lay sisters), it had an annual income of six thousand ducats and every farmer who worked in Avila with a pair of oxen and collected as many as fifteen *fanegas* of wheat was required to deliver to it three *celemines* each year.[16]

The first Abbess of Santa Ana was a certain Doña Illana Munoz, of whom, I am sorry to say, I know nothing except her name; but I have no doubt that she set a high standard, which has been consistently maintained by her successors in office, since it quickly became the custom for the rulers of Spain not only to include a visit to Santa Ana in the course of their royal progresses to Avila, but to select it as the scene for some special ceremony. Outstanding among these was the "breeching" of the Infante Felipe, who has come down in history as Philip II, and who was taken there, at the age of four, by his parents, the Emperor Charles V and the Empress Isabella, to be dressed by the nuns "in shorts with a sword." The visit of King Philip III with his consort, Doña Margarita of Austria, which took place in 1600, was also made an occasion of great distinction; and in the reception of these royal visitors our heroine, María Vela, took her appointed part as an outstanding member of the Community.

And now it is time to return to the second question which the average reader is likely to ask. I am sorry to say that, as far as I know, there is no detailed record of María Vela's personal appearance. We are told that she had very beautiful hands and that, as she was afraid these would lead to vanity, she did her best to keep them concealed under her scapular, but that this was not easy for her, because nearly every kind of work in which she was most actively engaged obliged her to reveal them: making artificial flowers, embroidering frontals, playing the organ, caring for the vestments and sacred vessels in the sacristy. We are indeed told that she earnestly requested her friend, María de Avila, to draw a veil over her face if she were overcome by rapture during a service, which she always hoped would not happen, or at any other time when she might be subject to general observation. But the raptures occurred with increasing frequency, as she grew older, and María de Avila was loath to comply because "on such occasions, María Vela became very beautiful." From this statement, we may infer that, except when transfigured because of her mystic communion with God, she was not characterized by exceptional perfection of form or feature. However, I think we may take it for granted that she had a graceful carriage and a pleasing expression, both because of her Castilian heritage, where such attributes are the rule rather than the exception, and because of her conventual training; while the loving-kindness with which she treated the novices in her charge, after she became their Mistress, and the outward calmness with which she was able to accept such "crushing mortification" as the tidings that she was about to be deprived of her best friend and wisest counselor—Francisco de Salcedo—must certainly have been reflected in her looks, to their great advantage. It may perhaps seem irrelevant to use a modern story as an example in such a case; but there is one which I have always thought very significant and, personally, I believe it is applicable: Abraham Lincoln once gave as his reason for refusing to appoint a man with powerful backers to a position of high office the fact that he did not like the man's face. "But he is not responsible for that!" the applicant's sponsors insisted. "Every man over forty is responsible for his face," Lincoln replied quietly.

I believe this is very generally true. What we are, not what we pretend to be or would like to be, is unmistakably revealed by the time we reach middle age. María Vela was fifty-seven when she died. Long before this, the purity and exaltation of her spirit must have been manifest in her face.

Thanks to Vaquero, the third and fourth natural questions can be answered somewhat more explicitly. María Vela had made an almost miraculous recovery from an attack of pneumonia which gave every indication of proving fatal, and was actually well enough to assume the care of another nun who was ill, when she was suddenly smitten with a *dolor de costado*—a pain in the side—which would appear to have been pleurisy. According to the custom of the times, she was bled until what remained of her strength must have been drained away from her; and since pleurisy is extremely painful, she must have suffered a great deal. But her spirit was serene and one of her most beautiful visions—that of a jeweled crown which the Saviour Himself placed upon her head—occurred at this time. When the Community entered her cell in single file—again, according to custom—she received its members with quiet courtesy and without any sign that there was only one among them whom she really wanted with her at the end. Her last wish was fulfilled; María de Avila was the only person with her when she died.

Almost immediately thereafter, the convent was besieged with crowds, clamoring to see "the saint" and importuning the nuns for relics. They had not foreseen such a tumult and such an outcry; moreover, it was natural that they should resent intrusion upon their first mourning. In their bewilderment and sorrow, they turned to Vaquero for advice. Wisely, he told them that the populace might be allowed to enter the courtyard, if this entrance were made with faith and devotion; but he countenanced a minor deception: María Vela's clothes could be changed and those which she had actually worn kept for the Community. Hence, it was fragments from those of another nun which were borne away as relics. The Bishop—*Don* Francisco de Gamarra—decreed that the burial should not take place in the cloister; this time, there should be a departure from custom. Her tomb was to be at the foot of an altar in the chapel—an altar dedicated to Our Lady of the Sun, to whom María Vela had always shown great devotion;

moreover, her body was to be placed in a casket, which had never before been done at Santa Ana, either. The Bishop himself officiated at the funeral, in the presence of all the great of the city, as well as those humbler folk who, a day or two before, had stormed the convent gates, but who were now pacified; and, before this service, as many as was fitting were permitted to see María Vela in her cell, where she lay as if asleep on her narrow bed, with a crown of flowers on her head and branches of palm in her folded hands.

It was by order of this same Bishop that her casket was later removed to a tomb far more ornate and more loftily placed; and it was also during his tenure of office and only two years after María Vela's death, that the so-called "ordinary process" for her beatification was conducted by him. No lack of competent and willing witnesses appeared to testify—by actual count, no less than thirty-nine; and far more than the requisite number of miracles were recorded. Over the door of the cell in which María Vela died is an extremely interesting primitive painting, which shows a certain Josefa Martin of Muñoyerro on her sickbed, gazing entranced at an apparition of María Vela. This picture bears the inscription:

"Josefa Martin, V. na de Muñoyerro, estando a la muerte, su hermana Ana Martin, la ofreció a la venerable mujer fuerte, Dª Mª Vela y llebandola su manta se la echaron sobre la cama con gran fé; se halló buena y en hacimiento de gracias puso este retrato. Año 1695." [17]

This inscription verifies the story told by Josefa's sister Ana that the latter had managed to procure a blanket once used by María Vela and that, as soon as this had been laid over the dying woman, the vision had been vouchsafed and the cure effected. Most of the other recorded miracles also refer to cures, brought about either through prayers for María Vela's intercession or the efficacy of her relics. Among these is the testimony of a religious at Santa Ana who three times recovered from grave illnesses through the latter means; and this same religious affirms that María Vela was often heard speaking to her friend María de Avila during Matins and singing in the choir during Benediction, and certified that "many other miraculous things" were observed after the Venerable's death. However, to this day, she has never been beatified. According to some authorities, the process of beatification was dispatched to Rome, but was lost in Alcalá de Henares, where its bearer, the Chief Accountant of the Count of Monterey, met with an untimely death. This theory is attested by an Augustinian of Rome, who was handling the cause. It has never yet been reintroduced and, naturally, this has caused great disappointment in Avila. It may, however, perhaps be mentioned in passing that such a delay is by no means unique. Francisco de Capillas, a Dominican martyred in China in 1648 and declared a Venerable, was not beatified until 1909; and the record of the ordinary process for the beatification of a group of Dominican Missionaries, martyred in Japan at the beginning of the same century, has only just been discovered in the archives at Manila, where it has lain buried all these years. Alonso Orozco, whose withdrawal to a monastery Philip II forbade on the ground that "saints could not be spared at court," was beatified shortly after his death; and more than three years ago, collateral descendants of his informed me that his canonization was now imminent and I have been on the alert for tidings of it, as I had been provisionally invited to attend the ceremony; but, as far as I know, further action is still in abeyance. Even Joan of Arc, now one of the two patron saints of France—the other is Thérèse of Lisieux, of whom I am frequently reminded by María Vela—was not canonized until centuries after her death. Natural as is the disappointment among those who desire to see María Vela raised to a higher rank, and greatly as they may feel she merits this, the aforementioned instances may be of some comfort, especially as the time when the findings of the ordinary process were handed in was rather unpropitious. The Pope, Paul V, who, in the world, had been Camillo Borghese, an outstanding member of that prominent Roman family, was not predisposed in favor of special recognition for Spaniards and, indeed, almost the entire College of Cardinals was intensely nationalistic, or rather, intensely Roman in its viewpoint and sympathies. Nevertheless, within the next fifty years—that is to say, during the reigns of Paul V and his successors, Gregory IV, Urban VIII, Innocent X, Alexander VII, Clement IX and Clement X—no less than seven Spaniards[18] were canonized, as well as Rosa de Lima, who, though herself a Peruvian by birth, was of pure Spanish blood. Moreover, Pedro Bautista of Avila and all twenty-five of his companions and protégées, some Japanese but the majority Spanish, who were crucified with him at Nagasaki in 1597, were beatified.[19] It is quite understandable that the Sacred Congregation may well have felt that sufficient recognition had been accorded to one country for the time being and that official action on their compatriots might properly be delayed until more nationals of some other country had been considered.

The definitions of beatification and canonization, given in *A Catholic Dictionary*, edited by Donald Attwater and published by Macmillan, also serve to cast abundant light on the subject. "Beatification," we are here told, "is the process by which enquiry is made into the sanctity of a deceased person and, upon proof thereof, permission accorded for his public veneration; this is usually limited to a particular country, diocese, or religious order and does not extend, without special permission, to the display of his image in church or to a Mass and Office in his honour. Beatification generally, but not necessarily, leads to canonization (q.v.), and both declarations can

now be made only by the pope himself. But the initial en-
quiries are made by the local diocesan who reports to Rome
and, if these are satisfactory, the cause or apostolic process is
introduced and passes into the care of the Congregation of
Sacred Rites, which subjects the life, writings and alleged miracles of the candidate to a most searching scrutiny; half a dozen
or more stages are involved and so thorough is the enquiry
that it usually lasts many years. The pope is the final judge
and if he is favourable, the solemn beatification takes place in
St. Peter's, when the brief is read, a picture of the *beatus*
unveiled and venerated, and the new collect in his honour
sung. He, or she, may henceforth be referred to as the Blessed
so and so. The pope is not infallible in beatifying."

Canonization is defined as, "A public and official declaration
of the heroic virtue of a person and the inclusion of his or her
name in the canon (roll or register) of the saints. Beatification
(q.v.) having been accomplished, it must be proved that two
miracles have been subsequently wrought at the intercession
of the *beatus*; the tests and examinations are as rigourous as
those which have gone before, and the miracles are discussed
in three meetings of the Congregation of Rites; there are required two things to be proved: that the candidate was formally or equivalently beatified, and has worked two (or if
equivalently beatified, three) miracles subsequent to beatification. The canonization is then carried out solemnly in St.
Peter's by the pope in person, whereat the bull of canonization
is read and a Mass sung in honour of the saint. Canonization
involves that the saint not only may but must receive public
honour; a day is appointed for his feast and a liturgical office
composed therefore; his relics are publicly venerated, churches
and altars dedicated in his honour, statues or pictures displayed
in churches, and prayers to him made publicly. This judgment
of the Church is infallible and irreformable. Owing to the
amount of careful work involved and the sumptuous scale of

the final ceremony, canonization is an exceedingly costly process. This is probably the chief reason why so large a proportion of canonizations are of priests and religious, many of whom were public characters and whose cause is supported by the resources of a diocese, nation or religious order. It must not be supposed that a person was not a saint because he had not been canonized (i.e., declared or certified as such): some of our greatest saints were never formally canonized; but at least since the 12th century public veneration without the permission of the Holy See has been unlawful. The first solemn canonization was of St. Ulrich of Augsburg by Pope John XV in 993."

When we ponder the statement, "half a dozen or more stages are involved and so thorough is the enquiry that it lasts many years" even for beatification, we can better understand why there may be many delays before this can take place, especially if the calendar is already crowded with objects worthy of honor. This understanding is further intensified when we ponder the statements, "owing to the amount of careful work involved and the sumptuous scale of the final ceremony, canonization is an exceedingly costly process. This is probably the chief reason why so large a proportion of canonizations are of priests and religious, *many of whom were public characters and whose cause is supported by the resources of a diocese, nation or religious order.*" María Vela was never a public character, and the diocese, nation and religious order to which she belonged are not wealthy as wealth is reckoned nowadays; indeed, Spain's "Golden Centuries" were already on the decline before her cause could have been officially considered in Rome. It ill beseems a stranger within Avila's hospitable gates to suggest what should or could be done there, in either temporal or spiritual matters; but such a stranger may perhaps be forgiven for saying that she has long been puzzled by the lack of public acclamation given San Pedro Bautista,

who certainly is the most arresting figure the province has produced, next to Isabel of Castile, Teresa de Ahumada and Juan
de la Cruz; and that she is equally puzzled because more than
three centuries have passed during which María Vela's writings have not been accorded the universal public recognition
of which they seem to her so eminently worthy, and which
might so logically lead to her beatification. If, in any slight
measure, this stranger has been privileged to bring such recognition about, through the co-operation of the Cistercians of
Santa Ana and the Dominicans of Santo Tomás, she will feel
that her long labors, leading toward this end, have been amply
rewarded.

Frances Parkinson Keyes

Palacete Montefrío
Avila, Spain
August, 1956—August, 1957

⎧ Sulgrave Club
⎪ Washington, D. C.
⎪
⎪ The Oxbow
⎨ Newbury, Vermont
⎪
⎪ Beauregard House
⎪ New Orleans, Louisiana
⎩ September, 1957—May, 1959

Hotel Wellington
Madrid, Spain
July, 1959

M.N. Saturnia
September, 1959

⚜ Chapter 1

How God began calling her to higher perfection from the first year of her novitiate; and what happened to her during the 20 years that her first confessor, God's servant, Gaspar Dávila, heard her in confession

I am writing this because you have so ordered under express obedience, although I have found it very difficult to do. I shall set everything down as best I can, with God's favor and for His greater glory.

After I made a General Confession the year I entered this convent—twenty-four years ago at the age of fifteen, on the Feast Day of the Presentation of Our Lady—Our Lord in His great goodness began to give me an immense yearning for perfection. I placed myself under the direction of my confessor, Father Gaspar Dávila, with complete confidence that, thereby, Our Lord would satisfy my longings. In the spirit of helpfulness, my confessor tested the effect of mortifications on all propitious occasions; and it seemed to him a good thing to have my aunt, who is now in heaven, act for him in this respect. So it came about that I could go to Communion only when she gave permission, which was fortnightly; and such was my custom during the six years that I was a novice.

My aunt exercised the same authority in respect to prayer and penance that she did in respect to Communion. I was not permitted to do penance without her knowledge, although my confessor sometimes secretly allowed me to do so. She restricted my periods of prayer to a scant hour and sometimes to as little as a quarter of an hour. Occasionally, she ordered me to say the rosary and nothing else. I always obeyed her without protest, but I shed many tears in secret, and begged the Lord that more time might be allotted me to serve His Majesty and suffer for Him. Since, after my mother's death, I prayed to be endowed with the virtue that most pleased the Lord in her, He gave me such a yearning for suffering that I thought it would never be satiated, even if I endured as much as one can in this world.

Since I was perpetually coddled and cared for, I was in continual torment; nor was I content when, contemplating the life and death of Our Lord and aspiring to imitate Him, I found myself so unlike Him. Consequently, I wept floods of tears, because it seemed to me that there was nobody unhappier than I; everyone else had something to endure, either mortification of the flesh, or the scorn of others, or poverty, or disease, any one of which I would gladly have undergone.

It happened that one Lenten season when I was not permitted to do any penance, I took the matter direct to Our Lord, entreating Him that He Himself give me a penance, since I could find no spiritual rest in so much physical rest; and He made me the gift of an illness that lasted until Eastertime, and with it great spiritual delight because I was suffering a little for love of Him. I was constantly aware of the love I owe Him, and this seemed to me the goal of my desire: to suffer for Him Who had suffered so much for me.

After some time, Our Lord began giving me the power for prayer of abstraction,[20] together with an ardent desire to have ample time to devote to prayer. I recall that, for a period of about twelve years, I was allowed only one hour daily. At night, I would perform my meditation,[21] seated on my bed, with a cord tied to my feet, hands and neck in such a way as to wake me if I became tired or sleepy. Since my desire for abstraction was so overwhelming, I often wept because I could not achieve more wholly that for which I yearned. When, as sometimes happened, my aunt became aware of this, she feared I might go to great extremes, even to the point of rapture; then she would try to divert me, by making me count the tiles on the roof, or move stones from one place to another, or sweep the floor, or net the corridors with thread,[22] or do anything to pass the time in some such futile way. Since I was always ailing, she would not let me join the Community at Matins and in the refectory and all this caused me much pain.

After my profession, Our Lord gave me courage and determination enough to conquer this obstacle; but neither the Prelate nor my confessor dared order that I do more than my aunt wished, lest she be distressed.

I also had to bear another cross which was still heavier and which affected me sorely: Our Lord was favoring me with supernatural grace and leading me along paths of love and confidence, and my confessor was not treading these same paths. He took the morsels in which I most delighted from my mouth, clipped the wings of my flight and the freedom of my spirit. He always preferred that I should be timid and fearful. I saw clearly where security lay, but stopped without daring to take advantage of the privileges now offered me. I had some conversations about this with Our Lord, all very tender and satisfying, and they fortified me and spurred me on to follow the road of obedience and mortification. My confessor ordered me to resist these impulses, saying that they were all an illusion of the devil and he forbade me to do anything without his approval.

I continually concentrated on the verse of Scripture which came to my mind when I began my meditation. My confessor tried to deprive me of this resource also, saying that I was trying to enter heaven by way of the roof and should leave such matters to the guidance of the church; and he prompted me with proffered reflections. But for me there was no entering in the way he suggested. I was on the lookout for anything else that might be offered, but until I was given permission to enter by any way I could, I did not dare try to do so, barring the reception of special favors.

When I told my confessor of such things, which were beyond my control, we quarreled, so that sometimes I let them pass without mention. On one occasion, he said that I should not think what I was doing was pleasing in God's sight. This made me so sick at heart that I had no strength for doing good; I asked why I should kill myself by doing what I undertook only to please God, if this were not pleasing to Him.

On another occasion, I was suffused with tenderness by the words, "Shew me thy face, let thy voice sound in my ears: for thy voice is sweet, and thy face comely" (Cantic. 2, v. 14). It seemed to me that the Spouse was speaking these words to my very soul, saying that, because of His goodness, He had cleansed it of the stain and ugliness of sin and beatified it with His grace, so that He might look upon it and rejoice in its beauty.

All this, I told my confessor; but I had to pay dearly for doing so, because he distressed me greatly, saying that pride alone made me think God was favoring me with such graces;

and he said more in the same vein, leaving me desolate and confused. But I never failed to be obedient in all things nor to believe that it was right for me to obey; for I learned in prayer that this is the true way: to obey with submission of mind and will, taking as example Christ Our Lord, from Whom we must draw these lessons and other virtues. Therefore, I continually gazed upon myself in that mirror—the Life of Christ—so that I saw my deficiencies and was given not only a great longing to adjust my life to that of Our Lord, but courage whereby to mortify myself.

So it was that my diligence and care were to deny my own will and opinion, and I had at hand an exercise affording me ample opportunities in this respect: whenever I went to meditate—by this time, the allotted period had become two hours, morning and evening—I would begin by asking my aunt what I should do. In this, I mortified my mind, because it seemed to me utter nonsense that, since this hour had been designated for praying and the voice of God within me was calling me to prayer, I should inquire of her who could not know my inmost soul what I had to do. I said this to my confessor. He approved my method and was heartened to have me follow it, thinking that by this means I approached prayer without exercise of my own will, but submitted myself wholly to the will of another, and that thus I practiced humility and could hope to know God's Will. All this was hard going for me, and filled me with such deep repugnance that, during the ten years that I followed the practice, I could never overcome my revulsion; not even once, I think. Sometimes it was a source of great affliction not to be assuaged. I kept trusting that God would grant me the favor of lessening my repugnance, but He did not choose to do so, and thus He kept me humbled by consciousness of the little I could do for Him, inasmuch as I could not even pray to Him without restraint, although everything had come to me from His hand.

After my aunt's death, I offered to make any sacrifice which the Lord might require of me, in order that He might grant her the grace of taking her out of purgatory. On the night I made this offer, I woke up in a state of very great joy, with these words in the forefront of my consciousness: "The Lamb that was slain is worthy to receive power, and divinity, and wisdom, and strength, and honour, and glory, and benediction" (Apocal. 5, v. 12). Since I had gone to bed shedding copious tears, imagining my aunt in the midst of purgatorial sufferings, this message gave me to understand that by virtue of the Blood of the Lamb, she had been pardoned and was already rejoicing in the Presence of Our Lord. Then the tribulations which I had voluntarily sought came upon me and for some three months I suffered greatly, without any relief. After this, Our Lord began showing me more frequent favors and, since I could not communicate directly with the priest who was then my confessor, because, during the past five years, he had been giving me only written counsel, I took, with his advice, Father Salcedo as my confessor and with him I was to deal for twenty years.

Chapter 2

What happened during the time that she confessed to her second confessor, who was Father Francisco de Salcedo of the Company of Jesus, a great religious as all those who dealt with him well know

When I began going to Father Salcedo, I was so ill that I did not follow the Rule of the Community. I seldom attended Matins;[23] I went during the day when the tremors which I suffered left me. Because of my weakened condition, I ate meat, with permission, even on days of abstinence; but Our Lord filled me with unsatisfied yearnings. And thus I might have gone on for a long time, with no one to help me, and nevertheless have eventually overcome the obstacles which prevented me from fully following my profession. (For five years, I had worn nothing but serge, though no one knew this except Doña María.) But, fortunately, I read in the Works of Holy Mother Teresa of Jesus how much it harmed us to complain of petty maladies and how everything depends upon having a great determination and trying to persevere, trusting in Our

Lord; so I confided in Father Salcedo and, with his advice to guide me, I began to lead a new life.[24]

Every day, His Majesty gave me greater faith and greater courage and, together with these, the bodily strength to do everything which the Order prescribed in regard to fasting, attending Matins and fulfilling other obligations. In addition, I managed to devote seven hours daily to meditation, most of this time on my knees, to scourge myself every day and on some days to wear haircloth. I followed these practices from All Saints' Day to Easter of the Holy Ghost and, when I felt inspired to do still great penance, permission was given me. In consequence, I wore haircloth daily, scourged myself three times every day, and set apart only four hours out of the twenty-four for sleeping. On Communion days, I slept on my knees.

During this period, God's favor was continuous. I experienced levitations, and their coming was preceded by signs such as yearnings of the spirit which made me weep and moan and, at times, made me feel as if an arrow had pierced my heart. My confessor gave me orders that, when such emotions overwhelmed me in the presence of others, even though this happened during the Divine Office, I should go to my cell and remain alone. And I did so when I could not remain seated, feigning sudden illness.

On numerous occasions, I heard Voices, learning from them and even without them, but because of them, many things about attaining greater perfection. They rebuked me for my faults, encouraged me to work, consoled me in my afflictions, and clarified my doubts with such unconstraint and affection that nothing could shake my conviction that they came from God. Such an assertion might scandalize many, unless they remember the infinite goodness of the Lord. Through this alone, He communicates direct with His creatures, deigning to deal with them and speak with them, not considering the many demerits of their souls. Let Him be blessed forever and glorified in His works.

Since Father Salcedo saw that the number of Mercies I received was increasing, he wished to consult Father José de Acosta, Rector of Salamanca, about them. So he went to see Father de Acosta, and showed him the notes I had written in accordance with my confessor's orders, setting down everything that had happened. This was during Lent. Father Salcedo had been my confessor four months by now, and all this time God had been showering me with Mercies. After reading my papers, Father de Acosta approved the spirit which they revealed. And though later on he knew of the various and contradictory opinions which have been held with regard to me, he never doubted that my guidance was from God.

I myself had many fears but, when absorbed in prayer, the Voices reassured me, though, afterward, the fear returned. However, since my confessor told me to persevere, I maintained silence on the subject, except for asking the Lord to enlighten him about my fears; and, while he was in Salamanca, I obtained permission from the Lady Abbess, *Doña* María de Mercado—may she rest in peace—to mortify myself publicly, in the way which she herself imposed on me as a penance, in Chapter.[25]

Some religious were scandalized. Father Alarcón learned of this and did not wholly approve, so the public mortifications were discontinued. I had begged for permission to practice these because, at that time, I was very desirous of being despised and rebuked. And it all came out well, as Our Lord ordained that it should; in the very midst of the scandal, when even from the pulpit I was called childish and foolish, and told I was offending God, I had faith that I was pleasing Him. And, though grieved at the scandal, I soon recovered from my sense of humiliation, for God consoled me by encouraging me not to give up the practice of such mortifications, whenever I had permission for them.

While I was following this way of life, we arrived at the Feast of Catherine of Siena; and, as I was meditating on the mercies which God had shown this saint, the Voices[26] said to me, "I will give these to thee, also." I trembled as I replied, "Only if I served You as she did, O Lord!" Then again I heard the Voices saying, "That is not what counts. What matters is that, unworthy as thou art, I shall treat thee as if thou wert deserving."

After the experience which befell me on St. Catherine's Day, I earnestly entreated Our Lord to give me, as He had given her, a new heart. I was filled with longing to imitate her virtues. Hence it seemed to me that whatever prompted me inwardly was directed toward imitation of her, as, for instance, silence, prayer, vigilance (like her, I did not retire to sleep until the clock struck twelve), a penance of three daily scourgings, sleeping on a cork[27] and a diet of herbs. Afterward, I found that I could sustain myself for several days on the Blessed Sacrament without other food. A great debility that brought me to death's door was cured without need of nourishment. On the contrary, it left me doubly strengthened in spirit and body and full of peace and joy. After many trials, I came to realize that Our Lord permitted these in order to try my faith, for when faith failed me and I ate to keep up my strength, I was inwardly rebuked; nor did I become as strong as when I fortified my faith and suffered joyfully, hoping that the Lord would be pleased and show me favor, as many times He did.

One day, just after Communion, the flavor of the Sacramental Species lingered on my palate, and it seemed to me that as long as I was conscious of this, there remained also the Holy Body of Our Lord Christ. The same thing had happened three years previously, in the period when I was directed by Father Gaspar Dávila. Because of this, no power could force me to eat on the days when I took Communion; in fact, it was a source of great anguish to do so while my soul was in retreat, gazing upon its Spouse, Who desired its company, occupied with loving Him and thanking Him for so great a mercy. I grieved to forego such a great gift by taking other food, as happened when I was ordered to eat or drink and, occasionally, the Lord would choose that the savour should not leave me until evening, although I was forced to eat.

Soon this experience was repeated at the time of another Communion. When it was time for me to go to the refectory, I became abstracted and could not do so. It seemed to me that Our Lord wanted me to let the day go by without eating, but I found a thousand difficulties in the way, since I could not fast unnoticed. Yet I believed the saying, "If this is My desire, who can resist Me?" and I recalled how Elias had been sustained by a hearthcake and thereafter had walked for forty days.[28] How much better then could I be sustained by the living Bread of the Blessed Sacrament![29] This thought, together with other pertinent considerations, convinced me that I was doing God's Will. My head was swimming, but I lifted my eyes to the image of St. Catherine that stood before me, and I recalled that the same thing had happened to her and other saints while they were fasting and still they had not slackened.

On this day, the Lady Abbess told me to go to the refectory without fail, for, unless I did, my absence would be noticed. I replied that, sometimes, I found myself unable to go. She understood that when such was the case it was because of an abstraction and, accordingly, gave me permission to absent myself. I turned to the Lord and said, "Lord, Lord, what has now been aroused?"[30] And the Voices said, "Do not be afflicted; follow My Divine guidance and pay no heed to what is said by others." It happened many times that, when I was confronted with some affliction or difficulty, I sought refuge in prayer and then became confident that I need not be confused or fearful, because I could have faith that the Lord would smooth my path.

These things happened while Father Salcedo was away.

Meanwhile, one day as I was reflecting that these fainting spells would probably not recur, since Our Lord had achieved His purpose by then, namely, my return to the habits of fasting which He had indicated, the Voices said to me, "Henceforth thou shalt be wreathed with a crown." This crown, they said, was to be of thorns, like St. Catherine's, which pricked and hurt; but in my case the thorns would be the contradictions which I was to suffer, not only from men and the devil, but also from God Himself. I accepted the crown, saying that from God's hands, I would receive thorns as willingly as flowers; and it seemed to me that it was His Divine hand which placed this crown upon my head.

One day I sought enlightenment from the Eternal Father concerning His Beloved Son, while gazing at a portrait which showed Him disfigured by agony, and which seemed to speak, saying, "Look on the face of thy Christ" (Psalm 83, v. 10). Then these words came to the forefront of my consciousness, "This is your hour, and the power of darkness" (Luke 22, v. 53). And then I realized that it was not only by the Eternal Father's Will, but by the power of the devil himself that Christ was delivered into the hands of sinners, who put Him to death with many kinds of injuries and torments. Then I understood, if the Master must suffer such things, what can the slave expect? If this happens to the innocent, how can the guilty complain? The Voices clarified my understanding, making me see that the Lord had permitted the devil to test my faith; and that only lack of faith would make me break my fast, since God's Will was that I should have no need of food on the days I took Communion; that I should have no fear of losing my life under the utmost stringency; and that if my strength failed, He would redouble it.

When Father Luis de la Puente arrived, I told him my life history. He considered everything very carefully and read all the papers I had written. At last he decided that my spirit was good, with no apparent intervention of the devil, although I might possibly have imagined some things. He further said that I should not continue to fast on the days I took Communion.

On another day, when I asked the Lord not to deny me His Presence because I carried out the orders of others in regard to eating and caring for myself, I realized that God abhors the gratified flesh, and delights in flesh mortified, chastised and afflicted for the sake of His love. This lesson Christ Our Lord taught us in His Divine Person, for He never spared His Sacred Self. During His Holy Life, He underwent hunger and thirst, heat and cold and weariness, for our salvation. Such also was the spirit of the saints. At this point of my reflections, the Voices told me, "Having only this knowledge—that mortification and austerity of life are pleasing to Me—the saints undertook tremendous endeavors; thou, with so many indications of My Will, dost nothing." I answered that my will was not lacking, but that I was not permitted to follow it lest I lose my life, and the Voices said, "Thou hast ample proof that thou canst trust Me. I have sustained thee throughout an entire year by My truths and I will sustain thee for ten years more if thou wilt have faith."

When I entreated the Lord to enlighten my confessor as to what His Majesty desired, and not to lead us into such confusion, the Voices told me, "That is not fitting; by these very means thou art to be tried on the forge of My love, whereon are tested faith, hope and charity, patience, humility and obedience." They said that I should be strong as a rock amidst the tempests of the sea, and that even though my hopes were apparently shattered, I should believe that the Lord would fulfill His promises.

The Lord so disposed matters that, at this time, which was Lent, the Provincial of the Society of Jesus stopped by. He was esteemed as a saintly man. Father Salcedo felt it wise to inform him of my problems and, this being done, the Provincial came to see me and told me that there should be no more tests, that it appeared to him it was very clearly God's Will that I should forego my noon meal on the days I took Communion; not secretly, as heretofore, but publicly, after asking permission from my Prelate. This I did and, at first, she gave permission; later on, she was reluctant to grant it, both because of my weakness and because she found the whole problem so extraordinary. Therefore, the Lady Abbess who, by this time, was *Doña* Isabel de Vivero, would not give her approval until she had reported to Father Juan de Alarcón and to her own confessor, Father Pedro Martínez. In this way, the whole question became a matter of public knowledge, because these two priests, who said it was the devil's work, were scandalized with the accounts of my fasting. Finally, I fasted for several days, without physical suffering and with great inner peace, although some of those who knew what I was doing opposed it. However, they raised no open objection, because they saw that I kept up my strength and attended to my duties without shirking any of the work assigned to me. Our Lord was not satisfied with this state of things, so that Lent He permitted me to begin experiencing the trouble with my jaws which was to give rise to much thought and talk.

It was on the second Sunday of Lent, as I was about to go to Communion, that my jaws were first locked, without my knowing how this had happened. They remained so for a short while, but were unlocked at mealtime. I think that everything was all right throughout the week until Friday, when they were locked again; and this time my hands, too, were clasped as if tied with a cord. I began to feel deeply distressed and entreated the Lord for permission to receive His Body; but the Voices said to me, "Why art thou afflicted? Hast thee not surrendered thy will to Me?" Then I recalled how they had told me that I must be a martyr to love; that the Divine love itself was to be my executioner; that all these things were sent to me as tests; that I should trust in His Majesty, Who knew what was best for me; and that, even though I did not take Communion, He would not deprive me of the virtue of the Sacrament. He also gave me to understand that He wished me to be guided by His Will in this as in all things; and that, on the day when He wished me to communicate, I would know it by the fact that there would be no hindrance to my receiving Him. To this, I responded that my confessor would not permit me to go to Communion on successive days. The Voices answered that I should report the Lord's Will. I was left with inner quietude and peace in the belief that the Lord desired me to be so tested.

One day, while I was reflecting on the fact that the Dominican Fathers had been willing that I should receive daily Communion, provided I did not fast too rigorously, it became clear to me why the Lord had made use of this strict fast and that it had to be thus: that the meal should be at sunset, of bread and herbs only, as I had been given to understand many months previously, and that, in this, I should imitate St. Catherine. I was greatly moved while contemplating the Divine plan as revealed through these words, "O the depth of the riches of the wisdom and of the knowledge of God! How incomprehensible are his judgments and how unsearchable his ways!" (Rom. 11, v. 33.)

There were days when the Lord wished to give me permission to receive Him and Father Salcedo never refused to let me go to Communion if there were no obstacle. Consequently, he decided to inform the Father Provincial, without whose authorization permission could not be granted, of the situation. Meanwhile, I was obliged to suffer whatever God permitted. At that time, as I implored the Lord not to allow the fact of this fast to be made public, but to mitigate its rigors, as Father Alarcón had instructed me to do, I understood the Voices to say, "If they give thee Holy Communion every day, thou wilt be enabled to eat every day in the way I have told thee; when I do not wish thee to eat, I will let thee know."

After this, I was commanded to take Communion only three times weekly, by order of the Dominican Fathers, so that I would not be fasting so much; and they told me that if I could not communicate on those days, it would be in order that they might understand nobody can resist Divine Will. Then it came to pass that, during all of Holy Week, I was unable to communicate. There were those who were scandalized, saying this was the devil's work. In this regard, Our Lord made me comprehend that, if I resigned myself to the Divine Will, the devil would be powerless. It is only when the soul tries to assert itself independently that the devil can seize upon it for his own deceitful ends.

On Easter Day, when I was wondering whether or not I should be able to take Holy Communion, I realized that I would be unable to do so until my Spiritual Fathers were in accord with Divine Will; and so it was. I can recall having communicated only once until the week of the Ascension, when it was agreed that I might receive Communion on fifteen consecutive days as a test. It was later learned that, on the very same day that this decision was reached, a similar permit had been signed at Salamanca. The Father Provincial and his companion, who had also spoken with me and who were acquainted with my problems, met there with Father Luis de la Puente and the Rector, Father José de Acosta. In view of this permit and sanction from the

Dominican Fathers, Father Salcedo decided that he might allow me to communicate every day, first carrying out the fifteen day test to ascertain whether or not the impediment of the locked jaws, which for so many days had prevented me from taking Communion, still existed. All agreed to this. Meanwhile, I implored the Lord for permission to communicate on the designated days, saying, "Lord, Lord, since You are such a great advocate of obedience, my failure to obey is the worst charge which they could bring against me." I understood the answer to be, "What if I wish to remove thee from the common rule?" And I understood further that, if Communion were given on these days in order to see whether the impediment were still there or not, I should be undisturbed, though the impediment would remain until the test was made. With this in mind, I tried to approach Holy Communion, but to no avail.

At this time Father Salcedo departed, leaving word with Father Torres to obtain permission for these fifteen days from the Archdeacon of Avila who presided over the vacant See. Permission was granted, and Father Alonso Dávila, who took Father Salcedo's place, authorized me to carry it out. And so it was that I could receive Communion without difficulty, and ate more herbs, and felt so strong and well that everybody was astonished and was obliged to admit that this was God's work. Even Father Torres, who had been one of my greatest opponents, was convinced.

On St. Catherine's Day—one of those occasions when I was communicating as a test—the Voices told me, "Now thy troubles will begin." The year was 1598. The permit had almost expired, and I was willing to undertake any burden in order to obtain its renewal.

When the fifteen days of consecutive Communions had ended, the Community began to be scandalized because I ate at night, and it was regarded as a singularity, and not an evidence of good spirit, that I should miss going to the refectory; it would be better for me to act like the rest. Furthermore, the fainting attacks returned, overcoming me at my place in the choir. A great turmoil arose, but when I remonstrated with the Lord for permitting hindrance in my exercises, I understood the reply to be, "This is done to show the strength of My arms, prevailing against those that resist Me." When I begged Him for permission to eat with the Community, since this was what seemed best to everybody and would restore quiet, the Voices said to me, "For who hath known the mind of the Lord? Or who hath been his counsellor?" (Rom. 11, v. 34.) It was then given me to understand that the main point was not the fast itself, but the encouraging example which might be set for others by me. He had permitted the murmurs of protest in order to test me; in His Own holy life He had scandalized many persons; His saints had undergone similar trials; I was not to blame if I could not follow the rule, since the decision as to that was not my own; the Holy Ghost who had ordained the Community practice for the sake of others was the same who had willed that I should dispense with it; and my case was by no means unique; for instance, St. Euphrasia, who was a nun, had not eaten for an entire week and had been criticized on that account; and religious in other convents had likewise fasted during long periods when they could not follow the customs of the Community.

It was no lack of esteem for obedience which made me implore permission of Our Lord to go into the refectory with the others, for I fulfilled, without argument, every command my confessors gave me; but they could not make up their minds to give the indicated order in this case because, whenever I attended regular meals, my health failed again and my jaws became locked.

With great insistence, I besought the Lord not to permit me to be deceived regarding what seemed to be His Will by removing me from the jurisdiction of my confessors. I told Him that I esteemed the Mercy He was showing by His wish to guide me; but that, since my desire was for the very thing which He had signified to be His Will, I wished that He might inspire those who commanded me to follow it; for such was the order He had established in His Church and such the road followed by the saints. The Voices explained it should preferably be said that, first of all, the saints were ruled by the Divine Spirit; then, having achieved sanctity and having learned to trust completely in God, they recognized the authority of His Majesty. But I had not yet attained this happy state. Therefore, I should not feel that I was lacking in the merit of obedience, since it was the Lord's Will that, for the present, I should obey the orders of others on earth, even though these were contrary to what the Voices told me.

I was assured by the Voices that, when I obeyed in this way, I was exercising a very high degree of humility; because, though knowing God's Will, I yielded to man's opinion; and that, when I met with hindrance in carrying out the orders of the Voices, I should regard this as a test, since fears would then overcome me, causing the soul to hasten with greater fervor in its search for light, and to exercise faith, confidence, resignation and humility; so that not only I, but those who had dealings with me, would derive profit from the obstacles in my path.

The more assurance I received through prayer, the more I feared lest I were being deceived or were following my own will, when I found that I could not obey. Consequently, I clung to God, beseeching Him that I be not misled and that my confessors be enlightened. One day, while thinking about a very saintly Discalced nun, I asked, "How is it, Lord, that You have assured her of her way, whilst You desire mine to be uncertain and dubious?" I understood the answer to be, "Why shouldst thou find it dubious? I do not draw thee away from the rules of the saints; from ordinary regulations, yes; because I have willed for thee this singularity. If what thou doest were contrary to what the saints did, that would be dubious." I replied, "Lord, what afflicts me is not to comply with the rule of obedience to the Superiors, since it is through them that You generally show Your Will."

I was having severe fainting spells at that time, and the Lady Abbess, seeing me so stricken, commanded that I should at least eat eggs and other delicacies, even if I would not eat flesh food. My confessors, who were then Father Alonso Dávila and Father Salcedo, felt sure that these attacks were not natural, but that they were permitted by Our Lord in order to test me. These priests so informed the Mother Superior, with the request that she should not deprive me of my fast. She herself did not feel it wise to grant this request, though she grudgingly did so, limiting her permission to eight days. She was always timorous and never permitted me to persevere in any one direction; and I had many critics, who thought I was following the bent of my own inclination, and who even said I failed in obedience to my Prelate and that I did not wish to observe the customs of the Community. The Lady Abbess was not pleased with what I did, so that even though everything was done with her express permission, she told those who spoke to her about it that she did not like giving this. Hence they inferred that I was acting against obedience, under orders from my confessors.

Matters were at this pass when Father Gonzalo Dávila happened to stop by at the convent. I was very ill at the time, quite unable to walk, a condition I believe came about because I was not allowed to fast. After Father Gonzalo had informed himself thoroughly, he pleaded with his sister, the Abbess, to permit the resumption of the fast and to convince the Community that such was God's plan. She gave the necessary permission and I was fully recovered before he took his departure. He was amazed by this and thereafter became my staunch advocate. The Prelate's satisfaction did not last long, however, since she consulted friars who had a different opinion and gave heed to them. She never reached a conclusive decision, and the Lord permitted my sufferings to continue.

And since I had been so ill that I could do nothing, the Voices said to me, "I have never failed thee; why should I fail thee now?" And, as I pressed Him to show His power, I remembered that, even when He lived on this earth, Our Lord did not perform all His miracles suddenly or by the mere force of words. Some He wrought slowly, prompting the very persons for whom He performed them to do their part as well. This had been the case with the blind man whose story is told in the Gospels, whose eyes Our Lord anointed with clay and whom He had then sent to the pool to bathe. I realized that perhaps He wished to deal in the same way with me: that, just as the clay might have deprived this man of sight if left on his lids, in like manner, I could be brought to death by counsels that I should not eat, when my spells of weakness and fainting were the means He was employing to restore my health. It seemed to me that I should take water in which an herb called hyssop was boiled and that, by these means, I should be cured at last. I did so and after I had drunk the mixture twice, the fever left me. This change was accepted by everyone as an indication of God's Will.

After I began to feel better, I regretted having escaped death; and one day as I lamented while I prayed that it seemed impossible to endure this exile for years, without the enjoyment of His Presence, the Voices told me that there was greater perfection in resigning oneself to living as long as God willed, even when experiencing a vehement desire for the joys of heaven; that we should accept our earthly burdens and imitate Saint Martin who said, "Lord, if I am still necessary to Thy people, I do not refuse the labor." I then was comforted. Another day, thinking it was possible that I still had some years to live, I understood the Voices to say, "Why art thou distressed, since thou hast My Mother? If thou art ignorant, I am Infinite Wisdom. If thou art weak, I am Power Itself. To thee, I will be all in everything." From that day onward, I have not been troubled.

After this happened, the Voices told me that Our Lord was about to punish a person who had strongly opposed me. I was grieved and said, "Lord, he was not to blame, for he had good intentions." And the Voices said, "He is to blame for not revering God's works." I pled that he might be forgiven and not suffer for my sake, even though I understood that the offense was to His Majesty and not to me. In great affliction, I tried over and over again to intercede for the sinner, asking that I be permitted to suffer for him, since I would willingly try to atone for him, and begging that he might be pardoned. Seemingly, my prayers were heard, for only a fortnight after Our Lord had restored me to a state of health, which enabled me to follow all my exercises, a serious illness befell me on the Feast of St. Simon and St. Jude, which brought me to the point of death. For many days, my life was in danger and five times preparations were made to give me Extreme Unction, since it was expected that I might expire at any moment. But I was not anointed because I did not wish it; I kept repeating that it was not yet time; and, though I was dazed and hardly knew what I said, I was right. This illness caused everyone in the Community to lose faith, even those who had been my most staunch supporters. They went around tattling to each other that I was deceiving myself, that my self-will had almost killed me; and these tales were coupled with other amazing stories, which were bandied about, both inside and outside the convent, and which greatly pained Father Salcedo. He alone continued to stand up for me, and the Lady Abbess, confirmed in her previous opinion, was very angry with him and with me. There was hardly a soul in the convent who did not attack me and even those who believed in me did not dare to say so. *Doña* María was the one who suffered most, partly because she thought I was dying and partly because the angry Community was blaming her for helping me toward everything I desired; and the general opinion was that my situation was leading me straight to hell. The proof of this lies in the fact they told my confessor he should ask Cuevas—may he have eternal glory!—to warn me that I was in a state of mortal sin. I finally recovered, but the general opinion about me remained the same. Our Lord continued to make me suffer: throughout my long illness He had remained shut away from me, forgetful of past Mercies.

While I lay on my bed, still very weak and warned that I would have a relapse if I should try to rise from it, the Voices said, "Unless thou rise, thou wilt never be well," and they added that, if I did not try to do so, I would suffer new seizures. So I asked for help with dressing, since I was not strong enough to dress myself, and that first day, I felt very ill. But I trusted in Our Lord and soon I was feeling better; the pain was greatest on the days when I was forcibly kept in bed.

About this time, Father Luis de la Puente chanced to come here. He was informed of everything that had happened, with special stress on the general opinion that I should not be allowed to do anything in the way of penance, and that all the advice I thought I was receiving was an illusion caused by the devil. But, once again, he spoke in my behalf and asked the Lady Abbess to permit me to give up meat as soon as my health improved. He dared not press her further, since this was a sore point with her. I was slowly getting better and, by the beginning of Lent, I could go to the choir; but I was not granted permission to abstain from meat; on the contrary, I was required to take it three times a week.

On Friday of the Cross, after Easter Sunday, I abstained from meat secretly, since it was useless to seek permission to do this from the Lady Abbess. The friars and the nuns advised her to give me some work in the convent which would divert my mind, so that I would forget everything else, and she sent me to the bakery. I accepted the duty, which offered ample opportunity for mortification, since I could not hide the impediment in my jaws. I had to speak to the baker and everyone else, and they all talked as they pleased, freely offering their various opinions. Some said my handicap was caused by illness; others by debility; still others, that it was all pretense on my part. The latter urged Doctor Madrigal to try opening my mouth, which he repeatedly refused to do, because he believed the impediment was God's work. At last, however, he decided to try and exerted so much strength that it made my teeth grate; but he not only failed to pry my jaws apart; they became the more tightly set and he the more confirmed in his opinion. On this account, he continued to defend me and urged his friends not to strive against me.

Some days went on in the same way and, during this time, Father Frias happened to stop by. Father Salcedo told me to speak to him and also gave his own account of my problems. Father Frias did not deem my meditations to be in the right spirit. He said they sounded to him as if I were brooding over sermons on the subject of penance; and he asked me what sins I had committed for which the Lord wished me to atone. He advised me to appear as much as possible as I had for twenty years previously, and I believe it was likewise he who advised me to give up my meditations for a month at least. I listened to him, but since I was not under his obedience, I was not distressed by what he said, though I tried to do what he had enjoined. Then the Voices admonished me, "No, My daughter, do not so. Do not withdraw nor leave off conversing with

Me. How canst thee bear the toils and tribulations that beset thee if thou lackest the help given thee in prayer?"

Father Salcedo thought it best to leave me while Father Frias was here and before the arrival of the Father Provincial who was expected soon. Father Salcedo was convinced that, because some clerics felt he had been mistaken in the way he handled my affairs, and had so informed the Provincial, the latter would forbid his dealing with me further. Likewise, Father Luis de la Puente, seeing the Abbess and the Community, as a whole, displeased with Father Salcedo, considered it unadvisable that this guidance should continue and, on that point, everyone was agreed. So, finally, one day, in the presence of Father Frias and in mine, Father Salcedo summoned the Lady Abbess and told her that he was tired of testing my spirit and that he had no courage to torture me any more; he felt a new adviser should be summoned who could do more than he. He advanced many other arguments, to all of which I listened with as much outward calmness as if none of these concerned me, the while I was left with no one but God to support me in my hour of need and adversity.

⟡ Chapter 3

How Father Salcedo ceased to be her confessor

Our Lord showed me the Mercy of giving me to understand that I should be no more affected by having people speak well or ill of me than if they were speaking of someone else. I was able to say that I never knew where they attempted to strike me because they never reached my heart.

After Father Salcedo left me, my jaws were locked for three successive days. During the first two, I felt no weakness, despite the fact that I ate nothing whatsoever; but, on the third day, after Communion, I fell down in a dead faint. The nuns rushed to my aid and carried me to my cell, where they made me take a little broth, but my teeth were so tightly clenched that no one could understand a word I tried to utter. I remained in a state of great affliction throughout the day, because I did not know what to do next. At last, since night had already fallen, I decided to send for the Lady Abbess. I told her I had learned that the locking of my jaws would be relieved, and that I should be able to eat, if she allowed me to resume my exercises. In view of my dire necessity, she gave the requisite permission for that week, which was the one that immediately preceded the Feast of the Holy Ghost. Thereupon, I recovered instantly. She was bewildered and so were her friends who were waiting for her at the door; they looked at one another in amazement.

On Pentecost, after Communion, while I was in a state of great abstraction, the Voices told me, among other comforting things, that the impediment to my jaws would not return as long as I had no Father Confessor, and that I could carry out any orders given me by the Prelate. I told all this to the Lady Abbess, as Father Salcedo had enjoined me to do, believing that it would tranquilize her; but I found that the only result was mortification and suffering for me, since she regarded it either as a jest or as a figment of my imagination. On the Feast of the Blessed Sacrament, she told me to speak with Julían de Avila. (May he have eternal glory!) I bowed my head and welcomed him, though I knew him to be one of my severest critics. During the two hours I spent with him, I gave a full account of everything I could remember, but he thought none of it important and was only confirmed in his previous opinion. He told me that everything I had said to him was founded on illusion and that I should recognize this fact; he said that, if I failed to do so, he could not feel sure that I would be prepared for a good death; and he said much more which deeply disturbed me. I was left in a state of great anguish which increased when I learned that the Lady Abbess wished him to be my confessor. My only recourse was to turn to the Lord and entreat Him to so enlighten me that he and I might understand each other. I had great hopes His Majesty would do this, even though it might cost me dearly. Father de Avila commanded me to resist the inner Voices and regard them as a deception, but I could do neither, despite my every

effort. He said that, considering the things I had myself imagined or that were put into my head by my confessor, he was
surprised that I had not become a Lucifer. He ordered me to
eat meat and to take Communion only three times a week; but
when I told the Lord how I was deprived of receiving Him, the
Voices said, "That is the case now; the situation will change."

The Father told me once, when I said God wished to
take a hand in guiding me, that even a person of little intelli-
gence would know this statement came from the devil. The
Voices told me to remind him of the verse, "He that dwelleth
in the aid of the most High, shall abide under the protection
of the God of Jacob." And the Voices further told me to
meditate on the verse, "His truth shall compass thee with a
shield." I was given to understand that His truth would be my
defense, that the darkness and doubts which assailed me
should not trouble me, neither should I fear the vainglory of
good works signified by "the arrow that flieth in the day" nor
"the noonday devil" transfigured into an angel of light; against
all these He would defend me and serve as my shield.[31]

When deprived of penances and fasting, I became very ill,
and implored the Lord in the name of Holy Mother Teresa
of Jesus and of the saintly Father Pedro de Alcántara to restore my health, so that Father de Avila might himself witness the Mercies the Lord had showered upon me, for I understood that He would do this for the glory of His saints, if
permission were granted me to carry out my penances and
abstain from meat. Permission for this was not given, though
it was for other things, and I began to get better.

In spite of this convincing proof, a fortnight later the
Father again ordered me to go to *Doña* María's cell and tell
her to have a meat stew prepared for me; this, I was told, I
must eat, because it was what I needed. I obeyed and soon
afterward, on that same day, my jaws were so locked that the
bone was thrown out of joint. The Father believed that my

discontent with him was the cause of my illness, so, after he had been my confessor for about two months, he sent me word that he would be taking leave of me on the Day of the Transfiguration.[32]

I then asked the Lord to so enlighten him that he would do what was most pleasing in His Majesty's sight and that all this conflict might be ended once and for all. The Voices told me that it would not be ended under his guidance, but under that of Father Salcedo, for whom this victory was reserved because of what he had undergone in trying to conform to Divine Will.

After the Father left me, since I was too ill to attend Choir, all the nuns in turn took great care of me and all gave me advice. Most of them thought I should be guided by the Dominicans. The Lady Abbess laid no orders on me, but it was understood that she was of the same opinion. Consequently, I decided to ask my brother if he would speak to Ledesma and request him to take charge of my affairs. My brother agreed to do so, since Ledesma was his friend. The latter came to see me one day and I was with him for perhaps a quarter of an hour. I do not recall having conferred with him about anything in particular, except Holy Communion. Since, for many days, I had been able to communicate only occasionally, he told me he would come again and do what he could. It seems, however, he concluded I was out of my mind; he said as much to my cousin, Father Francisco Vela, who told my brother. Into such hands was entrusted my spirit, and there were other things which caused me even greater mortification.

Father Ledesma never came back to see me; I was glad that I was in no way responsible for his staying away, because the nuns thought I wished to confide only in those who agreed with me. At this time, the Lord oppressed me with a feeling of abandonment, and to this was added my dread that my critics might be speaking the truth, that I might indeed be deceived and under the devil's dominion, forsaken by God. This seemed to be confirmed by the fact that I had nobody to advise me and that no one wanted to take charge of me. These and a thousand other things became so strongly implanted in my mind that I did nothing but weep, without finding consolation in either heaven or earth. Both seemed closed to me.

Father Domingo Bañez came by and the Lady Abbess ordered me to see him. I gave him an account of some special things that I had set down in writing. He told me that I was following a very dangerous road and that I should do what the Prelate commanded; in short, that in spite of my good intentions, I might be deceived and, therefore, err. I told him about some of my experiences while fasting and he did not believe me. My response was that if he did not believe what I was telling him, there was no use in my being there and so I took my leave of him and withdrew.

Then I was ordered to speak with Father Labata of the Society of Jesus. He told me to take a slice of melon with sugar, but said it would be better not to mention this, since everybody might be horrified. He assured the Lady Abbess that if I communicated twice a week, that would be sufficient. Father Bañez had said three times a week and Father Alarcón once a month.

After many days, during which I suffered from a deep sense of abandonment and inner anguish, I was rebuked for the discouragement and lassitude which this gave me. As I recovered, this verse sounded repeatedly in my ears, "Arise, why sleepest thou, O Lord?" (Psalm 43, v. 23.) Little by little, my heart was softened and enlightened by this message, for I saw that I had erred in allowing myself to become oppressed by the diligence and solicitude with which I sought to rise above the affliction which overwhelmed me, and that it was better to hope in the Lord's promises and have faith in

His works, with humility and resignation and in silence. As I became aware of my error, I said, "Lord, when You fail me, good counsel also fails me. 'And turn not away thy face from thy servant: for I am in trouble, hear me speedily' (Psalm 68, v. 18)." As I came to an end, I heard these words, "Do not be afflicted. I will be everything to thee; if thou hast Me, thou wilt need no one else."

On another occasion when I was grieving, because there was no one to whom I could relate any of this, the Voices asked, "If I Myself desire to teach thee directly that which I used to teach thee through human agencies, why shouldst thou be disturbed?" It was borne in on me that I received this message because I was continually writing letters, asking that Father Salcedo might be sent back, so that he could again be my adviser.

For eight weeks, I was not once able to receive Communion. As there was no one with whom I could discuss the grief this caused me, I hoped that Our Lord would remedy the situation; and He did so, for the gift of prayer suddenly returned. Many and continuous were the Mercies I received. I felt at peace, lacking nothing and not troubled by what I had suffered in the past, nor by the problems of the present. My levitations were numerous and public; I was not able to resist them. This caused me some anxiety and I begged the Lord that they might take place more privately. The Voices said, "Leave this to Me; do not resist." Another time, they asked, "What is it to thee whether people speak well or ill of thee? If they speak well, Mine is the glory." They said further that I needed only to be receptive of these evidences of Divine favor and that most persons would show more gratitude than I did.

Three days later, it was decided that I was possessed of a devil which had to be exorcised. I was not upset by this, but offered myself for the treatment with great joy and inner peace. My confessor at the time was the Father Chaplain who shared the general opinion that I was possessed. So one day that summer, when he was saying Mass in the chapter room and I had been prevented from taking Communion, he did try to cure me by means of the required treatment. However, he must have considered the cure had been unsuccessful because he had tried it only once. Consequently, he decided to treat me for nine consecutive days. After High Mass, he would approach the Communion window, toss a stole about my neck and recite every exorcism in the missal. I would make my responses with complete serenity and, when he had concluded, return to the choir. There I usually experienced a levitation, by which Our Lord consoled me and gave me greater courage to suffer.

On the Feast of the Presentation of Our Lady,[33] when I approached the window to undergo this cure, my jaws became locked, as they had been twice before on that same day when I tried to communicate. When the Chaplain saw my condition, he said it must be the doing of the devil who could be cast out only with prayer and fasting. He told me therefore to fast and pray, by which means I might have riddance of the evil spirit. Meanwhile, God was consoling me, for the Voices told me not to be troubled, since it was well that all this should come to pass, in order that He might be glorified in me. Upon hearing this, I was levitated to such a degree that it seemed as if my head were nailed to the window. God's servant opined that this was epilepsy and that I should take rum. During this abstraction, it appeared to me that Christ Our Lord was deigning to transform me into His Own likeness: His Majesty had been accused of being possessed by the devil; so was I. He was treated as if insane; I was thought mad. It was said of Him that He stirred up the rabble and that He was an eater of flesh food; of me, that I made a disturbance in the convent and regaled myself under pretense of fasting. Him they tried to slander and ensnare with His Own word; what

I said was twisted as my hearers pleased. He was deemed a blasphemer Who desired to become the Son of God; it was said of me that I was stiff-necked and proud, that I desired to be a saint and esteemed as such. He was so hated that His enemies wished to cast Him out of this world; mine wanted me to be outcast and nameless on earth. But "the stone which the builders rejected, the same is made the head of the corner" (Mark 12, v. 10). Hence, since I was like Him in the one respect, I yearned to resemble Him in the other also. I deemed myself so favored in thus sharing the insults and injuries which had been His portion, that I wished them to be the cause of my death. Accordingly, I said that this was my choice, meekly accepting the levitations even though they scandalized others. Gradually, however, the levitations came to be regarded in their true light and it was seen that the Lord was favoring me; because, however much I dissimulated so that they might be attributed to illness, I could not hide the truth completely. I was watched too closely for that.

Since I was not cured after three weeks of the treatment, I requested permission of the Lady Abbess to communicate daily during one week. I recalled to her memory the fact that I had been thus cured in the past, and suggested that we might try this method again if she agreed. She said that she would consult the Chaplain or, better still, that I should do so. When I did, he spoke to me with great severity, saying, among other things, that if the trouble with my jaws could be so readily cured, it seemed like something I had up my sleeve to use as I wanted. Finally, he said he would consider the matter. After a few days, he returned, saying that he had looked through many books without finding anything that would prohibit me. After that, his attitude changed and favored my feeling in regard to frequent Communion and defended me when anyone expressed a contrary opinion. Whenever I could not go to Communion, he explained to me that

it must be the devil who was hindering me and told me to receive Communion daily that week. The Lady Abbess con-
curred, so there was no hindrance. The nuns were so filled
with joy that they all congratulated me, being now more than
ever convinced that this was God's doing and not the devil's,
as they had once thought.

Meanwhile, Father Tomás was informed about me, and he
condemned the spirit in which I acted. I decided to speak
plainly to the Abbess, placing myself in her hands and trusting
Our Lord to so move her that she would order what was for
His greater glory. The Voices had given me to understand
that I could approach her with perfect confidence. I told her
that, with the approval of my brother, Father Lorenzo, I was
performing certain penances, since she had not specifically for-
bidden them. She replied that she had become aware of this,
by noticing that I was stronger and that I was attending Choir,
and she gave me permission to do everything I had done formerly. However, she said I should do all this secretly, so as to
scandalize nobody. I was very happy and thanked the Lord for
fulfilling His promises.

◄§ Chapter 4

How she was advised by Father Salcedo anew

On another day, after Prime, the Lady Abbess sent for me. She told me she had been unable to sleep all night, because she had been worrying about me. She said she knew how much it would upset me not to have anyone with whom I could discuss my problems, since, obviously, Francisco Díaz was not equal to handling them; and then she offered to send for Father Salcedo occasionally, and see to it that I could speak with him secretly, if I thought I would derive any solace from doing so. I replied that, if she would grant me this favor, I would be satisfied with seeing him once a month. She summoned him immediately and, to the great surprise of us both— and we did not cease giving thanks to the Lord on that account—she herself kept watch at the door. Thus I spoke with Father Salcedo often until Lent. Then the Abbess decided that she herself would also confer with him and give him an account of her soul. She was so pleased with the outcome of these conferences that she encouraged him to see her frequently, and the fact that he did this gave me a pretext for seeing him, too. Things went on like this until the Feast of the Visitation, when Father Salcedo went away.

Since my public levitations continued, and were especially frequent at Divine Office, Francisco Díaz thought they were the devil's doing; he said that, if they came from God, they would not occur at such a time. As I was required to attend the choir and fulfill my duties there, I told him that in similar cases a test had been made under obedience; and I asked him to suggest that, when I experienced a levitation during Divine Office, the Abbess should order me to come to my natural senses; if I then recovered these, it would be clear that all this was God's Will.

On the Feast of the Three Kings, my heart was troubled lest I should not undergo this test successfully; but I was told not to worry because God would provide for my welfare, as He had done so often before. This counsel comforted me and it proved to be true. Every time the Lady Abbess ordered me to recover consciousness, I did so; she had only to send a nun to me, who gave the command in her behalf. This happened repeatedly: sometimes when I went to Communion, sometimes when I was reciting the Office and, on still other occasions, when I attempted to seat myself in the choir and was forced to remain standing. This favor from God enabled me to recover the good opinion of others, which had been lost when they thought I persisted in disobedience.

After Father Salcedo's departure, I wrote to him every week, and this correspondence gave me strength to go on, although there were many times when I suffered fears and doubts before receiving his answers. Meanwhile, I had several bad falls, when I was least expecting that such a thing would happen; I would collapse while going through the cloister or the refectory or in the choir. Sometimes I hit my head so hard, in falling, that it is a wonder my skull was not fractured. But when I began falling in this way, the Voices told me not to be alarmed, that Our Lord would help me and that no harm would come to me. All would be in accordance with these words: "When he shall fall he shall not be bruised, for the Lord putteth his hand under him" (Psalm 36, v. 24).

ᵴ Chapter 5

How she began to confess to Father Jerónimo de San Eliseo, Discalced Carmelite

I spent my days in this way until the Feast of the Three Kings, when Father Jerónimo came here. He preached several sermons and the Lady Abbess conferred with him and was much pleased. She thought it would be a good idea for me to talk with him also, and indicated that I should do this. I did not feel like discussing my affairs with anyone. However, since I had many things to explain and could not find peace of mind until I revealed my thoughts—apart from the fact that such was the Prelate's wish—I decided to tell him about the most important things that had happened to me. He heard me out and gave me considerable consolation, saying that all had been in the right spirit and that he would so maintain, in the face of every opposition. He gave diligent care and attention to my needs, as his Community was not then opposed to such action on his part. He soon convinced the Lady Abbess that my fasting should be done openly and that my fare should consist of herbs. He tested me several times by having me break my fast and eat meat; there was the usual result: I immediately fell ill and my jaws became locked, so that I could not communicate. This worried him to such an extent that one day he ordered me to go to Communion even though my jaws were clenched, and said I should bear in mind that my failure to do so would be a very bad sign. I was sorely troubled and, being fearful that Our Lord would not show me His mercy in this case, I wept bitterly while imploring Him with the utmost faith, that He permit me to receive Him. In the end, I was able to do so. The Voices told me that, because I had revealed so much faith by my obedience, the Lord would show me mercy by removing my impediment. And thus it has been from that time forward; I have never again had to forego Communion on account of it.

Then I again began to faint and to fall frequently. Sometimes these attacks came upon me as I was about to go to Communion, in which case they prevented me from doing so; at other times, they occurred after I had received it. However, I did not lose my feeling of inner peace, but remained tranquil and resigned. Of course, this happened only when there was light in my soul, for when that failed, which was frequently, everything was in darkness.

That Lent, I asked the Prelate, *Doña* María Mejía, for permission to perform a penance to atone for a sin I had committed. She ordered a public mortification, thinking that the nuns might have forgotten the one I had performed in the past, and that it would be well to see how they received another. I talked the matter over with my confessor, who looked upon the idea very favorably, and ordered me to enter the refectory with a rope around my neck, to relate my faults openly, and then to lie prostrate until the Prelate should give me a signal to retire. I did all this and thereby caused considerable commotion. When Father Alarcón was informed of it, he wrote a letter expressing his vexation; this was read by Father Jerónimo, who commented upon it, as he held a contrary opinion. For some time it had been my wish to wear a coarse habit, such as is prescribed in our Rule,[34] and to take off my clogs. I conferred with my confessor, who told me to request permission in a letter to the Bishop and offered to deliver the letter himself, since the Bishop is his close friend. He said that if I had the Bishop's authorization, no one would dare oppose my desire. I wrote the letter, adding a petition in which I asked to be excused from eating meat. The Bishop received it kindly and replied that, as far as such abstinence was concerned, no permission was necessary, since the Rule prescribes it. As to the other requests, he said he was really desirous of speaking with me, so he would take action upon his return from a trip he was about to make. He asked Father Jerónimo some questions, and said he was glad to admit that, hitherto, he himself had not been well informed about me. However, time went by and the Bishop did not come to see me. He seemed to have forgotten all about his promise. I spoke of the matter to some of the older nuns, who were of the opinion that it would be a very unusual thing for a Bishop to pay such a visit; therefore, we gave up hope of it for the time being and Father Jerónimo enjoined me to forget it.

Some time later, Father Tomás de Jesús came to town, and Father Jerónimo asked me to see him without revealing my identity. I conversed with this Father for two hours, telling him all about my experiences. He said that he found nothing wrong in them; rather, he surmised that, in the past, the Lord had been leading me on toward attainment of the summit of love, and that my present state was such that, if properly guided, I would reach a high state of perfection, though, if not so directed, I was in danger of a serious downfall. He told me that I should not be concerned, either about my health or my penances, but to make Divine union my goal and my aspiration and to do this in a spirit of devotion rather than in one of anxiety. He urged Father Jerónimo to make me eat eggs and fish, saying that it was more important for me to be strong enough to pray than it was for me to fast.

At this time, Father Jerónimo went to Salamanca, but he left orders for me to follow these instructions. Soon I had a fever which forced me to retire to my cell, unable to take a step. The Lady Abbess, in view of my condition and her past experience with it, told me to adopt whatever measures I thought would cure me, adding that she did not like to have me remain secluded. Then the Voices assured me that I would soon be well if I were given permission to fulfill my promise of taking off the clogs, of dressing in coarse cloth as the Rule prescribed, and of fasting on bread and water in Advent and Lent. I told the Lady Abbess, in the presence of *Doña* María de Mercado, that if I were granted permission to fulfill these vows, I believed that Our Lord would give me health. She hesitated, because she thought there would be murmuring about the dress; but *Doña* María encouraged her, saying that, since it was in accordance with our Rule, she should not hold back on account of criticism. The Lady Abbess agreed, and on that same day I was strong enough to attend Office in the choir. I also resumed my accustomed diet of herbs.

This took place on the Feast of the Holy Cross.[35] On St. Francis' Day,[36] I appeared clothed in the habit which, here, we call *aljuba*; it is made of coarse stuff and is worn with a thick serge cowl and without clogs. Disapproval of my appearance was manifest on every face and many criticized it as a singularity. One sister even put on her cowl as a joke and went to converse with the sick nuns in mockery of me. This was a source of great mortification; but since it was my desire to be despised and to appear as the least in the Community, it did not make me suffer. On the contrary, I rejoiced in the opportunity.

I wrote of all this to Father Jerónimo, who had known nothing whatever about it. He wrote back, expressing his gratification, and said that when he ordered me to eat eggs he had merely been taking someone else's advice, since that was not his own opinion, but that, henceforth, he would ask nobody for advice. All the rest, he said, was well done and he sent me his blessing and gave me permission to undertake whatever I thought was God's Will; he was sure that everything would end well, provided I had the help of the Lord. This consoled me, and I enjoyed great peace for several months. As for my critics, when they tired of voicing their opinions, they left me alone.

Later on, several other religious, among them *Doña* Juana de Toledo, decided to make *aljubas* and wear them if they could have the Prelate's permission to do so. I myself made the one for *Doña* Juana and clothed her in it. On the day she appeared wearing it for the first time, the entire convent rose up in wrath against the Prelate because she had consented to such a proceeding and against me for having started it. The scandal was such that the matter was reported to the Dominican Fathers, and their Prior came to the grille for the purpose of issuing orders to our Community. He summoned the Prelate and many religious and told them that singularity should not continue; that the Prelate would be in a state of mortal sin if she consented to it; and that we must all take off the offending habits. The Abbess ordered the others to remove theirs, but she did not think this necessary in my case since I had been wearing mine for so long. The nuns, however, were not satisfied. They thought that, unless I took mine off, the others would begin wearing theirs again. Since the Prelate remained unconvinced, my fellow nuns sent word to Santo Tomás that

I alone was not willing to obey. The Lady Abbess learned of this and deemed it wiser for me to lay aside the offending habit in order to avoid further controversy. She sent me an order to this effect one day just as I was about to receive Holy Communion. I decided not to communicate until I had followed her orders and immediately went out and clothed myself as formerly, even to the clogs. The Superiors ordered me to take these off again, to add sleeves to the thick cowl and to make a skirt from the *aljuba*. I followed their instructions and this is the habit I am now wearing. Gossip was rife within and without the convent, as if I had clothed myself like a scarecrow, disfiguring the habit of St. Bernard. Word to this effect was sent Father Salcedo, who wrote me an indignant letter and was not appeased until he came here and saw me at the grille, first in the habit that had been devised and then in the usual garb. This disturbance took place at about the time of the Feast of the Three Kings.

Since there was no one to advise me, and since I was in great need of counsel, I begged the Lady Abbess to send for Father Eutropio, Prior of the Discalced Carmelites. Although we became good friends, he never knew nor wanted to know that I was *Doña* María Vela. Twice during that Lenten Season he visited me. I would have liked to have him take charge of me, but he did not want to do this.

Then, about the time of Pentecost, I underwent another trial. Since Francisco Díaz was insistent that I should not go to Communion and the Lady Abbess wished to have me do so, she sent for the Prior, and he comforted me greatly by directing that I should by no means omit this practice. He said as much to Francisco Díaz and I received Holy Communion, but the Chaplain was not pleased and this displeasure had the depressing effect of increasing my scruples. He said that I might not be making good confessions, since God usually sends afflictions, such as mine, in punishment for bad confessions. The Prior was absent at the time and I was desolate. I was forced to speak to Father Villena, who comforted me as best he could.

At this time, Father Jerónimo returned from Salamanca. Before I learned of his arrival, the Voices had told me that I should not be free from this affliction until he ordered me to communicate. That very day, Father Villena conferred with Father Jerónimo, who told him to command me, under obedience, to communicate, since this was the only cure for my trouble. For some time Father Villena was undecided what to do, but finally he wrote, giving me the order. I replied that I would make the effort, but that I had been given to understand I should not be able to communicate until Father Jerónimo's arrival. He wrote in reply that, in order to inspire me with greater confidence, he was letting me know that he had given his instructions with Father Jerónimo's approval, and he repeated them. On the following day, I was able to communicate and Father Jerónimo came to see me, but I was unconscious, having collapsed immediately after Communion. He sent orders that I should arise and come to him. I did this at once and told him everything that was happening. He encouraged me to suffer and put an end to my scruples. In three or four days, it pleased the Lord to have my trouble disappear. Later on, I was to suffer abundantly, for the Carmelites were denied permission to come to the convent, a decision which the Prior took to heart.

One month before the Feast of St. Bernard,[37] the fainting spells returned just as I was going to Communion and the Voices gave me to understand that I would be unable to communicate until St. Bernard's Day and then only at the command of the Father. There was nothing to be done, either by writing myself to the Prior or by having the Lady Abbess request him to see me at least once. I decided to write to Father Jerónimo and send the letter through Father Villena, who would ask him to answer me. Father Villena did indeed kindly take the note and brought back the reply, in which Father Jerónimo expressly ordered me to go to Communion, adding that he understood the Lord had punished me because I slackened in my exercises. On the same evening that this answer arrived, the Chaplain had told me I should inform the Lady Abbess that, in his opinion, I should be exorcised as before. She laughed at this and said it was not to be mentioned again. It was Our Lord's pleasure that, the next morning, I was enabled to take Communion easily; and thereupon all real anxiety about me came to an end, though hitherto every one of the nuns had wished to become my adviser, when I was bereft of Father Jerónimo.

Later on, permission was obtained for Father Jerónimo to hear my confessions once a fortnight, but after all the trouble about it, he stayed here only about two months more.

⚜ Chapter 6

How her confessor left, and what happened to her until she had a permanent confessor once more

On Wednesday of Easter Week, Father Jerónimo went away. I was so tired of seeking a confessor that I simply gave up. Since my brother, Father Lorenzo, was here, I consulted him about my problems and followed his advice. By the time he left town, I had become acquainted with you, although I did not yet owe you obedience. Instead of feeling troubled about not having a confessor, I rather enjoyed being free to seek counsel wherever I could.

Before my brother's departure, which took place around St. John's Day,[38] the Inquisitor came to this town and this convent to read the edicts.[39] I felt no anxiety as to what he might be told about me. The Inquisitor delegated his powers over the convent to Father Alarcón, to whom all the nuns went with their problems—most of which, I understood, concerned me. The Chaplain warned me to be on guard, since certain religious had made remarks about me which he had believed at the time, and he supposed they would say the same things to Father Alarcón, whom he advised me to consult in self-defense.

I replied that, since my conscience was clear, I felt in no need to defend myself; I was willing they should say what they pleased. His answer was that, under such circumstances, it was still right for me to go and unburden myself. I did go to Father Alarcón and he said that I did well to present myself since, otherwise, I might be deemed guilty. For his part, he had been confirmed in his previous opinion that I was meddlesome and caused scandal in the convent; that many nuns had come to him with adverse reports about me, but that he had given heed to only seven, namely the following:[40]

I

That the nuns should not commend themselves to the saints, since these did not hear our prayers.

Il

That, since God inspired me with knowledge of whatever He wished me to do, I needed counsel from no one else.

III

That I did not wish to submit myself to obedience because God, Who is above obedience to superiors and confessors, governed me Himself.

IV

That I did not care about praying aloud because silent prayer sufficed.

V

That my works were not to be done in secret, but publicly, so that everyone could see them.

VI

That I would deem it a privilege to be brought before the Inquisition.

VII

That when I was very weak from illness, I said to those who urged me to eat, "Why not leave this in God's hands?"

VIII

That when asked to pray for a soul's conversion, it had been revealed to me the soul would not soon be converted and, consequently, I had ceased praying for it.

I answered to all this that I did not recall having said any of these things, although some statements of mine might have been misinterpreted. With regard to the first charge, namely that I had alleged the saints do not hear our prayers, it was my recollection I was requested one day by a religious to recommend the recovery of some sick person to God, because He Who hears His saints would restore the invalid's health through their intervention; and I had replied that I had heard Father Julían de Avila say, when Our Lord does not wish to grant what we ask through the intercession of the saints, He sees to it that they do not understand our prayers; and, in that case, they will not intercede with Him. I had said this and nothing more. As to the other charges, I might have said something on which to base them, but I did not remember having done so. When Father Alarcón heard my explanations, so at variance from the tales which had been brought to him, he was astounded and decided to pay no more attention to the other accounts. I took up a certain problem of mine with him and then we discussed other matters. In the end, he talked freely with me, admitting that, in the past, he had acted and spoken in accordance with the indirect information he had received. I felt no resentment and we parted as good friends. A few days later, he wrote me the letter which you read and in which it is made abundantly clear that Our Lord always comes to my rescue in my hour of need.

Soon after leaving the Father's presence, I began to feel greatly depressed by sadness and a sense of darkness. It seemed to me that, since so many persons condemned me, I must be guilty without being spiritually capable of realizing this and, if that were the case, all my striving for perfection was futile and might as well cease. This conviction was torture to me; the devil assailed me with thoughts that my plight was hopeless, and I did nothing but weep, without knowing what to do nor where to seek counsel.

It seemed to me that I was the target for fiery darts which I could not withstand, that heaven and earth had both rejected me and that hell was opening to receive me. After a night spent in such a state of affliction, I could not calm myself sufficiently to take Communion the next morning. The nuns, who were all watching to see what I would do next, asked the Lady Abbess to lay her commands on me in the name of obedience. But I replied that I could not obey until I had spoken with Francisco Díaz and they left me alone.

After High Mass, I talked to him in detail about my troubles. He was moved to compassion and comforted me greatly. Our Lord put words into his mouth to restore my soul. He instructed me to take food and to rest, since he realized that, aside from being enfeebled by the tears I had shed, I was almost at death's door from sheer anguish. I think that this was one of my darkest hours.

With this, I make an end to my tale of trials and tribulations; of other burdens still heavier, you are already informed. I will only add that all those, both priests and lay persons, who looked at me askance, were nevertheless guided by good intentions and truly desired what was best for my soul. Therefore, through God's mercy, I have never complained of anyone nor shown any resentment or sorrow nor lost my peace of mind. Of these failings I have never had to excuse myself. May the Lord be blessed in everything and may He use my sufferings to give me strength for whatever lies in store for me, so that He may be glorified in it all. And may you, my Father, plead for me. May Our Lord be with you and increase your knowledge of Divine love.

❧ Chapter 7

In which she tells how she came to know Dr. Vaquero and by what means he treated her in matters concerning her spiritual welfare

You have ordered me to continue the story of my life. I shall try to do this, with God's help, though I find it difficult; I do not know why. Let me begin by saying that, on the first day I spoke with you, your spirit and mine seemed in such complete accord and I felt so deeply satisfied and so encouraged, that I hardly recognized myself. And all because I had found that for which I had yearned so long: someone deeply experienced in all that pertains to the spirit and in supernatural prayer. However, in spite of this great consolation, I had no thought at the time of giving obedience to anyone; I only thought that, when oppressed by doubt or conscious of need, I would call upon you for advice. I considered that Our Lord had shown me a great favor in making you willing to hear and counsel me. It was with this feeling that I used to converse with you when you came to see *Doña* María, more on her account than on mine. Nevertheless, Our Lord soon began to manifest the esteem and love in which He holds your soul; and it appeared that mine, however arid and distracted it might be, needed only to compose itself and withdraw within itself to perceive this. For, one day when I asked the Lord to enlighten me—that was my practice because, as I said, I then owed obedience to no one—He turned a deaf ear to me, even though I importuned Him repeatedly. At last, after Communion, the Voices told me: "This is my beloved Son, in whom I am well pleased: hear ye him" (Matthew 17, v. 5).

I understood that these words were addressed to you and that it was His Will I should hearken to them and obey you; that by these means He would give me the light which I sought. For many days, I remained in a state of great wonderment, and whenever I besought His Majesty to indicate His Will, the Voices repeated what they had said before, until at last I resolved to resist no longer; I saw clearly that it would please Him if I placed myself in your hands. Therefore, I begged you to be so good as to take charge of my soul and you, with that charity which Our Lord has given you, received me without heeding the trouble which this might cause you. And it has been clearly indicated that such were His Majesty's wishes, for when I thought the matter over during Meditation, saying, "Lord, it is You Who has placed me in his hands," I was told, "Bear in mind that, even when I seem to leave thee, I am with thee; because I have given thee into the care of another who can guide thee." I was greatly comforted by this merciful message.

For several months, though I could give you an account of those matters which seemed most important to me, I could not actually go to you in confession, because it was not considered prudent at that time that anyone should know you were advising me. I merely kept to the usual routine, without making a change in my way of life. Following the Feast of the Purification, I suffered great aridity of spirit; and after Easter Sunday, I retired to my cell for eight days, and did not leave it from the time of the noonday meal until I went to Matins the following morning. At this period, I suffered from a sense of abandonment and melancholy and emerged from seclusion more depressed than when I retired.

◄§{ Chapter 8

New attacks of fainting on going to Communion

Meanwhile, I again began to experience such great faintness in going to Holy Communion that I was prevented from receiving it. At times, I collapsed before reaching the Communion window. Nevertheless, I had great confidence that, if you were to order me to do this, I could; for, besides the promises made to me by the Voices, you have also given me to understand that, in the case of such a command, I should be able to carry it out. You did not share my confidence, but were proceeding rather slowly, until I decided to write you, suggesting that the remedy employed by Father Jerónimo was made under obedience. The note in question brought about a decision on your part and, without my knowledge, you issued an order to me, under obedience, while you were praying in a place unknown to me and, at that precise moment, I was able to go to Communion without fainting or falling. I immediately improved in health, though I had been very ill and, moreover, was left with such a sense of interior peace and buoyancy that, until you came and told me what you had done, I wondered how so sudden a change could have been possible. I think the period while I enjoyed good health and peace of mind lasted four or five months. Then I again began to fall down whenever I attempted to approach the Communion rail, until you ordered me not to collapse or, if I fell, to rise again.

I also suffered from periods of faintness and many physical indispositions which, at times, forced me to retire to my cell. You did not seem much concerned about the faintness, for it disappeared or was alleviated when I resumed my special diet. I overcame the other ailments when you commanded me to go back to Choir and my other exercises. This took place many times, to the astonishment of everyone at the convent.

⚜ Chapter 9

How she openly took Dr. Vaquero as her confessor for the rest of her life

After having dealt with you in secret for some ten months, as I said—and keeping the secret in a house like this was as miraculous as any of the rest—I learned that Father Jerónimo was coming back to town. On the one hand, I wanted him to find me permanently settled with you; but, on the other, it was essential that Father Julían de Avila, under whose obedience I still remained, should give permission to that effect. Both you and I, in view of past experiences, had misgivings on this score. I decided to speak to him, trusting that he would agree, if such were Our Lord's Will. I informed him of my resolution and asked him to give me a confessor to whom I could entrust my soul, which I was placing in his hands. He was pleased to learn that I had no wish to return to Father Jerónimo and told me that he considered you more than sufficient for my purposes, and that he would enjoin you to take charge of me; but he said that, in this case, I must prove myself to be a woman of strong character;[41] that if I placed myself in Dr. Vaquero's keeping, I should not seek another's. This I promised to do and, with God's help, I shall comply.

I ceased to be discomfited and confused as soon as I was able to deal with you openly and confess to you whenever I could see you. In this way, I was offered a good opportunity to mortify myself, for the saintly Father directed that Francisco Díaz should also take part in guiding me. But, thanks to the Lord and your wisdom, all difficulties were smoothed out.

Soon afterward, around Pentecost, I made a general confession, which I deemed necessary in the light of what might happen later. My faith in obedience, my love for it and confidence in it, were becoming stronger; and Our Lord wished to test these by letting the evil spirit torment me, whether in preventing me from going to Communion by causing attacks of faintness, or in raising scruples and causing confusion which might undermine my obedience to you. But as all this was not sufficient—for the Lord in His infinite goodness enlightened me to recognize these devilish tricks—the demon tried several times to put an end to my life. First, he fractured my skull on St. Benedict's Day, when the silver crosier fell from its place and cut deeply into my head. It was a miracle that this did not strike me dead then and there—or so thought the surgeon, who said I had my cranium cracked. But as the Lord was preserving me for greater toils, He healed me that night by miraculous means. I begged the Blessed Virgin to help me and placed a rosary of yours on my head; then I retired to prayer and was told that this Lady would care for me and cure me through the owner of the rosary. On the following morning, the incision in the head was closed. Only the gash left by the crosier was open and this healed without forming pus or giving me fever. Before the month was over, I was back at Matins and attending to my obligations.

Not long afterward, since this stratagem had not worked, the malign spirit devised another: namely, to constrict my throat with the quinsy, so that I would feel as if I were being choked. This was especially noticeable one night in Choir, when all those around me thought I was dying. Thrice before I could see you, I suffered such attacks. You diagnosed these forthwith as the devil's doing and ordered me, under obedience, to be up and about. They did not recur for some time.

Around the Feast of the Three Kings, I felt a great pain in my side and thought that my end was near. The Voices told me that I would not die, but would be healed by obedience in the same way as on previous occasions, and they said to you, "The God of gods shall be seen in Sion" (Psalm 83, v. 8), and they also told you that you would witness marvels. I interpreted this as meaning that Our Lord would cure me through you and felt sure that such was God's Will. Therefore, my only desire was for you to believe this, too, and order it under obedience. But you, like a very prudent man, bided your time. Rashly, I believed that you were lacking in faith, resisting God's Will or delaying its enactment, so as not to arouse comment by this unusual method. I was a prey to anxiety, thinking that every other consideration should be overborne in order to carry out God's aims, never realizing that I was trying to cloak my own selfish will.

While I was revolving these thoughts in my mind, you wrote me that I should endeavor to comply with the Divine aims, for you believed me to be faltering. You also believed that God would then disclose what was best for me and that, in due time, you would call on me. And you gave me to understand that I was not yet prepared to receive God's wonders. This note dismayed me, because though I neither recognized nor understood any such lack of resignation, I strove, by acts of faith, to comply in every way—all to no avail! The detainment was not by force of will, but simply by God's grace, when He was pleased to grant it at His Infinite goodness.

That night, not knowing the why or wherefore, I found myself without these troubled and restless thoughts, careless of my cares,[42] resigned to God's purpose and not leaning so heavily on what had been revealed to you or to me, or even on obedience, where I had placed so much faith. These things no longer seemed to me to represent God's Will. This conclusion was contrary to what I had been given to understand. And I was disconsolate in the belief that, through some fault of mine, obedience and the Will of Our Lord had not been in concurrence.

To go back to my story: for about two days, I had enjoyed this state of mind. Then, on the Feast of the Purification, you sent me word to dress and come to the confessional. The day before was the twenty-first that I had been in pain, for I had suffered a new attack and had been very ill. I received Holy Communion with a sense of supreme peace, and went to the choir to sing the Mass and play the organ. Then I went to serve at the refectory, greatly to the surprise of all the nuns and the still greater surprise of the doctors. Eight days later, Lent began and I abstained from meat and never missed my duties in choir. Blessed be the Lord in all His works!

During Easter week, I began suffering again from attacks of faintness when the bell rang for Matins. I could not go to Choir nor even get up until after Mass and, consequently, I could not receive Holy Communion. You let me suffer, although you fully realized that this was a ruse of the devil. I endured with a sense of peace and inner joy whatsoever Our Lord desired of me. This must have upset the enemy, for he threatened me with the tribulations which I have endured for fifteen months in all, and I can think of no other reason. This deadly foe has employed a variety of inventions and ruses to

separate me from God and from the obedience I owe you.
But it has all been like raining pitchforks on his own head, to
his greater confusion. For, by virtue of Christ Crucified, Satan
has been despised, confounded and conquered by the Lord's
ministers, while the devil has gnashed his teeth and shuddered
at the power which God has given His Own.

After this futile threat on St. Philip's and St. James' Day,[43]
I suffered no more fainting attacks, but when I rose and went
to confession, my spirit became so confused, as I left the confessional, that I did not know what I was doing, nor could
I calm myself or shake off a sensation of sadness. I surmised
that some great toil was in the offing, so I went back to the
confessional and told you what I was experiencing. You ordered me to go to Communion; but I wished to receive at
High Mass and collapsed before it started. Although I was
resigned to the Divine Will, I was afflicted in the usual way.
Every day, my ailment became worse and, with it, my fears
and distress and, for thirteen days, I could not communicate.
You were very kind to me, coming to see me every day and
consoling me by saying you had been told I should not fear,
since the Lord would supply me with fortitude. You sympa-
thized with me, but you were also concerned lest, if the ailment were to last a month, it would bring my life to an end.
I think it was Divine Providence that restored me to health
for a few days, in order that we might unbosom our feelings
to each other and gladden our hearts, so that our wills would
be better disposed to welcome the tribulations which were to
pour down upon us, for, so far, I had received them half-
heartedly.

After thirteen days of great affliction, on the Friday before
Pentecost, you came to say Mass, determined to give me Communion, full of confidence that I would be released from my
handicaps and able to receive. You ordered me to do so under
obedience and I communicated with a sense of great peace.

The clouds were lifted from my soul and the light came back. With the purpose of encouraging me to suffer and to trust that, in His goodness, He would not abandon me, the Lord was bountiful in His Mercies during Communion. But I felt certain that He would not relieve me of my tribulations altogether.

They were absent for fifteen days, but returned on the Saturday within the Octave of the Blessed Sacrament, more furiously than ever before. I was so confused and ashamed that I did not dare raise my eyes to the altar and continually burst into tears because of the great torture this caused me. Finally, on Wednesday, I was put to bed, for my weakness was such that it seemed I was about to expire. The nuns sent for you and I confessed to you from my bed, for you greatly feared I would give up the ghost. On Friday, you came back to give me Communion and say Mass. While we were both giving thanks to the Lord, you were asked by the Voices, 'Why shouldst thou be concerned if I am pleased to see her suffer?" And I myself was told, "My grace is sufficient for thee." [44] I felt greatly consoled and encouraged to suffer. For this was the Lord's method: as you were always depending on prayer and trusting in His Majesty, He hastened to enlighten you in your doubts and difficulties, giving you words of comfort and assuring me of His Divine help and favor and giving me grace to persevere. This kept me from becoming the prey of manifold troubles, though they were increasing in number and quality, for the evil spirit "goeth and taketh with him seven other spirits more wicked than himself." [45] They exhausted me with their shadows and with the memories of persons and things past and I was in constant fear of offending the Lord, although I called upon Him continually for aid.

On the Eve of the Visitation, when I had cast out the shadow of that evil spirit, he came back, under the guise of silence. This caused me great distress, for it was highly important that I should speak out; a prolonged silence could well be the cause of my perdition. This was precisely what the demon wished to bring about. He put such difficulties in the way of my speech that I remained mute for three days. On the fourth day, I became the prey of scruples, but did not report this. So I told you I could not make even a short confession, still less explain my troubles. I begged you to ask the Lord for enlightenment. As usual, His Majesty hastened to our aid and you told me that clarification had already been granted. I was filled with wonder that you could so cheer and console me, as if all this were your own immediate concern. In short, it was God's mercy and His work.

As a result, the enemy was so enraged and resolute that he caused you to fall downstairs and bleed profusely, for the Lord was permitting him greater scope. And Our Lord accepted the act of charity which you offered, together with your blood, for the good of my soul. Despite this accident, you made an effort to see me, for you were more concerned over my ailments than your own, but the enemy was not content with his first attempt against you: nine days later, he caused you to fall down another stairway and break two bones which, when poulticed, made you suffer great pain. I felt this deeply because I knew that it was on my account you were obliged to endure so much. Nevertheless, I realized that, in the end, such suffering would bring a higher reward to you and greater confusion to the evil one; for you emerged from this trial more vigorous than ever, and determined to help me in my afflictions, even though they should continue for a lifetime. That is what you have been doing these fifteen months past, hastening to my aid every day, overcoming difficulties and bearing with my peculiarities and melancholy and all the rest. I hope the Lord is preparing a well-deserved reward in heaven for this patient endurance, because you are moved to do these things by sheer charity and by the desire to please Our Lord. You have given ample proof of these generous motives. May the Lord's name be praised!

My difficulties increased a hundredfold. Often my strength was so drained away that I had neither the capacity nor the vitality for more burdens.

But, on the Feast of St. James,[46] Our Lord chose to favor me by removing the handicaps I had suffered, so I was able to receive Communion at the second Mass and felt so strong that I was convinced I was again perfectly well. I, therefore, deemed it to be God's Will that I should descend to the lower choir, where I performed my normal obligations at Terce and, later, at Vespers. On the following evening, the Feast of St. Anne,[47] I was present during the entire Office. I was also able to take Communion on that day. Then the tempter began to insinuate that I need not write you because—since the Lord had relieved me of my handicaps—He wished to start a new order of things. In this, He would be my guide and I could and should take Communion freely. There should be no objection on your part to this schedule—also said the tempter. If there were, I would again be unable to communicate. I suspected that this advice might be another snare of the tempter and decided to write and ask your opinion. I went into no details; I said only that I was well again. You ordered me to communicate and, accordingly, I went down to the choir.

For a whole year now, it has always been necessary for you to impose obedience upon me in order to enable me to confess; and on many occasions, the command has not, in itself, been sufficient. For, when I began my confession, or even when I knelt in the confessional, the enemy would knock me down, so that only by dint of your order I could rise, trembling and shedding tears all the while. I found it difficult to utter even a few words; you had to do most of the talking.

The same thing has happened with regard to Communion throughout the past year; when you were not at hand, I have seldom been able to receive. One favor the Lord has granted me for the assuagement of my troubles: the enemy could not prevail if you wished to exercise the power the Lord has given you. The stubborn enemy has come back many times and, as many, has gone away, helter-skelter. I suffered an attack thrice the same morning and thrice rallied in the name of Christ Crucified. Often, when I have tried to receive the Host from your hands, the enemy has wrenched back my head; and were he allowed, he would toss me a hundred leagues hence. However, he could do no harm unless he were given license such as he has been permitted when, by assuming different disguises, he wearied my soul.

On St. Matthew's Day,[48] some eight days before the Feast of St. Michael, I suffered an attack which I thought would lead to my death. The tempter took advantage of my melancholy state, insinuating that I had already fallen into his clutches and that I would die in mortal sin that very night. I seemed to be surrounded by a legion of evil spirits which were walking about my bed to watch me die and take me to hell. I was in a state of both physical and spiritual turmoil, striking out aimlessly and calling aloud in a way that made everyone at my bedside weep. Yet no one sent for you, since all felt you would come early in the morning anyway. The result was that my agony increased; I felt sure day would never dawn for me and I shouted that if you did not arrive, I would surely go to hell. When the nuns finally recognized the state I was in, they managed to get the door open and send for you, late at night though it was.[49] Indeed, the Lord's Will was made manifest that I should confess and become calmer.

Several days earlier, I had wished you to say a Mass for me, believing, as I did, that the Holy Sacrifice could put an end to all my troubles. This Mass was postponed about fifteen times, from day to day, one of them the day when I was so ill. Finally, on the Eve of St. Michael,[50] you said a Mass for my intention; by Our Lord's mercy I was well and at peace for the next four weeks, as if surrounded by the light of His love. When, at this time, you were considering whether or not you would allow me to go to the choir, you were told by the Voices, "Leave her alone. What is it to thee? Let others judge as they will."

At the end of those four weeks, my soul began to be clouded by a lack of quietude, sure portent that trouble was again at hand. You tried to console me by saying that such trials purified the soul and that I should submit to the Divine Will accordingly. Fatuously, I answered that, by this time, I should have already been purified sufficiently. You reproved me for my arrogance and the Lord punished me by permitting the devil to torture me anew. On the Feast of St. Simon and St. Jude,[51] I was surely bereft of my senses, for I desired neither to see you nor to speak with you. There were many such days which, of course, was exactly what the devil desired; he might well have brought about my total perdition, had it not been for the fact that I had vowed obedience to you. Against this vow, neither all the difficulties which beset me nor the machinations of the evil one could prevail. Despite his efforts to silence me, I was obliged to acquaint you with my condition. And immediately the clouds of my disquietude lifted; my sense of devotion returned and the sun of peace shone anew.

Around this time I experienced great joy because of the tidings that I might expect my death any day, if I were properly disposed. But, since I still lack the preparation that Our Lord wishes for me, the day has not arrived, nor will it come until the Lord Himself thoroughly cleanses and prepares the house of my soul. With these thoughts, at the same time joyful and sorrowful, I have filled my days.

On Christmas Eve, you directed me to come down to the choir. I attended Vespers and Compline and, in the early morning, I was getting ready for Communion when I began to fear that I might not be able to receive it, though my spirit was at peace. I went to confession at the confessional,[52] but on going back to the choir for Communion, I had an attack of faintness that prevented me from receiving. The nuns notified you and you said Mass in the high choir and gave me Communion. This was the first time, among the many to which I have referred, when it seemed as if someone pulled back my head and hindered me from reaching out to receive. It was as if the Lord were pleased to see that I received it only from your hands.

On New Year's Eve, I thought my end had come. When you arrived the next day, to hear me confess, you found me so weak and emaciated that you feared I was dying, although, in fact, I felt as greatly at peace as if I did not have to render an account to God. But my time had not yet come and I remained here to endure more suffering. My pain was excruciating as I watched new visions of the Crucified Saviour drift shadowlike before my eyes and I was told that I could not now excuse myself from worshiping Him. Then I was led to understand that I might have committed an act of idolatry, since the vision could have been the devil in disguise. In my desperation and anguish, I was the embodiment of a lost soul. I cried out to the Lord in my despair, but my supplication went unheard; rather I felt that I had been cast out from His Presence. Had you not been here at that time, had you not written to me and talked with me and strengthened me with the faith which your words always gave, I am convinced that I should have lost my mind.

In the month of May, about the time of St. John's Day,[53] the statue of Our Lady of Sanzoles[54] was brought to town. You decided to say a Mass for me and to offer your life for mine. Your prayers were heard. While you were stricken with a high fever, my health improved over a period of several days. But soon my physical sufferings returned and would have overwhelmed me if I had not been able to retain my peace of mind. I entreated the Lord, both in your behalf and in mine, and His Majesty listened to me. Your condition improved and, although for a fortnight you could not move about, I bore my sufferings more patiently. The tempest had spent itself, even though I was unable to receive Holy Communion; that I could never do when you were away.

On Ascension Day, I obeyed your injunction to go to the choir, but returned so exhausted, after forcing myself to take part in the Divine Office—which lasted many hours—that I was obliged to keep to my bed for three days.

Then came the Feast of the Blessed Sacrament. As a general rule, it is on the holiest days that I suffer most, in order that I might esteem more highly the favor He wished to grant me. That night I was in a state of great affliction; and while I besought heaven to help me, it occurred to me that if you would give me a written message, ordering the tempter to leave me, he would do so and that, thus, the Lord might be willing to free me from the clutches of the devil for at least two or three days. I turned this idea over and over in my mind, though fearful of displeasing the Lord with my procrastination. But at last I wrote you a note, saying I felt sure I would get well if you would be kind enough to send me that slip of paper. You placed this plea in God's hands so promptly that I was relieved of my trouble, which did not return—except for two days while you were in Madrid—for three months and a half.

That journey of yours lasted for fifteen days. The day before you left for the capital I was given up as lost; my condition had never been so critical. By God's mercy, you had not yet departed. I was almost out of my mind because of the clamor when you came to the grille the evening before and expressed regret at being unable to see me. The tempter began whispering to me that I was too much attached to you, that this attachment kept God from operating within my soul as He could if it were void of all earthly affection; and the tempter pretended that only therein might lie my offense. I was calm and at peace when these insinuations began and, consequently, could not immediately persuade myself that these were reproofs from an evil spirit. The belief that it was otherwise, however, became a torture for which I could find no relief, except continual weeping. After all, you know better than I the plight in which my soul found itself; how close it was to being wrecked and lost, and how and with what difficulty I was saved from that dark storm and brought back into the light.

Coming back to my story, you finally left for Madrid and stayed there for a fortnight. During this whole time, I was unable to receive Communion, since, though the devil's hands were otherwise tied, he was at liberty to prevent my receiving the Sacrament. Consequently, I could communicate only when you were present.

On St. Lawrence's Day,[55] you sent the second note, which was like the first, except that in this one you mentioned only the Holy Eucharist. From that time forth, I could take Communion even if you were not there in person, and I have gone on being able to do so up to the present time; but I could not go to confession in spite of all my efforts. Once, as I was beginning to confess to another priest, I was thrown to the ground.

This is the present state of my soul. I am expectant of whatever the Lord may ordain for my life, since my whole desire is to love Him with the utmost purity and complete detachment from all earthly things. May His Majesty accomplish this in me for His greater glory! [56]

*

I wish to jot down here the illuminating thoughts Our Lord has been shedding on my mind and yours, from the beginning of these troubles, through the intercession of Our Blessed Lady, in order that we may be prompted to praise the Lord for the protection with which He has shielded my soul.

Remonstrating with the Lord for my desolation, I was told, "What consolation did I have on the cross?" Asking Him to make it possible for me to receive Him, He replied, "She who is My true spouse is contented to do My Will."

Many times, I was told, "I shall give thee fortitude. Be not affrighted. I love Her more than I love thee. 'It is hard for thee to kick against the goad' (Acts 26, v. 14)."

"I will come and heal him." [57]

"Fear not that I will desert thee until thou attainest perfect resignation."

When I begged the Lord that I might be able to receive Holy Communion, I was told, "This is the best way of purifying thyself."

To show me very clearly how different are the Lord's ways from ours, the Voices reminded me of the verses in the Psalms:

"Who giveth snow like wool: scattereth mists like ashes.

"He sendeth his crystal like morsels: who shall stand before the face of his cold?

"He shall send out his word, and shall melt them: his wind shall blow, and the waters shall run" (Psalms 147, v. 16-18).

By this, the Voices meant to convince me that my soul could be tried, if the Lord wished to purify it as were the three youths—Sidrach, Misach and Abdenago—who were thrown into the furnace of Babylon, which had been heated seven times. The Psalter might well have read: "Who shall turn snow into fire and fire into snow?"

God lets me know how much He loves my soul and how greatly He rejoices at having made it conform to His in order that it may help carry His Son's cross.

I was told, "God is faithful, who will not suffer you to be tempted above that which you are able." [58] This is especially true of one who has always wished to serve Him; and He would wish you, my spiritual Father, to fly to my rescue.

Christ Crucified was represented to me, meaning that He wanted my soul to be crucified also.

"I have told thee already that there is nothing to fear. I may let thee die to give thee a new life in Me."

"This is the change of the right hand of the Most High" (Psalm 76, v. 11), meaning to say that one must be first tried in a crucible to be purified.

"He who does not carry his cross is not worthy of Me." [59]

"The gates of hell shall not prevail against it" (Matthew 16, v. 18).

"Just as the body cannot live without a head, the soul cannot live without one who governs it."

"Is not the Lord in the midst of us? no evil shall come upon us." [60]

The Voices told me that Our Lord desires you to comfort and strengthen me, and help me to bear this cross, and they asked how should His Majesty fail one who wearied only in striving not to offend Him?

My soul was portrayed in the mighty arms of the Lord, Who said, "Who then shall separate us from the love of Christ? Shall tribulation? or distress? or famine? or nakedness? or danger? or persecution? or the sword? (As it is written: *For thy sake we are put to death all the day long. We are accounted as sheep for the slaughter.*) But in all these things we overcome, because of Him that hath loved us." [61]

"Is it not thy joy to suffer for My glory?"

"Thy labor will not cease. But I will give thee My Mother for thy comforter and companion."

I should have perpetually in my mouth the invocation, "Mary, Mother of Grace, Mother of Mercy."

How could He abandon one whom He had chosen? Fear was my safeguard; without it, I should have been endangered.

"Did My words fail thee, perchance? 'He shall cry to me and I will hear him: I am with him in tribulation, I will deliver him, and I will glorify him' (Psalm 90, v. 15)."

I was shown a towering cliff lashed by furious waves that could not destroy it.

"Tell her to fear not, for My hand is powerful: 'For my hand shall help him: and my arm shall strengthen him. And I will cut down his enemies before his face; and them that hate him I will put to flight' (Psalm 88, v. 22 & 24)."

I saw the rock so tall that its summit was lost from sight.

"Thou shalt see My Will fulfilled in her. She is My beloved; who shall separate her from me?"

When I asked for health, I was told, "Thou art more pleasing to Me as thou art."

"Let her be; disregard the judgment of others. What does gold lose by passing through fire?"

When I said that I was unworthy to be His spouse, I was shown Christ bound to the pillar and told, "The lashes were still more unworthy of God."

When I asked the Lord to remove a certain temptation, I was told, "Every temptation is dangerous without My help."

"The greater the peril, the greater the victory."

"Bid him be strong in suffering."

"Now thou art My true daughter."

Showing me Christ Crucified, the Voices said to me: "If I give thee what I took for Myself, how can I show thee better the love I have for thee?"

"Tell her that I shall be her faithful friend."

"Before wheat is placed on My table it must be ground."

I saw the rock risen from the waters soaring toward heaven.

I saw myself dangling by a hair over hell, but the hair was strong because it was in God's hand.

The Voices told me, "If any stain has remained on thy soul, all that thou sufferest against thy will will purify thee."

"The rose looks best amid thorns."

"Many waters cannot quench charity, neither can the floods drown it" (Cant. 8, v. 7).

"Thou hast handed thy heart over to Me; I hold it in My hand. Therefore, thou shalt not sin, since thou hast My grace."

"I would have thee repay what thou owest Me by giving Me thy trust as thy sincere friend."

"Fire has not touched thee. 'The fire had no power on their bodies, and not a hair of their head had been singed, nor their garments altered, nor the smell of the fire had passed on them' " (Daniel 3, v. 94).

"I gave thee My promise never to fail thee, and now I give it again. I shall be thy right arm. In My strength, thou wilt conquer every enemy, and in My virtue thou canst accomplish everything."

"Now is the time of testing; thus gold is purified by fire. Here thou shalt die completely, so that thou mayest live for God."

"In this way, thy betrothal to Christ will be confirmed and thou wilt be united to Him for all eternity."

"The longer the trial, the more is God glorified."

"I do not wish to heal thee, because I wish to see thee delighting in Me."

"Whenever thou perseverest in calling Me, thou wilt find Me."

"Though I afflict thee, I do not forsake thee; and if I could,

I would be sorry for thy afflictions, because I love thee so much. It becomes thy soul so that it may be purified and shine brightly without any stain and join Me in heaven. This is the purgatory thou asked of Me. This will be thy bliss and thou shalt enjoy Me forever."

Chapter 10

She resumes the story of her life and tribulations

I have written the foregoing account at your express command. Two years and four months ago, toward the end of Lent in the year 1608, I completed the final section of this story of my life. Our Lord has been pleased to prolong my days to the present time, so that I might suffer the more for His sake. Blessed be His Holy Name!

Now, while I am still yearning for the Lord to bring this exile to an end, you charge me to continue the narrative. Although there is no lack of material to make a long story, my memory is failing and I have not been keeping notes, so there is very little that I can say. With God's help, I shall set down everything I remember.

On Easter Sunday, after Holy Communion, desirous of suffering affront and contumely in imitation of Our Lord, I was given to understand that, if I continued to bear with resignation troubles like those of the past, I should have my wish fulfilled; and it was further revealed to me that I should set little value on suffering in this life. I volunteered to undergo whatever trials were given me, if it were by His Will and with His help. This was like preparing myself for war, because, before that day was over, tribulations came back as in the beginning, with every aggravating circumstance. The little strength I had left began to fail me when I tried to follow the Community. I was forced to retire to my cell and, with utmost regret, to go for confession and Communion in the high choir. Before long, I found myself once more unable to receive the Lord unless you were present.

I recall one of these days you wished to make an experiment in order to ascertain whether all this was imagination on my part. Without my knowing anything about it, you commanded the adversary to depart. You issued the command under obedience, but without making the act of faith, which was your usual practice. The command had no effect, and my jaws remained locked. You gave the order once again, but accompanied it this time by a strong act of faith; and I was cured. Only then did you reveal to me what you had done. We both marveled greatly. Blessed be the Lord forevermore!

The same thing happened with regard to my fainting. Whenever I was conversing with you and waiting for the Chaplain to bring the Blessed Sacrament, I collapsed and fainted. Then you would order the tempter to depart and tell me to recover my strength, and I would do so. This occurred on countless occasions. If you had not been present so to help me, I should have been unable to receive the Blessed Sacrament for months on end. Since all doors were closed to me, and God opened no new gate, this was, for the time being, my last resort. Because it was so extraordinary, a few persons took notice of it, and raised the question as to whether it was well done. They began gossiping about the matter to such an extent that it caused us no little grief. You had taken every precaution to avoid becoming conspicuous and were hesitant about being present when I took Communion. However, when you saw my great tribulation on the one hand and, on the other, my extreme need for the Divine food of the Eucharist, you dared not leave me, since, whenever you did so, I was unable to recover. There was an instance of this on the Octave of the Blessed Sacrament, that is, on the day when we celebrate this feast in the convent here.[62] You had just left when the Chaplain brought up the Sacred Host. Immediately, I felt faint and dropped my head, nor could I raise it for Communion. Simultaneously, I was afflicted by such a racking cough that the congregation in the church noticed it. I was taken to my cell, which you had to enter in order to heal me, by bidding the enemy to leave me. When he presses me so hard, I fear that he will smother me, as would have happened on more than one occasion if God had permitted it.

The tempest passed and my health improved. However, my inner peace did not last long. Because you saw that I frequently had to forego Communion, unless you were present, but recognized at the same time that, since your presence and commands were so much out of the ordinary, they might occasion scandal, you decided to consult another religious, a very learned and spiritual man. He replied that so long as the Prelate—the Abbess—did not decide otherwise, you should not abandon me, because I was in great need of your assistance. He said that you should pay no heed to the inconveniences, but should continue as heretofore. You were satisfied with this advice. But a few days after this, the Abbess, for good and sufficient reasons of her own, related all of this to another learned religious of the same Order, and advised you of that fact, saying that it was necessary for him to confer with you. After the conference, he decided that it was best for you not to be present when I took Communion, even though I were to remain an entire year without communicating; and he told the Abbess not to give you permission to enter within the walls, even if I were dying.

I did not know about this at the time. I knew only that you left me alone, and I bowed to the Divine Will, in the belief that His Majesty would find some means of having me receive Him when He wished. I could not communicate for many days; not until I fell ill with a tertian fever and was thus doubly affected: by illness and by not daring to ask for you, nor even to show resentment for things past. Finally, without my having requested it, you came to give me Holy Communion when my illness grew acute. I recovered sufficiently to leave my bed, but my spiritual troubles waxed greater and I felt an over-whelming need to converse with you. However, since it was so soon after you had last visited the convent, it was deemed best that you should not go to the high choir; so I felt utterly desolate, since it seemed to me that you held yourself aloof and did not wish to aid me as had been your custom. I thought, too, that it would give my enemies a new weapon to see me left thus alone. The result was that, at last, one day I became so desperate, I felt that I was in hell itself. I flung myself about in my bed with such violence that I was actually injured and thought that my life was at an end. In desperation, I begged the nuns to send me a confessor, even if it were the Chaplain. And, when they saw the state I was in, they made a concession and called you in, with the result that I immediately began to improve. This was on the Day of St. Francis.[63] Eight days later, I think it was, you said Mass in the high choir, and I took Communion, which I had not been able to do for many days, because I would fall in a faint on the way. Consequently, I always had to take Communion with another nun beside me. Six or seven weeks must have passed thus, during which time I could do nothing but wait for God to clear a new path for me in the stead of the one He had barred.

My condition was so piteous that the Lady Abbess was eager for someone with the gift of casting out evil spirits to see and cure me. The religious who, as I have already said, brought things to this strait, now so advised her, in view of my dire need. She probably believed all this, but did not wish to seek out such a person herself: she wanted you to find him and bring him over. As you were far from believing that I could be cured by such means, you wished to do no such thing. You yielded only in so far as to let someone else make the experiment, which was very kind of you. Finally, to end the deadlock, *Doña* Isabel de Vivero volunteered to find the exorcist. She brought in a certain religious from the Antigua Convent of the Order of St. Benedict, who happened to be in town. He had effected many cures, and had healed many persons possessed of evil spirits. This holy man said Mass, and brought the Blessed Sacrament to the high choir for my Communion. I collapsed, as usual, unable to move from my place to receive it. He put a stole on me, and began the exorcism which continued for a long time, while he called on the demons to leave my body. All to no avail. I felt at peace as I listened, unperturbed, to his invocations, never doubting that Our Lord would do what most befitted His glory. In the midst of all this, you came up and aided him, responding to his prayers and invocations, until he had recited all he knew. Finally, astounded at finding there was no change in me, he withdrew to a corner of the choir and left the matter to you. Then, trusting in Our Lord and for His glory, in the presence of that religious, you employed your usual formula to command, by the power of Christ Crucified, that the evil spirit leave me in peace and begone to the infernal place to which God, by His judgment, had condemned him for his rebellion; and you commanded as well that I be left free to speak and to do whatever was ordered. At that precise moment, I recovered, and could answer every question asked me, to the great wonderment of that religious. The Lord be blessed forever!

You were heartened by this remarkable favor the Lord granted us and, a few days later, ordered me, under obedience, to receive Holy Communion, even if you were not present. Our Lord was pleased to grant this favor and, for some time, I was enabled to communicate. But, as it is the Lord's desire that I be detached from everything, always pending on His Will and ready to comply in perfect resignation with whatever He wishes me to do, sometimes His Majesty gives the enemy permission to place obstacles in the way of my taking Communion, whether these be falls and faints, or the inner tribulations that are more painful still. So it is that for two years, come November, ever since the incidents which I have just related, I have often been unable to communicate for a fortnight, or a month, and occasionally for five or six weeks, in spite of trying every day and receiving daily commands. And this is the case until the hour arrives which the Lord has appointed for showing me this favor. With respect to confession, it has twice happened that, when you were absent, or ill, and had ordered me to go to another priest, as soon as I prepared to go, I was seized by a tribulation that closes all avenues. For you have ordered me to confess to no one else when the prey of this trouble, inasmuch as you deem it a lesser evil to wait than to acquaint someone who might be prejudiced against me. So it seems to be Our Lord's Will for me to be guided by your hand in everything.

Addenda to Chapter 10

Since you order me to forge ahead and record some of the Mercies that the Lord in His Infinite goodness has bestowed on my soul, I will mention a few among the many which He has deigned to grant so unworthy a being, to my confusion and His glory.

The greatest of these Mercies has been to enlighten me with regard to my predestination: this He has done three times, on different occasions. The first was when I was absorbed in deep meditation and recollected these words: "Yea I have loved thee with an everlasting love, therefore have I drawn thee, taking pity *on thee*" (Jerem. 31, v. 3). The light He shed on my soul with this verse was so powerful that I was transported with rejoicing and rapture and aflame with love for Him who has so bound me to Himself.

The second occasion was when I was singing these words of St. Paul at the choir lectern: "For the word of the cross, to them indeed that perish, is foolishness; but to them that are saved, that is, to us, it is the power of God" (1 Cor. 1, v. 18). These words again shed the same light on the fact of my predestination. I did not cease to thank the Lord, marveling over and over with lips and heart at His works.[64]

The third time was about five months ago as I sang the Matins on All Saints' Day. When I read underneath their picture[65] in the psalter, "These are the beloved sons of God," [66] I saw myself as one of those happy souls who are so fortunate as to be the children of God and I was so overcome with joy that only through a great effort could I force myself to finish the Matins.

On the Day of the Expectation of Our Lady,[67] it occurred to me that some day I might lose God's grace and friendship. In my anguish, I could not restrain my tears, and I cried out to the Lord, begging Him to let me die a thousand deaths and to suffer hell itself in this life, rather than to deprive me of His grace. This state of mind lasted for about a quarter of an hour. Then an inner voice seemed to bid me weep no more, telling me that such a deprivation would not be possible.

After a short while, I asked, with a burning heart, "What does this signify, Lord? What do You want of me?" And I was told, "This signifies that fire will never fail on the altar of thy heart." I interpreted this to mean so long as I did not fall into mortal sin, and the Voices said to me, "If thy faith were strong enough, thou wouldst behold wonders," which I understood to mean that I had been granted the gift of perseverance. I esteemed this gift so highly that I was beside myself with joy and hardly knew what I was doing. I could only say, "Is it possible, Lord, that this be true? Wherefore is a humble being so blessed?" This abstraction lasted three hours and I was enrapt with extraordinary joy for several days. I kept repeating this verse: "Let them say *so* that have been redeemed by the Lord, whom he hath redeemed from the hand of the enemy."[68]

One day after I had received Holy Communion, Our Lord gave me full knowledge of that supreme communication of the Divine Nature among the Divine Persons: How the Eternal Father, understanding Himself and comprehending His whole Infinite Being, begot the Eternal Word by way of understanding, to Whom He communicated His Own Nature, of Which He had that Divine concept. In like manner, the Eternal Father, seeing Himself in His Eternal Son, and the Son in the Father, and loving Their Infinite Being, which is one and the same, breathed forth, by way of love, the Holy Ghost, communicating to Him the same Nature, which is one and the same in three distinct Persons. Consequently, if something of His Infinite perfection remained to be understood by the Eternal Father, it would remain to be communicated to the Word; and if, between the Father and the Son, there should remain something of Their Infinite Being not embraced by love, it would remain to be communicated to the Holy Ghost. This bespeaks imperfection, which cannot be in God. That knowledge increased my love and left me with a desire for the aspirations and acts of charity which, it seems to me, unite us immediately with God.

While in a state of suspension, with my will kindled by Divine love, I was told, "Believe it is I Who work within thee." I replied that I could believe it was indeed God Who did this, by reason of the effects which I saw in myself. Then the Voices enlightened me with regard to the mystery of the Incarnation, showing me how God had determined that the concept of Divine understanding, which is the Word, should be inscribed in the most pure person of Our Lady, so that God would be revealed to men. "And the Word was made flesh." [69] Reading this written Word from the page of His humanity, one could see tears, blood and death, but reading it from that other page of His Divinity, one finds its message to be God's fortitude, because with such frail weapons He had conquered death and hell. I was also given to understand how, in all the works of Christ Our Redeemer, His Divinity shines forth; what God is in Himself and what He is with respect to us; and many other things I cannot now recall.

I heard a preacher say in a sermon that God loves with an infinite love all that He has created; and that He cannot love anything outside Himself, but must love all in Himself and of Himself. Later, when I was at prayer, Our Lord showed me the Mercy of explaining it thus: God contains in Himself all created things, and in Him they have life, the very life of God. "In him was life, and the life was the light of men" (John 1, v. 4). After having been given form and substance, they are still in Him because, since God's Divine Presence pervades everything and He cannot depart from Himself, everything remains within Him. Hence it is that God cannot love anything outside Himself. And because the creation of beings required all the power of the Father, all the wisdom of the Son and all the goodness of the Holy Ghost—the attributes of the Holy Trinity—He needs must love them all with Infinite love, for He loves Himself in them. It is as if an artist were to paint a beautiful and much admired picture, into which he has poured all his art: what he chiefly loves in it is neither the board on which he has painted nor the figure he has depicted, but his own genius and skill. So we may say that he loves himself in the picture. But if the picture were his own portrait, he would esteem it even more highly; and if he could infuse life into it and make it another living self, his delight in his handiwork would be boundless.

This then, as it seems, must be the difference in the pleasure and gratification which the Maker receives from dumb creatures which are merely His blurred image, His footprints, His shadow, and from human and angelic beings that are His living semblance. That pertains to the natural order. If this image be given the life of grace, whereby he lives the life of God, he will resemble ever more closely and share ever more fully the Divine perfections as grace increases. What pleasure will his Maker derive from having created so perfect a masterpiece! But since God's love, being Infinite, cannot increase, and since it is the same love which He has for Himself, the statement that God loves some souls more than others must be interpreted as referring to the special signs of love He gives to some and the particular grace He shows them.

I was also made to understand that love on the part of man must correspond to the Infinite love of God and be supernatural. This is what Christ Our Lord meant when He commanded us to love Him with our whole heart and mind and soul, not merely on the natural level that cannot touch God's heart, but on the higher order of grace. It seemed to me that what His Majesty desired of us was a kind of disposition to detach our love from earthly things and offer it wholly to the Creator. Then the Lord, with the breath of the Holy Ghost, swiftly kindles in our hearts that same fire which burns in His Own.

I also understood that the value of grace is infinite, because it is communicated to us through the merits of God made Man. God is rightly ours through grace, which is a participation of His Divine nature, in the image of Christ Our Lord.

One day, just after Communion, I began to desire ardently that all souls should come to the fount of living waters, which always remains full and overflowing, no matter how many partake of it. I recalled the words of St. John, "Adore God" (Apocal. 22). And those other words came to mind, "All you that thirst, come to the waters" (Isai. 55, v. 1). And it seemed to me that these waters became an ocean in God's immensity, and that just as one drop of water cast into the ocean and mingled with the rest loses the name of drop and acquires the name of ocean, so our souls, cast into immensity and commingled with God, acquire a new form without losing their identity. It is as if they were deified, in accordance with the text, "You may be made partakers of the divine nature" (2 Pet. 1, v. 4). I was given to understand that this means we may accompany Our Lord in His Divinity, just as we accompany Our Redeemer by imitating His mortal sufferings.

Hereupon, an abyss of mysteries which I know not how to describe was revealed to me. It seems to me that the Divine participation through which the soul works with God follows this pattern: He communicates to the soul His Own fortitude —"Put on strength, O thou arm of the Lord" (Isai. 51, v. 9). This strong arm represents Christ Our Lord as a human being. His greater strength is in His Divinity. By employing the might of His arm, according to these words, "He hath shewed might in his arm," [70] His suffering and death were caused; but He was still enabled to resist the proud of spirit and overcome agony, death and hell. In like manner, the soul, clothing itself in strength by virtue of Christ's merits and striving to control its inordinate desires, will vanquish its spiritual enemies.

The soul also partakes of Divine wisdom, another gift of the Holy Ghost, and this remembrance of God so enlightens the understanding as to bring a lofty concept of that incomprehensible Being, that Divine wisdom, together with the gift of the Holy Ghost which illumines and tests the soul by fire. Thus it kindles the will with Divine love, so that the soul becomes a living image of God, not only as One, but as Three.

I was likewise shown the charity and mercy of Christ Who humbled Himself for our sakes—according to St. Paul: "But emptied himself, taking the form of a servant, being made in the likeness of men" (Philip. 2, v. 7). Though equal to God, He took the form of servant and sinner. In like measure, the soul should imitate Christ for another soul's benefit, whenever opportunity offers, even though transformed in God through contemplation—even to the point of demeaning itself by dealing with everyday matters and thus penetrating to his heart. The foregoing were among the many thoughts that came to me in meditation and kindled my resolution. When God offers them and the mind accepts them without questioning, they do not lack ardor, but, rather, awaken the heart.

Pursuing this line of thought, I realized that God had shown me this Mercy in order that I might perceive in whose hands He had placed me: those of him[71] who was then guiding my soul. For, in prayer, we glimpse the highest mysteries and from it derive praiseworthy concepts; and we savor truth with a different salt from that found in books. Our father, St. Bernard, said that oaks and beeches had been his teachers in the Sacred Scriptures.

One day at prayer, while I besought Our Blessed Lady to be my teacher, so that I might employ my time in the manner most pleasing to Our Lord, it seemed to me that she prayed beside me on my left hand—that is, next to my heart—while my guardian angel stood on the right hand and whispered to me the words that were the beginning of our salvation: "Behold the handmaid of the Lord; be it done to me according to thy word" (Luke 1, v. 38). It seemed clear to me that she meant God is greatly pleased by the two virtues of humility and resignation. I accepted her message and, though bathed in tears, I saw, as by a dazzling light, that it is the hand-maiden's obligation to serve without recompense and I re-joiced that this was so, saying, "God, I would choose to be Your handmaiden or slave rather than mistress of all the world." I was given to understand, also, that, besides serving as a slave, I must show the spirit of a loving daughter, eager to do her father's will; and, while not expecting any reward for my services, I should cherish the hope of sharing the heritage which he bestows upon his children. Then I per-ceived that God had dealt with me as Moses had with the Ethiopian woman;[72] for, though I was a slave, ugly and de-spised, He had made me His betrothed and brought back my lost beauty at the cost of His blood. These thoughts burned in my soul like live coals.

One day, as I meditated over the saying of the Holy Mother Teresa of Jesus that we should not lose sight of the sacred humanity of Christ, Our Lord, since it could not dim our view of His Divinity, a voice said in my inmost heart, "Who can help thee cross this bridge better than I? 'I am the door. No man cometh to the Father, but by me'" (John 10, v. 9; 14, v. 6). And He showed me the bleeding wound in His side, giving me to understand that only through this narrow passage can one enter His Sacred Heart, rejoicing. This filled my own heart to overflowing with love of Our Lord and I was more than ever grateful to Him and felt my strength renewed to suffer for His sake.

Another day, while in suspension after Communion, I imag-ined that I was in the arms of the Lord and that He drew me to Himself with a bond of union and love even closer than theretofore; and I thought He told me that, thenceforward, I was wholly His and He mine, and that there would be nothing hidden between us; that I should have no care for myself, since His Majesty had me in His care, but should seek to glorify Him in all things. And it seemed to me that Our Lady was at my right hand as if rejoicing in the favor Her Son was showing me; and that I knelt at Her feet, asking Her benediction, which She gave to me, saying, "My blessing and that of My Son descend upon you, My daughter." Meanwhile, I experienced inexpressible joy and glowed with Divine love. I was left with a sense of my own lowliness and unworthiness which lasted for several days, during which time I said to the Lord, with love in my heart, "My Beloved, the chosen spouse is in Your hands." I found immense consolation in the thought that He would raise so abject a creature to such a place of dignity.

On yet another day, as I knelt in prayer, I saw in an imaginary vision[73]—the previous one had been intellectual—Our Blessed Lady with Her Son in Her arms, drinking at Her breast. She invited me to partake also. I was overcome by timidity and reverence, together with a burning desire to receive the Mercy They offered me, for I saw that the Child was turning His eyes toward me lovingly, taking His lips from Her breast, and making room for me beside Him. Yet, trembling in all my being, I dared not approach Them until finally the Child, extending His arm toward me and beckoning, said, "Look, this is what I wish." At that, I threw myself down beside the Virgin. I felt in my spirit a great consolation and tender joy. The Voices gave me to understand that, with that Divine sustenance I should be rid of the fainting attacks from which I suffered; and so it was for some four or five days. God's Presence was with me for a long time, especially when I remembered how the Child had left His Mother's breast to offer it to me. I recollected that Our Lord had embraced His Cross and denied Himself for the time being the glory that was His in order to win it for me.

One evening as I stood at Compline, I experienced levitation and my spirit soared to heaven. I saw in a vision a throne of majesty and was given to understand that "The only begotten Son Who is in His Father's bosom" was seated upon it. Prostrate before it were the twenty-four elders of whom St. John tells us,[74] worshipping in silence the Lord of so much Majesty and Glory. I, too, wished to prostrate myself, adoring Him as they did; as I made this obeisance, I felt profound reverence, which I hoped to have permeate my soul forever. Then it seemed to me that a multitude of blessed spirits were singing, "Praise and honor are becoming to Thee, Lord." [75] Longing to embrace Our Lord and rejoice in His glory, I found that I embraced instead Christ Crucified. This meant to me that, in mortal life, I should neither wish nor strive for aught else than to see Our Lord, scorned and suffering on the Cross; and that only in the future life would I enjoy Him All-Glorious. I accepted this, and offered myself as companion in His sufferings. I was left with a feeling of heartfelt gratitude and profound inner peace.

One day I was reciting Prime and remembering it was at this hour that Our Redeemer was carried with bound hands through the streets of Jerusalem from one court to another. As I began my meditation, with eyes of the soul, I saw those beautiful pierced hands, without being able to envisage the rest of His Majesty's Sacred Person, despite my fervent yearning.[76] Then it seemed to me that He graciously heeded my desire. He said to me, "From bleeding hands what can you expect to receive?" I replied that I would accept His blood joyously, could I but rest in those hands. This was a prophecy to me of the sufferings that were to come, and that have come. It all caused me to feel deep devotion and, for several days, those Divine hands, beautiful as in my vision, were laid upon my soul.

One morning as I made ready for Communion, I was unable to concentrate. I besought the Lord to let me feel Him in my heart, since I could do nothing without Him; and it occurred to me that He was withholding Himself now so that, later, His Majesty might let me know His Will. After Communion, I went to sing Terce. There I felt the old yearnings that used to come when He wished to grant me a levitation. I asked permission and retired to my cell, where I began to pray. The yearning increased. I entreated the Lord to make known His Will, for mine was ready to comply with His in everything. Thereupon I saw clearly the face of a friar, shielded by a black cowl, gazing on me with glad eyes. I realized that it was my Father, St. Benedict. He did not utter a word; and I was at a loss to understand the meaning of it all. Then it seemed to me that Our Lord complained of the ingratitude of sinners, saying: "Those who love Me well should weep with Me because there are those who forget all I suffered for them, and who do not even wish to hear about My passion and death, and take My Holy Name in vain. It is My Own Christian people, who were baptized in My blood, who trample it underfoot, who despise and abandon Me. 'They have forsaken me, the fountain of living water' (Jerem. 2, v. 13). It wounded My soul in the hour of My passion to know how few would avail themselves of the abundant opportunity afforded by so copious a redemption, when I prize souls so highly that I would have undergone all of that suffering to save a single one. Think how great is the dignity of the soul! I, the Infinite Wisdom, gave My life to redeem it. Yet men know not how to esteem and evaluate their own souls. They should grieve also because there is hardly anyone who loves Me for My Own sake; they are so self-centered and short-sighted that they seek naught but their own interests."

I came to understand these and other mysteries, but I was grieved to feel the desire dying down again so soon in my own heart. The Lord rebuked my lack of warmth and by means of such humiliation made me return to His Presence and with as much loving-kindness as before. He stated clearly what I had not understood respecting the vision of my Father St. Benedict's wisdom, and said that, as He was weary of the world's ingratitude, the saint had told Him, "Lord, this daughter will help You mourn the ingratitude of man, for You have made her after Your Own heart." Then it was that He had complained of the forgetfulness of man; and He repeated to me all that I have just related.

On another day, when I had placed the Host on the altar before consecration, I attempted to visualize the Lord crowned with thorns and with His holy hands bound to the pillar. Ardently, I besought Him to let me come nearer and receive Him. The Voices asked, "Why shouldst thou not suffer a little for Me Whom thou seest before thee afflicted and wounded?" And I was given to understand that His Majesty was longing to come to my soul even more fervently than I to His, and that since He had revealed Himself to me with bound hands, I should deliver myself, similarly bound, to His Divine Will. After consecration, my hands and jaws were locked. I was profoundly moved because I had received this Mercy; and when I declared I had no other pleasure than His, I heard a voice say, "Now thou shalt behold My face." And gradually, as if emerging from amid shadows, a heartrending figure appeared to me, streaming with blood from the thorns; and I heard the words, "Behold the Man." All through the day, I could see Him beside me and speak to Him as to the Spouse of my soul.

On another day, when I had sought permission to omit Communion, because of being otherwise occupied, and when the Mass, to which I was listening from the high choir, had almost reached its close, I felt a vehement impulse to take Communion. At the same time, I felt that I was being forced to go down to the lower choir in order to communicate, and was told that I should not fail to do so by reason of any occupation whatsoever. The compulsion became so strong at last that I went tearfully down for Communion, and found that there was a consecrated Host for me. While I was giving thanks for this singular Mercy, I heard a voice say, "Thou hast pleased Me more than if thou hadst anointed all My wounds."

Once, after sweeping the choir, I was dusting a statue of *Ecce Homo* and was told that if I desired to heal His Majesty's wounds and alleviate His suffering, I should strive for the welfare of souls and their spiritual growth, since these, with their sins or negligence, had given Him that form.

While reciting Hours one morning, I saw with the eyes of the soul a hand pierced by a nail, and I heard these words: "Be not afraid lest I forget thee. I have thy name written upon My hands. See Me thus designated as thy Redeemer." I then began to wish that my heart might be affixed by a nail to Our Lord's hand. Next it seemed to me I saw that hand streaked and stained with blood, my heart nailed thereto; and I felt that the blood coming from that sacred hand was mingled with blood issuing from my heart. I was given to understand that the Lord merged the suffering and desolation which I was undergoing with His Own, in order to make them more pleasing in the eyes of His Blessed Father. This thought left me prayerful, thankful and resolute to suffer.

While in suspension, I was told that my tribulation had not been in vain, since I had my heart nailed to Christ Our Lord and could not be separated from Him nor would He abandon me. "No man shall pluck them out of my hand" (John 10, v. 28). It was always my understanding that this nail signified the scorn and contradictions of the earthly lot. I thought, too, that the Eternal Father, when He looked upon the face of Jesus Christ, looked likewise at Our Lord's hands and was pleased to see my heart held there.

On the occasion of another suspension, a great light revealed to me the abyss of baseness which is attachment to earthly creatures. Because of my unworthiness, I felt abashed that anyone should care for me and esteem me. It was clearly evident to me that this lack of self-knowledge is the source of our resentment for insult or injury. As a matter of fact, we do no wrong in despising one who deserves nothing but contempt; instead, we do justice by giving him what he deserves. This truth was engraved deeply on my mind. I am far from attributing to myself any good quality, even in earthly matters, because I perceive very clearly that whatever is mine was bestowed as a gift. I am happy in my poverty and in the hand of God, from Whose bounty I expect all gifts. It seems to me impossible that in this light, there could be vain complacency in the soul; if it rejoices at all, it must rejoice in God, to Whom all its gifts belong. I was made to understand several things with respect to self-denial and poverty of spirit; among them, that this poverty consists in a total renunciation of our personal freedom to God's Will, in such degree as to think or desire nothing, however good in itself, without first ascertaining whether Our Lord wishes us to think it or desire it. We should regard ourselves as God's chattel for Him to expend and distribute at His pleasure. I hardly know how to express this: feeling something is very different from saying it. Those truths illuminated my soul with so powerful a light that it seemed to me I had never before approached such profound knowledge; and I asked myself, "Who could teach what you have learned here in so brief a time?" The Lord be blessed forever. When Our Lord wills to grant me this Mercy of suspension, He prepares me for it with this enlightening thought:

without His help I am as naught, and can neither know nor do anything but sin, which is extremest misery.

On All Saints' Day, while in a suspension, I was given light regarding what goes on in heaven. I saw the blessed as if submerged in that ocean of bliss which is the Divinity, and I joined them and was borne along by the current of that mighty river flowing from the Throne of God and the Lamb. I was given to understand that all who enjoyed this bliss had followed in the footsteps of Our Lord and washed their robes in His blood (Apocal. 7, v. 2); that now they had forgotten their toils and tribulations and wished they had suffered much more. It seemed to me I heard these words: "If thou, with this sight of a mere morsel of our joy, forgettest all your present sorrows, how must it be with us who enjoy immeasurably this supreme good?" This heightened my concept of that Incomprehensible Being, "Thou that sittest upon the cherubims" (Psalm 79, v. 2), Who is alone all knowledge and all wisdom. If the loftiness and dignity of that Throne can be neither attained nor comprehended even by the highest and wisest of the angels, what must the Lord Himself be! All these thoughts kindled the fire of Divine love and brought me rapturous joy.

One day while the other religious were going to Communion and I tenderly entreated the Lord that I might do the same, it seemed to me that He Himself was giving me Communion with His Own hand, invisibly—"He Himself is the Host and Priest"—and that my mouth was filled with the Species, by which I understood that in a most secret and holy way, He was communicating to me the virtue of His precious blood. I was filled with joyous serenity and could only believe that the Lord was with me even while I wondered how this could be, since I had not received Him sacramentally. Soon, I realized that to God nothing is impossible if He wills to do it. Then

I had that sign, about which I have already written, of the bodily Presence of Christ Our Lord which lasted throughout the day, so that it seemed to me He was continually at my side.

The Mercy I am about to describe was granted by Our Lord. It is the greatest, or one of the greatest, I ever received: it lasted for days and it seems to me that it still permeates my soul.

While I meditated on how this vision of the power and the glory of God is but an indication or vestige of what happens in heaven, and pondered His mercy gratefully, these words came to me: "He will make my feet like the feet of harts: and he the conqueror will lead me upon my high places" (Habac. 3, v. 19). And I reflected that the Lord had brought my desires to the utmost perfection and had established and enthroned my spirit on the loftiest peak of the highest hills, so that the soul, superior to all spiritual things and to itself (since in this loftier level one does not look to one's self, nor remember one's self, but rather casts one's own desires into the heart of God) thus brings about a union with Him that only the Almighty can comprehend.

On the occasion of the death of a religious, I asked of the Lord, since I was not worthy to die in the martyrdom of fire, to grant me the grace of dying consumed by His love. At this very instant, I felt that fire blazing in my soul, inflaming my will and enlightening my mind. I felt that longing for God and that sorrow because of not yet having enjoyed Him; that desire for solitude and that eagerness to receive Him in the Holy Sacrament, that ambition to accomplish great things and suffer a thousand deaths, if possible, for love of Our Lord and salvation of all men; that yearning for the Creator to be beloved of His creatures and, above all, I desired that God be known and loved for His Own sake: these emotions and desires spring from the love of God. But they are of little worth in comparison with that void which the soul makes of itself, renouncing and stripping itself of its desires, affections and self-love. Upon that foundation of its nothingness, God will build, shaping and enlarging as He wills in accordance with His design for that soul and His other creatures. This is the meaning of "Open thy mouth wide, and I will fill it" (Psalm 80, v. 11). When the soul unites its own pleasures and desires with those of God, it is filled with a joy and satisfaction, a fullness and completion which can be compared only with the rejoicing of the saints and gives the greatest glory that His creatures can offer God; since thereby the soul, forgetful of itself, partakes of the heavenly bliss; and that, after all, is what the blessed do.

This is what you[77] wrote me: that the spiritual exercise, in which I was shown how the soul can better please God in this life, is so pure and true, so consonant with the Holy Scriptures and the highest aspirations of the spirit, it is, as you had told me on another occasion, the prelude to the soul's sphere of action in heaven. You said, moreover, that with the same words I had heard, not adding nor subtracting an iota, you had been given an identical interpretation of "Open thy mouth wide, and I will fill it," and that you had perceived how God bestows on the soul all these things essentially existing in Him as their source and origin, with its nothingness so complete that you were told, "Prepare thyself in like manner and I shall fill the emptiness of thy soul and thy nothingness." You said you valued this Mercy of the Lord's so highly that you desired we should never depart from it, since it leaves in the soul every day great devotion, great superiority over all things; such greatness of heart that it can hold a thousand worlds; such desire of pleasing God and conformity with His Will that whether the soul look up to heaven or down to hell or forward to death; whether it regard tribulation or prosperity; nothing deters it from peaceful union and identification with the Divine Will; and so far from one's own will that I cannot in the least explain what one feels on these occasions.

On Annunciation Day I was told, "Henceforward thou shalt be My spouse in an indissoluble bond and a closer embrace, for this is My Mother's desire."

Ever since that day, I have been told many things, and have been granted many Mercies, regarding which I have jotted down only the following notes:

"This is to be thy special requirement: to devote thyself to prayer, because My delight is to be with thee."

"Thou art Mine and I am thine. Rest in Me."

"I would bestow greater favors upon thee if thou wouldst surrender thy cares completely and cast thyself with utmost confidence in My arms."

"I pledge My word that I shall never fail thee."

"Arise, make haste and do not slacken. 'Thou hast yet a great way to go.' " [78]

When I besought Our Lord to teach me how to do His Will, I was told, "María, this is My Will: that thou be Mine, for I am thine; that thou belongest wholly to Me, for I belong entirely to thee."

When I had suffered great anxieties, I was told, "Thou hast not departed one iota from Me in thy tribulation; rather, thou hast come closer to me and are even purer than before."

"Sin hath not touched thee, for I have shielded thy heart with Mine. This hath not been the wrath of an angry Lord, but the jealousy of a loving Spouse."

"The more afflicted thou art, the more beloved. If I gavest thee My word that henceforward thou wert to be My spouse in a close embrace, I have kept it, although My embrace hath been from the cross with bleeding arms. Soon I will enfold thee in the arms of My Divinity."

"Purity captivates My eyes; humility My eyes and heart."

"I am enamored by that nothingness which thou knowest thyself to be."

"María, My dove, dwell in thy nest which is My heart; here wilt thou find the fire to renew thy plumage."

"Occupy thyself in love. Identify thyself with My Will by the nakedness of thy affections and desires. Desire only that which thou knowest would please Me."

"María, thou shalt be the instrument of My glory."

"When thou rejoicest, rejoice in Me."

"I bestow these favors on thee for My Mother's sake, and She is grateful to Me."

"From this nothingness, thou wilt soar to a loftier flight."

After I had suffered various travails of body and spirit, the Lord was pleased to alleviate them by granting me a prolonged abstraction, during which I was shown the value of troubles like these; in such manner that the essential meaning of the Cross stayed with me. It was revealed to me as a dazzling beauty, an infinite and incomprehensible Good. My soul, desiring ardently to possess that supreme Good, was shown Christ Crucified embracing me. I was given to understand this meant the Good sought by my soul was in Christ Our Lord, for He is of one substance with the Father; but that, in order to enjoy Him, I must enter into His heart by means of the wound in His sacred side, in conformity with Him in His suffering. Thereupon, I pictured to myself the travails of this Our Lord, in all of which He desired me to imitate Himself and be crucified with Him. I came to realize that in the very way that His enemies sought to abase and bury His name, His Father exalted Him, giving Him a name above all names (Philip. 2, v. 9); and I was given to understand that He would deal likewise with me. For, though it seemed in the eyes of the world that He was humiliating and abandoning me, in eternity my name would be among those of the blessed, and that His benediction would descend upon me.[79] "Come, ye blessed of My Father, possess you the kingdom prepared for you from the foundation of the world" (Matthew 25, v. 34). Then it seemed to me that the Crucifix by which I was embraced was being lifted on high and I was eager to follow. I understood from this that, in order to join Christ upon the Cross, one must forget self and all that is of this earth, bearing with resignation abandonment by heaven. With the many other favors my soul received, I became absorbed in prayer and remained abstracted throughout the day. The Lord granted me this Mercy, as He has done on numerous occasions, when I fell in a faint after Communion.

The following day, I received Holy Communion without fainting. I believe this was due to the intercession of Our Lady, the Blessed Virgin Mother. It seemed to me then that the Lord had received me into His arms to deliver me from all evil, and that He said to me, "Since I receive thee, why not surrender to Me? I do more in receiving thee than thou dost in giving thyself." I answered that I was nothing, could do nothing; that His Majesty should indicate what He required of me. Then I rejoiced in the text: "His left hand is under my head, and his right hand shall embrace me" (Cant. 2, v. 6). It seemed to me that through the wound in His side I drew the strength and virtue of His heart to vanquish my enemies.

The Lord be blessed forever because thus in His mercy He dries the tears of her whom He had justly stricken.

LAUS DEO

❧ Some of the Mercies Granted by God to Doña María Vela

(WHOSE LIFE IS HERE WRITTEN)

Which she herself recorded by order of Father Francisco de Salcedo of the Company of Jesus, who was her confessor at that time and who charged her to give him an account in writing each day of what she did and what passed through her soul

The account follows:

As I pondered on the Mercies Our Lord showed Mother Teresa of Jesus and on the fulfillment of all her requests, I reflected that, though my Mercies bear some resemblance to hers, the Lord does not grant my every supplication. Then the Lord said to me: "Thou dost not ask with confidence, and thou mayst do so, for thou seest that I speak with thee and I Myself teach thee, which is a sign that I love thee." Thereupon, I was emboldened to ask three things: first, that He should manifest His Will to my Father Confessor and, with regard to this, I understood that, although such was His Majesty's wish, this would not be soon fulfilled because it was well that He should first desire it greatly. Second, that He should change the heart of the person to whom I said, "By this I know, that thou hast had a good will for me" (Psalm 40, v. 12); though later it seemed that I had been wrong in this. My third request was that He give Your Reverence whatever you desire, since, among other advantages, that would serve to further my progress. He answered that this He could do Himself.

Sunday, after having received Holy Communion, I devoted a little time to unquestioning love of Our Lord. Then there came to my mind certain ways in which I find myself improved during the past few days: such as a great determination to do whatever I understand to be most pleasing to the Lord. It even seems to me that I am not free to resist the Divine Will. Nor do I care in the least what may be said about me, nor if others complain or are angry or resentful. Neither does it seem to me that anything could disturb me nor take from me this peace I feel. It is so strong a feeling that even though sometimes I wonder whether I am deceived, I am not disquieted. Also, I have courage to mortify myself in ways which it seems will be harmful to my health, and have learned from experience that, on the contrary, they tend to make me stronger.

With these feelings come oblivion of all things else, including those of human necessity, so that I do not seem to carry the weight of my body, nor do I feel its burden except when it hinders me at prayer from lifting my spirit unquestioningly to God. But, after having dwelt on all this, I regretted doing so, for it seemed to me that I had wasted time. And the Lord said to me, "Thou hast not done so. I wished to enlighten thee, so that thou mightst see what I have bestowed on thee and know that I am the giver." This so persuaded and convinced me it is God Who corrects me, teaches me and speaks with me that, despite my natural instability,[80] I know not whether henceforth it will be in me to waver as I have previously done. Thereupon, I said, "My Lord, would that I had loved Thee!" And He said, "Thou dost love." And so it seemed to me that my will was enkindled and even my senses to some degree suspended, though I cannot explain how this could be.

While I was at prayer on another occasion, the Lord did me the favor of elucidating a certain point in this way: God's love for His creatures, if it is to be measured by the gift, is infinite, as St. John seems to declare in these words, "For God so loved the world, as to give his only begotten Son" (John 3, v. 16). Therefore, He loves and values infinitely that for which He paid so infinite a price. For what has the creature in itself that God should love it with infinite love? It is not what it has of itself, which is nonexistence. Without God it would be nonexistent or, if existent, sinful. That which does not exist cannot be loved and that which is sinful must be abhorred. What He has in it of Himself are His omnipotence, His wisdom, and His goodness, each of which attributes is wholly God's. In Man, God loves His Own image, which is motive for greater love; and in the just man, his very life is communicated through the merits of Christ Our Lord. Therefore, this spiritual life of the just cost the Father the precious life of His only begotten Son, and cost the Son His Own life; and all this He deems good if, in exchange, Man, His Own image and creature, be renewed and perish not; but rather may mercy shine in Him, since in His superior image, which is to say the angels, His justice was achieved.

Our Lord also gave me to understand that the love which must correspond on man's part to this great love must be supernatural, as Christ Our Lord tells us when He commands us to love Him with all our heart, with all our mind, and with all our strength. For naught that is natural has power to wound the heart of God. This seems to me something like a disposition that His Majesty desires of us, freeing us from all love for creatures and gathering all for the Creator. Then the Lord comes with the breath of His Divine Spirit to kindle in our hearts the same fire that burns in His. I was likewise made to understand that the power of grace is infinite, because it is communicated to us through the merits of God made Man, because with it He is justly our God, and because it is a participation of His Divinity and a figure of Christ Our Lord.

Another day, after having received Holy Communion, I felt as if my heart, like the altars that held the Blessed Sacrament, was burning with a blazing fire and I lovingly entreated the Lord that some part of its flame might reach all souls so that they could be purified in it. My own heart was for some time in a state that made it seem as though it were being consumed with this great ardor, in such sweet delight that I trembled with ecstasy. Fortunately, nobody was aware of this. Later, when I took my seat to hear a sermon, Our Lord wished me to listen only to His Majesty, and then and there I became absorbed in thought. It was revealed to me how much I still fell short of perfecting the virtues which the Lord continued giving me. And I turned to His Majesty, shedding tears, though they were most sweet, as one who expected from His hand the favor of attaining that perfection. And the Lord said to me, "Do not grieve." When I replied that I would not grieve if His Majesty would take my heart and work within it, I understood that He wished me to follow His Divine indication and not to fail therein because of any human considerations, since by pursuing this path I should progress.

Later, at Matins, a thought came to me making me wonder if I had lost the grace and friendship of God and, in my grief, I wept as I besought the Lord that I might suffer a thousand deaths and hell itself rather than have Him permit such a loss. This state of mind must have lasted a quarter of an hour; and it seemed to me that an inner voice told me, "Weep not";

though it was impossible for me to obey. Shortly thereafter, I felt as if my heart were being consumed in flames and questioned therefore, "My Lord, what is this You wish of me?" And He replied, "This signifies that there must always be fire on the altar of thy heart." Wondering how this would be, I thought it meant so long as the soul did not fall into mortal sin, since I dared not believe it signified anything else. And the Lord said to me, "If thou hadst believed, thou wouldst see marvels." I answered that I believed Him all powerful to deliver me from falling into sin, but besought His Divine Majesty to give me permission first to make this known to Your Reverence and not to be angry with me, since I no more wished to anger Him than to tear out my eyes. The Lord did not leave it at that, but forthwith gave me so high an appraisal of the Mercy which He had granted me that I was transported with joy and knew not what to do or say, asking only, "Is it possible, My Lord, that this be true? Wherefore so great a boon for so vile a creature?"

There has remained with me a particular affection for those in heaven, because, if this be true, I may now consider that I belong there. Formerly, I went there very rarely, but now I go, I speak with everybody and beseech them all to supplicate the Lord to confirm my hope; and I constantly observe how they employ themselves and serve their God, so that here on earth I may do likewise: and I see that they are submerged and effaced so that now only God lives in them; everything pertaining to man has been consumed; they are transformed through love into Himself. With this, I yearn for the Lord to take my hand and oblige me to perform great services, and this I entreat Him to do.

On another day, after having longed to receive Holy Communion, I felt, while saying the Hours, that I must commune with myself and so, although I regretted to leave the choir, I went to the *ermita*[81] and there prostrated myself at Our Lord's feet. I remained thus for a while, my heart filled with such ardor that it seemed about to break its bonds; and made me breathless. Then I said to the Lord that I had come hither in obedience to His Majesty, that He should deal with me as if I were His, for this I now am, and in gentle protest I asked Him why He had taken me from the choir and told Him that His Majesty should keep these Mercies toward me until the hour of prayer. And I was given to understand He had done this so that I might see I had no part in making decisions, for when I least expected it a Mercy was granted me and, furthermore, on this occasion, He had willed me to see that He could regale me without sacraments. I remained for about half an hour in enjoyment of this Mercy; and as it was then time for Refectory, I asked the Lord's permission to withdraw. He said, "Thou leavest Me after all?" I answered, "O My Beloved, this is not leaving You, Lord, because You well know how willingly I would do without a meal in order to be with You, but as I do not have permission, my absence would be conspicuous."

While I was giving thanks before a crucifix for the Mercies His Majesty grants me, saying, "Wherefore, Lord, so much favor for me?" He replied, "Thou owest it all to this blood."

On another occasion, when I besought the Lord to enlighten a soul, I was given to understand that He encountered resistance there.

Again, when I was pleading for the same soul and for others, asking the Lord to truly convert them, it seemed to me that His Majesty uttered this complaint to me: "They have forsaken me, the fountain of living water" (Jerem. 2, v. 13). This so moved me that I mourned it with the Lord, and importuned Him anew until He said to me, "Ask, and then be silent." I understood that He told me this because I was doing and saying to others some things that had to do with His concerns, in order to help them if I could; and that, since the time for this had not yet arrived, the Lord did not wish me to discuss the matter except with Him.

On Easter Day, after having received Holy Communion, I was so weary at Matins that I could not properly pay attention, and all drowsily besought the Lord to keep me in His care, because, unless He gave me help, I could bear no more. As I began to withdraw into myself, recollecting that part of the sermon which concerned a child who communicated by signs, I felt that this was exactly what the Lord desired of me: that it would be more profitable for me to speak by deeds than by words. For a while my spirit was kindled and I continued to enjoy the Presence of God. I felt such quietude that it seemed to me I had never undergone that night of suffering. It has happened several times that when, because of a severe head-ache, I felt incapable of observing my hour of prayer yet forced myself to do so, I ceased to feel ill as soon as I withdrew into myself. I speak of this lest Your Reverence fear my health be impaired.

Your Reverence took up part of my time after I had received Holy Communion on Friday. I could not refrain from entreating Our Lord to give Your Reverence what He has inspired you to desire so much, because I believe it would be of great avail if you and I thought alike. Therefore, I confidently told the Lord that, until His Majesty should grant us this union of thought, I should not cease to importune Him, and that I could not help believing He wished to grant it, since He made me ask for it so insistently. Thereupon I was given to understand that He proceeded thus because He wished me to acquire the merit of charity. I was conscious of the Lord's Presence for a considerable time after this Communion; and though it was necessary to attend choir and play the organ—which duties are distracting enough!—it seemed to me that the solitude of my spirit was undisturbed by any exterior occupation. At Terce, when I felt that I was withdrawing into myself, yet could not leave the services, I solved the problem by remaining quiet and permitting myself to be led. This I did until I was obliged to sing a psalm. Meanwhile, such was the fervor I felt, that it seemed to me an interior voice was saying to me, "Yield thyself to ardor!" It is my opinion that there was nothing to prevent, except the obligation of returning to my Office.

Another day, I understood from the Lord it was His Will for me to obey Your Reverence in regard to Communion as in all else, and I wished that Your Reverence would remember this and mention the matter to Father Gaspar Dávila. The Lord said to me, "Bid him make haste." Uncertain whether the prompting was from God or from my own mind, I felt love enkindle me, but did not cease entreating the Lord to further declare His Will. Again I heard, "It is this."

At Sunday's Communion, I felt a burning strength of spirit, while my powers and senses were suspended longer than ever before. At the same time, marveling that Infinite Majesty should desire to enter a place so unworthy as my heart, I offered Him my thanks and asked, "What seek You, Lord, by such frequenting of the Sacraments?" It seemed to me that He replied, "This: that through love thou shalt be transformed into Me." I was also given to understand that, though He could achieve this end by other means, He chose that method so as to oblige me to serve Him the more in whatever His Majesty should be pleased to command.

Later, when we were reciting the Hours, and I was thinking how well the Lord had nourished me that week, He said to me, "I would have thee always thus." Since these words accord with my own desire, I feared that I might be speaking them to myself, while believing they were God's. But I have noted that they have a great effect on my soul. At times they kindle it in love; again, they move it to praise God or to revere that Infinite Majesty. On still other occasions, they tear my soul apart and annihilate it. This last is the impediment which Our Lord promised me to remove.

Another time, when I was indisposed, I understood—I do not know how—that it was Our Lord's Will for me not to complain. I said that I would very willingly do my best so long as I could move, which, as a rule, I cannot do on these occasions. And the Lord said to me, "Thou shalt be enabled." So it has been. The Lord relieved me of a pain in the thighbone from which I had suffered these eight years whenever I have had this indisposition. Furthermore, I have suffered greatly from the aridity of my prayers, even though my inner joy was immense. Now that I see what I can do of myself, I rejoice and say to the Lord, "At last, My Lord, there shall be harmony between us forever; therefore, set any price that You desire on this Mercy."

After I read a pamphlet that caused me some apprehension regarding these talks on Communion, I yearned to know God's Will and remained at prayer for an hour and a half, imploring Him to declare it. There was no way of withdrawing into myself. On the contrary, I was distracted, as I had not been for many days. Afterward, I again importuned the Lord to reveal His Will to me and heard Him say, "Why seekest thou to know it, since in so far as thou dost know, thou doest it not?" According to my understanding, His meaning was that I did not obey Your Reverence about Communion. In this state of uncertainty, I became absorbed as had been my wont, and the Lord told me that He had taken Father Gaspar Dávila from me and given me Your Reverence; that I was His and He could do with me as He wished. He desired me to obey you. While I was wondering how I could do this without causing complaint from the other person concerned, I heard these words, "I have already told thee to follow My Divine inspiration without fear of human considerations."

Thereupon I left myself in your hands, resolved to do whatever was most pleasing to His Majesty, come what might. I heard also, "How canst thou doubt that it is I? Who else could change thy heart one iota?" So it was that, despite being utterly unprepared for this Mercy, I found myself inspired and suspended. Blessed be God.

On the very Day of the Circumcision, I was considering how much the name Jesus, which means Saviour, had cost Christ Our Lord, and was longing for Him to grant me the Mercy of writing it on my heart, so that thereby might be wrought the salvation which it signifies. I was given to understand that if I wanted this, it too would cause me grief and suffering by eliminating all excesses and disorders of my sensual appetites, so that by this means I might acquire perfect health for my soul. Moreover, this must be through Holy Communion, whereby light would be given me to see my faults and imperfections, with strength to mortify them. Then Christ Our Lord would have complete dominion over the fortress of my soul, and would emblazon on it the arms of His Holy Name, before which trembles the abyss of hell. I besought the Lord to show me in what way He wished this elimination to begin. I understood it was to be in words: I was not to speak except when questioned, unless there were some special need. With His help, I prepared to obey.

Until Friday, though I was absorbed in devotion, my prayers were without form, since I was very distraught; however, I was resigned, as is my wont, to the Divine Will. That evening, Our Lord granted me the Mercy of achieving consciousness of my own unworthiness. I marveled that His Majesty should deign to admit me to His Presence and communicate so tenderly with me. For a while, I was enraptured; and, as I once more voiced my prayers, these words came to me: "To him, that overcometh, I will give to eat of the tree of life" (Apocal. 2, v. 7), and I repeated, "Rather, Lord, without it there is no victory," for I understand the fruit of that tree to be the uniter which we desire; and, as I continued my entreaties, I understood that so it must be, to conquer.

On Monday morning, as I had been ordered to take Communion, I first spent a brief time in prayer. Because I had been up since one o'clock, I was so tired that I could not kneel and decided to be seated. The Lord told me, "It would be better to prostrate thyself"; and so I did until the others came to communicate at Mass.

During this Communion, I felt a deep consciousness of these words, "If thou didst know the gift of God . . ." (John 4, v. 10). I marveled greatly, and understood from the Lord that, since He was beginning to show me new Mercies, I should strive most earnestly to serve Him. I was profoundly grateful and determined to mortify myself by speaking only when it was absolutely necessary. Later, I withdrew from the rest of the Community into a side chapel, so that I might listen to the sermon; and while I was there, I understood from the Lord that He had forced me to remain in the chapel so that I might enter the more fully into His love. Thereupon, I became absorbed and afire with such awareness of My Spouse's Presence that my whole body trembled uncontrollably. The thought of going in to table filled me with loathing, and the Lord said, "Thou seest that thou hast no need of food; resign thyself to Me."

I had two hours of prayer Wednesday morning before Communion, one on my knees, the other standing. I have never been able to recall what the Lord granted me then. I know that I was enraptured by Him, with a burning determination to serve Him; I also know that I received some instruction, but I cannot remember what it was. It seemed to me only that my every effort was bent toward entering into God's bosom and I recalled the words, "I shall die in my nest" (Job 29, v. 18). And there I found myself so favored and so guarded, and so far above all mundane events, that these last seemed a thousand leagues away. It was irresistibly borne in upon me that God loves me greatly, and I felt wholly confident that I could ask for Mercies, especially from the Saviour Himself. Furthermore, I saw that this favor had already been granted me; in the words of St. Paul, "He that spared not even his own Son . . . how hath he not also, with him, given us all things?" (Rom. 8, v. 32). This so pleased me that I said to the Lord, "Undoubtedly, Lord, I must come to You with small matters as well as great, since You can help me better than any earthly friend." His Majesty replied, "So I wish it to be. Who else can grant thee thy heart's desire?"

Later on, at Communion, I was deeply moved to reflect that this had been ordained with special forethought, and that thereby I was obligated to begin a new life. Thereupon the Lord reminded me of the many Mercies He had granted me in a very short time, especially the Mercy of assuring me that I was not to lose His favor. All this held me for a while so spellbound that, though I was in the choir and Mass was being celebrated, I was scarcely conscious of it. Accordingly, I resolved that, in order not to attract attention, I would go to my cell during Hours, until this rapture should pass away. These Mercies so transport the soul that, if God did not draw a veil over them, one who receives them could not live among other people.

On Friday, I had no time to meditate before Communion. I prepared myself by renewing my vows, as is my custom every Friday, since it was on that day that I first made them to God. After having received Communion and given thanks, I turned the eyes of my soul toward God and said, "Eternal Father, I possess My Beloved." The Lord responded, "I gave Him to thee"; and I understood that the very Son of God was giving Himself to me and that the Holy Spirit also was giving Him to me, since the gift had been made through love; also, that when the Son was given me, all Three Persons were given me, since all are of one substance with the Father, according to those words of Our Redeemer, "I and the Father are one and he that seeth me seeth the Father also" (John 10, v. 30; John 14, v. 9). Then it came to me that my soul had become a little heaven, because it had God in it; and that the angels accompanying the Lord were amazed to see Him in a place so unworthy, the while I was saying, "His blood embellished my cheeks." [82] Since they saw that this was so, the amazement of the angels turned to praise. Then my soul seemed to me a garden in which the Lord was walking, and which, by means of my Communion, He watered with His Blood, so that flowers might blossom and produce fruits of virtue. And I implored the Lord that the flower of silence might bloom with perfect beauty, the more to please His Divine eyes. Thereupon I seemed to understand it to be His Will for me to remain in the choir a brief period after Refectory. Since this is the hour when worldly people let their tongues wag more than ever by way of entertainment, He desired me to spend this time asking that a watch might be placed over my tongue. I understood also that I must refrain from saying things that might make others esteem me more highly. The Lord likewise gave me to understand that by means of Communion I should conform to His Majesty in love and suffering. After this, though deep in meditation, I became more enraptured and my hands were benumbed; thereupon I understood from the Lord that it was His Will for me to practice certain mortifications which I had elected to perform. These were: not to go near the fire in wintertime, unless it were absolutely necessary; not to wear a shawl; not to have a warm kerchief attached to my blanket with which to protect my face, which often swells with the cold; to rise immediately on waking, which is always before Matins; not to rest during any interval in my occupations that might occur before Prime, but to spend such time in meditation or in reciting the rosary.

Afterward, at Mass, while I was giving thanks for these Mercies and recalling that Your Reverence had written me—and how rightly!—that I should not be perturbed, the Lord said to me, "Take heed to do My Will in everything in which it has been revealed to thee. And when this seems hard, I shall be with thee and will help thee; in My Power thou canst do all things. Therefore be not troubled by what is given thee to do."

At Communion, on Sunday, I was so enraptured that it seemed to me as if God Our Lord held me more within Himself and my soul was mingled with Him in the most secret recess of His Divine Essence. For a while, I did not know what I was doing or, rather, it seemed to me that I was lost in love. My soul was left deeply satisfied and with a sense of wonder. Throughout the day I kept repeating to myself, "What is this?" and He answered, "This is My body."

On Monday, as Your Reverence told me that you had been pondering as to whether or not I had deceived you, your words left me somewhat confused and I spent the whole period of my meditation in praying that Your Reverence and I might be given light, lest His Majesty permit me to be mistaken because of my sins. Tuesday morning, while at prayer before Matins, I felt so deeply obligated because of present Mercies that I yearned to be consumed in the love and service of Our Lord; and I was overwhelmed with remorse to realize how imperfectly I was carrying out His Majesty's Will, as He Himself had revealed it to me, thereby obligating me that much the more. This is in regard to silence, for I cannot as yet quite adjust myself to what I understand the Lord desires of me. Later, in prayer, I felt this very poignantly; and it occurred to me that if I were indeed deceived, then I was in uttermost peril, mistaking the devil for God. Yet I am not alarmed, because I am certain that if I have given false information, it has been because of not knowing better, with no intention to deceive. It also reassures me that I have never taken credit to myself for these things; on the contrary, I have always feared them.

After this, I was possessed of a great desire to be less esteemed, since I perceived clearly the reason for this: it seemed to me just that all creatures should rise up against me, not only because my sins made me deserve the lowest place in hell, but also because I have not shown sufficient gratitude for the Mercies now granted me. I saw this plainly, and felt that one who had received such favors as I from God Our Lord should be far more advanced in His service. Here I recalled that the Lord had given me to understand it was His Will that I should conform to His Majesty in loving and suffering; and that He, Who had felt most keenly in His Passion the affronts and contumely offered His Divine Person, now again was affronted when one who was the cause of so many torments to His Majesty as I, nevertheless was loved, esteemed and praised. This, therefore, is what I must endure and bemoan, while yearning to receive the contempt and opprobrium which I deserve. To so receive them must be my joy, in order to avenge the affront to My Lord.

Hereupon it seemed to me that, while I should rightly be reprimanded for temerity and irreverence because of frequent Communions, I had not offended God by this misguided activity, since I had known His Will, but, on the contrary, had been zealous to honor Him. This meditation lasted for two hours, accompanied by sorrow and tears. Then I understood from the Lord that these things were not in the spirit of evil, since they bore the superscription and image of Christ Crucified. I responded, "My Lord, in this the truth can plainly be seen, but not so in other things, which might well be false."

On Wednesday, I felt less abstracted than usual, although more like myself when I received the Lord. After I had thanked Him and praised His Holy Name—for we were celebrating the feast of this—I remembered St. Paul saying, "He hath given him a name which is above all names" (Philip. 2, v. 9). I remembered, too, how His Holy Father had given it to Him because He had humiliated Himself in obedience, even to death on the cross (Philip. 2, v. 8), and that it is by such means that we are to prevail with God. I entreated Him, since the Father had left it all in His hands (John 13, v. 3), to be Jesus to me, bringing perfect health to my soul. Later, this verse came into my mind, "I have loved, O Lord, the beauty of thy house; and the place where thy glory dwelleth" (Psalm 25, v. 8). For it is He through whom the beauty of grace was given to men and angels, and in Whose countenance all yearn to see themselves; and none is ever sated with gazing upon it. I perceived also that the beauty of God on earth is the bread of the elect; and I felt so content that I invited all creatures, saying, "Rejoice with me, for I now possess what I awaited, embrace what I coveted, see what I desired." Although these words were with me throughout the day, I was not so overwhelmed as on other occasions; but that night when I began praying, I was affected with such vertigo that I judged from past experience I should not be able to continue longer; and I made a vow to be an hour and a half on my knees. While I was reflecting that days had passed since Our Lord had taken me to Himself, except when I was at prayer, I found myself so enraptured that I experienced almost no difficulty while praying and my vertigo passed. Again, I was lost in love. I do not recall anything that I heard; but, as I resigned myself to the Divine Will, I realized that, although I should feel greatly afflicted if deprived of Communion, this would not deprive me of peace. I would embrace the Will of God therein as readily as in regard to prayer. I kept more to myself than had been the case at morning prayer; and it is my experience that whenever the Lord fills me with ecstasy this lasts a long time. If I speak, I do not know what I am saying, nor do I hear if spoken to. In all respects, my soul seems not to be in its earthly dwelling place.

As I began prayer on Thursday, giving thanks to the Lord

for having granted something for which I had petitioned, as well as for other similar Mercies with which His Majesty had favored me, He said, "See what I do with thee!" And I felt a mounting rapture, the while my spirit was kindled by an ardent desire to be united with God. And it seemed to me that His Majesty was granting me this favor, lifting my spirit above itself, so that, rejoicing with Him, it kept uttering such words as Life, Love, Infinite Good—all without mentioning God by name, but by His attributes and perfections. This abstraction lasted only a little while, for shortly I returned to my normal state and was obliged to work in order to eat.

Friday, on the way to Matins, my companion told me that a friend of hers had gone to the choir the previous night, alone in the dark. This information was given me at the moment we entered the choir, and my first act, without thought of myself, was to give thanks to the Lord and to beseech Him to grant that soul light. I understood from His Majesty that He had done her this favor through me. That message from Him moved me deeply, and I would have liked to give myself over completely to praise of God. I prayed that, since He had deigned to hear me, He would finish in that soul the work He had begun.

Afterward, at morning prayer, when I entreated the Lord not to keep Your Reverence at a distance any longer, but to let you meet with His Majesty, He asked me, "Dost thou not see it is preferable that he remain at a distance, so that he may be the better prepared?" I responded, "You know well, Lord, that You can prepare him in an instant; do this, for Your Own greater glory!" With these and other words, I importuned His Majesty incessantly, until at last He said, "As soon as thy confessor finishes the book, I will do so in payment of the services he has rendered Me; for I hold the honor of My saints in high esteem." [83] These words did much to revive my soul, which had been somewhat arid. Then I began to withdraw into myself, filled with tenderness and recognizing my own unworthiness and the infinite goodness of God. Thereupon I recalled those other words, "If thou believest, thou wilt behold marvels." It seemed to me that I did behold them; for what greater marvel can there be than for God to stoop to nothingness, to the level of the very dust of the earth, and take a creature so lowly that she is an outcast from His house as an instrument for granting Mercies to one so superior to her in virtue? I spent some time in giving thanks, yearning greatly to please Him to Whom I owe so much. Afterward, I took Communion and was, to some degree, abstracted. I do not recall what words then came to me; but I know that in so far as I can judge, my trust and love increased. Blessed be God. Amen.

Saturday morning, I spent two hours and a half in formless prayer, but I was content with acts of humility and resignation. Even if I were enabled to possess all the virtues and heaven and God Himself, I should not want that boon unless it were given of His Own Divine hand and as a Mercy.

When I was at Compline and recalled what Our Lord had said with regard to that which touches Your Reverence, the thought came to me that, in order for you to believe it, I should ask the Lord to let me know some specific idea that is passing through your mind, so that, when I told you of it, your doubts would be set at rest. Then I was fearful lest this be a devil's trick, and cast the thought from me, humbling myself and entreating the Lord that He should not permit me to consent to such promptings, which are permissible only for very intimate friends.

Tonight, I told *Doña* María something that I had resolved not to tell her. Later, realizing I had not possessed the power to resist doing this, I was so remorseful that my entire morning prayer was an entreaty for the Lord's pardon. Though grieved to receive Communion so ill prepared for it, I finally approached the altar and received. Afterward, I besought His

Majesty to forgive me and not to hide His countenance from
me. I firmly proposed, with His help, not to suggest the favor
of ecstasy; but I was enraptured for an hour. I seemed to be
tenderly held in the arms of God, and He said to me, "I am
sufficient for thee, since I am sufficient for Myself. Seek neither well-being nor consolation from anyone but Me." I replied, "My Lord, do with me what You will, and let all my joy
and pleasure be from You, in You and through You." Again,
I heard the Lord saying, "Stay with Me, for I have come to
thee." I told Him this was my desire: to be at His feet, listening to His Divine words. Then He said, "That is what Mary
Magdalene used to do when she received Me in her house:
'Mary hath chosen the best part, which shall not be taken
away from her' (Luke 10, v. 42)." Here I said, "Nor from me,
Lord!" He responded, "Nor from thee, either." All this occurred in the hidden recess of my soul, where my spirit blazed
with inner ardor. My absorption was so complete that, in order
to return to earthly consciousness, I trembled from head to
foot, and could hardly raise one of my arms because of the
pain I had suffered from pressing it tightly against my breast.

It so happened that once in the choir, after great aridity at
prayer, by merely lifting my heart to God and saying, "My
Lord, what do I lack or desire beyond You?" I became abstracted from earthly things for more than an hour and remained without moving in one of the choir stalls. At such
times, I experienced deep yearnings to begin with and un-
bosomed myself not knowing what I really desired. Sometimes
I shed many tears and can do nothing more. But after the
Lord gathers me to Himself, I feel great quietude and peace,
free of that torment which caused the yearning.

The day Your Reverence left, I wondered fearfully whether
or not there were anything to shun in all this. It was not
enough for me to tell myself that the devil has no power over
interior things, for I have heard that he does have power over

the imagination. While I was at choir, saying Vespers, I told the Lord that, since Your Reverence was leaving, His Majesty should watch over me. And I was given to understand that I should not lack His favor. While I was still at Vespers, He enlightened me by showing that what passes through the imagination may be called exterior, even though not seen nor heard by the corporal senses; that interior experiences result from the soul's faculties and that in this realm the devil is powerless. Furthermore, I was made to understand that these experiences of my own were all interior, since they do not come from either imagination or speech. Afterward, I was in a state of abstraction for two hours. Under such circumstances, I never completely lose consciousness, but am benumbed. If I willed to resist the oncoming of this state, I could do so; but I permit myself to be borne along because my soul benefits greatly thereby.

On Monday, I did resist two or three times and, in consequence, was oppressed and felt great inner affliction. My spiritual Father wrote, counseling me to try not to give exterior signs of abstractions, and I asked the Lord what He ordained with respect to these orders that had been laid upon me. He said to obey them if I could. While I was wondering how it also was that I was ordered to place myself in God's hands, He said to me, "If thou art in My hands, how does it come about that thou art ordered to resist?"

One day at None, I lifted up the eyes of my soul and beheld Christ Our Lord on the Cross as He appeared when uttering the words, "Father, forgive them, for they know not what they do" (Luke 23, v. 34). And it seemed to me that He said this for me also, since when I offended Him, I did not truly know Him. I then felt a deep sense of consolation and tenderness and was profoundly grateful.

On another occasion, having read about the grievous sins of Mother Teresa of Jesus, I was reflecting how much greater my own sins have been and sorrowing because I had offended Him Who so supremely merits love and service. Then I was caught up into ecstasy, as is my wont. And it seemed to me that I besought the Eternal Father to forgive me through His Beloved Son and—as though it had been said for me—I repeated the prayer on the Cross. And it seemed also that He told me, since His Majesty was petitioning Him in my behalf, I could not fail to obtain what I sought. I was wholly consoled and wished to remain alone, giving thanks, instead of immediately going in to prayer with the Community. However, in order not to attract attention, I kept making an effort to regain normal consciousness. I reflected that if I were all that I should be, and set a good example to those around me, they would assuredly profit more greatly. Yet, at the same time, I was made to see that they would likewise profit if they could understand the Mercies which God grants me, and that I need neither flee nor hide because of His favor. I responded that His Majesty could easily perceive the obstacle: that even though one nun might profit, others, scandalized, would speak without reverence of His works. He told me that, in order for one person to profit, He would willingly bear all, and that I should set this down in writing, so that I might discuss it with Your Reverence as soon as I saw you. Then I was left in a state of rapture, my hands numb, but my spirit ardent.

Another time, when I was at prayer, my powers of memory and understanding were in a state of suspension for about half an hour. As I recall it, I was perfectly aware that my spirit was striving to love more and more, and I desired to penetrate further into that secret of the Divine Essence. God was thereby affording my soul a loftier appreciation of His Incomprehensible Being; and it seemed to me as if this were the shadow in which I saw the Throne of God. I could not see it clearly because of the secrecy which surrounds it and which no one can penetrate. It seemed to me that God alone could comprehend the excellence of a soul in a state of grace. Nor could I wonder that God loves it and communicates Himself to it, since it is deified by participation in the Divine Nature. I understood that He had thereby obligated Himself to love it, and that, in justice, He must fulfill this obligation. What bewildered me was that He had for some time abandoned it, thus permitting vices to take possession of it when it was to have been the garden of His delight. Then it came into my mind that the reason was to reveal the power of Our Redeemer's blood, which could so purify the soul as to make it capable of becoming God's temple.

On another day, after Communion, I understood from the Lord that, during the coming week, I should prepare for Communion, before I partook again. I asked His Majesty how to prepare, and He replied, "As thou art doing; by keeping from all communication with thy fellow creatures."

While I was pondering what measures to take, in order not to be present on a certain occasion, lest I be distracted there, it seemed to me that I saw Christ Our Lord place His hand on His Divine breast and press me to Himself, saying, "I shall keep thee from distraction." The gesture was so fleeting as scarcely to be glimpsed, but not so the impression that it left; that persisted a long time, and the words His Majesty spoke are graven on my soul.

When, during prayer, God grants the faculty of comprehending some particular truth, if it concerns a virtue or imitation of Our Lord, it is my habit to dwell on it a second time, even during the same period of meditation, so that I will not forget it. In this way, God illuminates the soul with His light. As the truth that He wishes to teach the soul is gradually revealed to it, the will is likewise kindled and, sometimes, it glows with a sudden blaze which illumines understanding. As long as the illumination lasts, that blaze of light is suspended in such a way as to be dazzling; but when it is taken away, I dare to say, "Lord, give me Your light as before; it is not seemly that this should be briefly dismissed." And, without effort, I glance at it again, asking the Lord's permission, and He allows me to see it more clearly, so that I may even be reflected in it. Far from diminishing the will to love, this light kindles it the more.

While I was considering how to carry out the commands laid on me with respect to limiting speech, I learned that my conversations were always to be about God, and that they should be infrequent, grave and modest. When I consulted the Lord as to how this was to be achieved, since I am not on the same terms of familiarity with all the Sisters, He replied that He would help me and that I could so spiritualize the conversations I heard, even the bad ones, as to derive from them the power to praise God and edify my neighbor.

On Monday, meditation held me enraptured for about an hour. At the end of this time, I strove to show my willingness for resignation more forcefully than ever before; and I assured the Lord that, if this were His Will, I would endure such abandonment to the end of my life. Then I reflected that, even though I should be consumed by the love of God, I could not satisfy my yearning to love infinitely; and that if I wished to find what I sought, I should fix the eyes of my soul on that Divine Essence which loves itself infinitely and incessantly, because it is itself the cause of His Infinite love and delight, ever present. I dwelt on this thought for a time, finding it a great solace, the while no indifference was left in me. Then, I know not how, I found myself love's captive to such a degree that I seemed deprived of freedom to cease loving; whereupon I remained at prayer. This feeling did not leave me throughout the day. And, as every act of power and sense was that of the captive, I deemed all came from the Lord. Hence, I was careful to do nothing save in His services; and although very exceptional occasions arose for me to talk, I was not thereby distracted.

During evening prayer, my outer, as well as my inner senses, were somewhat in a state of suspension, with resultant endeavors to show my love of God and my abhorrence of sin. Accordingly, I told the Lord I could see plainly that I deserved hell and that if I were to be damned, I hoped this punishment would come before I offended Him yet again, since the thought of this is a great torment to me. I told Him also that should I be doomed to separation from His Majesty forever, I hoped He would at least grant me the opportunity of suffering greatly for His love as long as my life should last. It seems to me, too, that if permitted to choose, I should elect to be the least in heaven, rather than to merit the glory of the highest angels because, by one offense against God, I had succeeded in lifting myself with such fervor.[84] All the foregoing, as it took place within my mind, was very different from what it is as here expressed. I was left with a deep yearning to suffer; and it seemed to me that if I should love more than all who have ever loved and should suffer everything they have suffered, I should desire no greater glory in this life nor in the life to come, because for my soul nothing else is so great as to conform with Him Whom it loves. In the midst of these reflections, I pondered whether I might have spoken fewer words than I did to a laywoman and decided that I could not have done so, since we cannot measure these things with complete exactitude. And the Lord said to me, "Daughter, that is not what offends me." I was deeply delighted and most grateful that He called me daughter.

Tuesday at morning prayer, as I reflected on the three burdens of the Cross, which are scorn, poverty and suffering, I reached the conclusion that one who loves justice needs must love scorn, since what is more just than for him who scorned God, himself to be scorned? And how can one who was the cause of such suffering and death deem himself undeserving of death? Can such a one fail to embrace willingly whatever suffering or torment may be allotted him? St. Bernard avers that for those who are grateful to the Lord it is pleasant to imitate the dishonor of Christ Crucified. Then I recalled how, by means of His blood, He washed away the obligation which, according to St. Paul, was contracted through sin and by reason of which the devil has power over us (Coloss. 1, v. 14). Other things that I do not recollect came into my mind, all bearing on the love of scorn and insults for the sake of Christ and in imitation of Him. I perceived clearly, as if by a great light, that all the good in the soul is of God, since it has of itself only power to sin; and even as I marveled to see this so clearly, I was told, "He who follows Me shall not walk in darkness, but shall have the light of life." Then, with the same clarity, when it seemed to me that true humility consisted only of this, the Lord said to me that it was not in this alone, but also in rejoicing that I could do nothing of myself, and that I must expect all from His Majesty; that this act of humility was contrary to the pride of Lucifer, who, though well aware that the virtues and powers he displayed were not his own, gloried in them as if they were, and neither reverenced his Creator nor was subject to Him. Therefore, the prayer left me glad that I could find happiness in poverty and in dependence on God, expecting from His Divine hand whatsoever I lacked, and acknowledging as His whatever gift He may have bestowed on me; in the belief that neither on the one account nor the other is there any merit in me, but rather so many demerits that, in justice, mercy should be denied me.

On Monday, St. Sebastian's Day, when I left the confessional to say my penance, I entered into a state of abstraction just as I was kneeling near the door to the choir. Since the bell was ringing for Compline, I should have liked to remain quietly where I was, in order to ascertain what the Lord desired of me; but since I was in sight of everybody, I did not do so, but forced myself to go into the chapel with the Community, although it was extremely difficult for me to move. I attended Compline and then stayed on in my stall for an hour, withdrawn from the world, and burning with fervor from Divine rays. While in this state, I told the Lord that, if He would be so kind as to transfer to Your Reverence these Mercies with which He favors me, all would still be well with me so long as He did not deny me His love. And I heard the Lord ask, "Dost thou hold My gifts so lightly?" I responded, "I hold them in most high esteem, but I hold You in yet greater esteem; and for this very reason I wish to see them bestowed on one who will know how to profit from them and to show proper gratitude." Then His Majesty said, "I have enough for all. I can give them to him without depriving thee."

On Tuesday, at Communion, with respect to the words, "Behold his reward is with him and his work is before him" (Isaias 40, v. 10), the Lord gave me to understand that this Mercy was Himself. In order to dispose the soul to receive it, He sent ahead the virtue of His immense sufferings and death, in which the soul had been made participant. Then there came into my mind that antiphon of St. Agnes: "He put a sign on my face, so that I should accept no other love but Himself." I understood that sign to be Divine Love by virtue of which the soul abhors and sets little value on what does not come from God.

During this Communion, I was conscious of Christ's Presence, as I was accustomed to be throughout the three hour period of my abstraction. I felt both inwardly and outwardly great reverence, together with the utmost peace and quietude. It seemed to me that everything had taken on new meaning and I was very much displeased when the bell rang for dinner. If Your Reverence had not ordered otherwise, I would not have entered the refectory, at least not from choice; for it seemed to me discourteous to dismiss the Lord from the dwelling place of my soul when His Majesty desired to remain within it. However, I went in to table, first asking pardon of the Lord and explaining that I did so through obedience. After the meal, I did not feel His Presence as before, but spent an hour and a half in prayer at the shrine. Later on, I prayed again for two hours, but all was desolation and aridity. Since I wondered if the Lord had been displeased by what I had done, I begged Him to declare His Will on that point. No answer came. Afterward the Lord told me that He had decided to absent Himself, so that I might serve Him in some way, instead of always receiving Mercies from Him. I myself had longed for such an opportunity, but had not desired that it be accorded me in this manner. I should have liked to be offered contumely and reprimand, so long as the Beloved was present, since His Presence makes anything endurable. However, His Majesty preferred a different method, which would make me suffer more greatly. I aver that resignation to the Divine Will is never more necessary than when a soul has attained enjoyment of God. Sometimes it suddenly feels as if it had never known Him through the experience of love. If, on such occasions, the soul is not dispossessed of itself, I prophesy ill fortune.

Later, at prayer, I felt very tired and besought Our Lord to strengthen me and give me fortitude to fulfill my spiritual exercises. He answered, "My saints endured great suffering and underwent great travail; but love can achieve all things."

Nor was I able Wednesday morning to enter into prayer. Instead, drowsy and absent-minded, I stimulated myself with words of love, which I am in the habit of using more in My Beloved's absence than in His Presence. When He is present, He so fills my soul with Himself as scarcely to give it opportunity to utter a word. When He is absent, my soul is more at leisure and entertains itself as it may. Thus I spent two hours.

Then I took up one of these sheets of paper on which I am writing, and began to read over the account of my Mercies; gradually my heart was so softened that I felt the wonted ardor and, at the same time, a deep obligation toward His Sovereign Majesty. Consequently, I remained in a state of abstraction all day; so much so that, though it became necessary for me to speak a few words, I did not thereby lose the sense of Our Lord's Presence.

At Communion on Thursday, after giving thanks and repeating the verse, "Lord, behold, he whom thou lovest is sick" (John 11, v. 3), I felt I had no need to be anxious, since I had both the Divine Physician and His remedies in my possession. Then I became like one mindless: unable to speak with God, insensate as a stone. I must have remained in this condition about an hour, trying to exert my will. It was useless. Then the thought came to me that God might relieve me of an illness from which I suffer and which considerably hinders my spiritual exercises. At such times, although I wish to carry out my obligations, the other nuns are always alert to prevent my doing so. Then I heard, "This time and no more." I did not understand what this meant. Precisely at that moment, I became conscious that I was afflicted by the illness of which I have spoken, although I had been unaware of the fact until I heard these words. As they were uttered, I recognized the infirmity and began to wonder whether or not that consciousness proceeded from God. I withdrew into myself, asking, "How, O Lord, have You entered the dwelling place of my soul and left me outside? Surely it is not Your desire to be with me, whilst I am not with You! Give me Your hand, Lord, that I may enter where You are. I cannot see myself without You, nor can You desire to be in my soul's dwelling place when I am absent." Immediately, I entered upon a state of suspension and felt that I was with Him Whom my soul desired. I was made to understand that if the Lord removed the impediment of my illness, it was in order that I should not have occasion to forego whatever travail was allotted me, nor should the other members of the Community have any reason to hinder me from doing so.

At this point, the Lord Our God enlightened me as to the special care with which He cherishes me and as to the confidence which I can feel in dealing with His Majesty. It seemed to me that nothing could be so hard that I would not undertake it gladly for His pleasure, in complete assurance that I could carry it through with His help. All this caused me such profound emotion that I felt as if my heart were being dislodged from my body. It made me moan a little. Then I understood from the Lord that I should forget myself once and for all and be mindful of Him only. I besought His Majesty not to fail me, so that I might obey Him, and He responded, "I shall not fail thee."

That night *Doña* María was ill and problems arose which made it necessary for me to talk. However, I did not limit my speech to what was strictly essential, but employed some unnecessary words, because of enjoyment in speaking. Afterward, I was most remorseful on account of this. Consequently, at morning prayer on Friday, I remembered my error and asked the Lord's pardon in great perturbation. On the one hand, I was aware of the Mercies which He shows me constantly, and the obligations which they entail; on the other hand, I perceived the scope of my ingratitude when I cannot refrain from even such an insignificant act as speaking a word.

I was given to understand that when God grants me a Mercy, He does not take into consideration what my defects are in His service, but is moved instead by the superabundance of His Own love and mercy. All this caused me to feel still more confused and I said with St. Peter, "Depart from me, for I am a sinful man, O Lord" (Luke 5, v. 8). I said in my heart, "It seems, Lord that You have forgotten what manner of creature

I am. What has light to do with darkness? Behold, I am she who breaks Your laws and transgresses against Your Commandments and fails to keep the pledged word." I spent an hour in shame and abasement before the Lord, deeming myself unworthy to receive His Majesty so often. If the decision were mine to make, I would neither do so nor dare to do so.

Later on, at Hours, I wondered if I had understood aright that the impediment of my illness was to be removed. Desirous of believing this, I besought the Lord, "Make it true!" Even as I uttered these words, I felt as though my spirit shook and trembled. I cannot explain this, but it seemed as if I were being reprimanded for my lack of confidence, though not with words. In fact, I could not perceive how and, in consequence, felt greatly perturbed. Afterward, while gradually growing calmer, I heard the words, "The Lord is faithful in all his words" (Psalm 144, v. 13), and they warmed my heart.

On Saturday, throughout the day, I had no feeling whatever, except desolation and anguish, either at Communion or during the hours of prayer. It seemed to me that the Lord was angry; and this wounded me to the heart! All day I went about my duties with this thorn in my spirit and found no solace anywhere. As I was going in to Vespers, this verse came to me, "The Lord is nigh unto them that are of a contrite heart" (Psalm 33, v. 19). Then, in a flash, I realized that the Lord was not as far away as I had imagined. But the consolation that this thought gave me lasted a very short time, and soon I felt as dull and insensate as before.

The Lord awakened me at two o'clock Sunday morning. I felt my accustomed fervor and vigor. The clouds had dispersed. For something like an hour and a half, I gave myself over to love and praise. Later, at early morning Mass, I recalled the Lord's promise to grant a Mercy to Your Reverence, and wondered again in how far it was to be believed. Then, as I heard those Gospel words, "Why are you fearful, O ye of little faith?" (Matt. 8, v. 26) it seemed as if the Lord were addressing them directly to me. This brought to mind other words which His Majesty had spoken to me, and which I had seen fulfilled, as well as promises of further Mercies. They all seemed darts that pierced my heart and proofs of the Lord's love for my soul. Thus I became submissive, humble and comforted; and for the time being I felt not a particle of doubt.

Since Your Reverence had ordered me to receive, I regretted deeply that I could not see you first, on Monday, to consult you regarding the state of my soul, so as to be prepared for Communion. I, myself, believed that I was not able to receive. Accordingly, I besought Our Lord, with tears and entreaties, to bring Your Reverence to me. However, when I realized that His Majesty paid me no heed, and that the hour for Communion was approaching, I felt tempted to petition our Abbess to excuse me from obedience. Nevertheless, I resisted this impulse and in the end obeyed, almost without realizing I did so.

After Communion, I was in a state of profound abstraction, during which the Lord punished me, first by a reprimand for having of my own volition resisted His Will. I was given to understand that what Your Reverence ordered had been at His command; that He knew my disposition with regard to Communion, and it was within His power to make me rightly disposed whenever needful. I was made aware that what He desired of me was that I be always submissive and confident, realizing that whatever He commanded me to do was His Will and that, moreover, it was beneficial for me to feel the weight of my Communions, even though they seemed to bow me down and make me fall into the depths of the abyss. I understood further I should never doubt that whenever His Majesty grants a soul Mercies, He also grants, at the same time, means for making good use of these Mercies. The Lord said to me further, "Thou art Mine and I am thine. Why are thou troubled?" He also gave me to understand that, even if I should desire to seek comfort by talking with Your Reverence, I should not request this boon with anguish, but should leave it to His Divine Will, since His Majesty would bring Your Reverence to me whenever it was best. He said that He was greatly pleased to have me relinquish to Him all my cares, both corporal and spiritual, without seeking human assistance for my desires and necessities. He told me that I should approach His Majesty confidently with every plea, as a child to a father. I responded to all this, "My Lord, would that not be to expect miracles?" He replied that it would not, considering my experience of His protection and care. The foregoing occurred while I was in a state of utmost abstraction, with arms folded and benumbed. This condition lasted for an hour and a half, during which time I became somewhat fatigued, since I was on my knees with my body bent. In my opinion, it is quite a hindrance not to lose consciousness completely under such circumstances. One is aware of pain and sounds and other extraneous things which prevent the poor soul from delighting in what is offered it. On this occasion, I longed for a complete loss of consciousness. I do not know whether or not that desire was wrongful.

During the prayer before Communion on Thursday, the Lord made me feel regretful that so few souls resolutely pursue ultimate perfection, and that occasion can always be found to cast off whatever burden God has willed to place on our shoulders. I longed to be among those who truly seek perfection, and asked Our Lord to grant me this Mercy on His Feast Day. I became confident that I should receive it. For half an hour after Communion, I was unable to withdraw into myself as I usually did, for this withdrawal cannot be achieved, however great the effort, unless it be God's will. However, I was not absent-minded, but rather engaged in acts of devotion and delight in the Lord's Presence. The words of the Spouse came into my mind, "His hands are filled with jasmine" (Cantic. 5, v. 14 and 5), and I recalled that these fragrant flowers were the gifts of heaven. However, I saw that they were shedding drops of myrrh, which signified the mortification, suffering and affliction God allots His Own. Since these came from the hand of Him Whose heart is wounded by love, it seemed to me that they could not be deigned hardships nor fail to be embraced with joy. These thoughts, and others which I do not recall, offered themselves, not while I was in a state of suspension, but during ordinary prayer. I noted how great is the difference in love's force and feeling when God gathers the soul to Himself, for then He seems to lift it to the very rooftops, where the sun blazes with all its strength and the view of heaven is unobscured.

Mass began when I had been at prayer for half an hour. I attempted to go to the choir, but the Lord decreed otherwise, for He began to draw me so close to Himself that it seemed best not to resist. Consequently, I remained for an hour and a half consumed by love. I was given to understand that the bestowal of this is the ceaseless labor of God Our Lord throughout eternity, and that His Majesty desires I should profit by it as continuously as possible. This time, because I had remained in a place which some of the religious were passing, I suffered much annoyance and no little embarrassment. Since the head must move as the spirit indicates, I endeavored, when anyone went by me, to turn in such a way as not to be noticeable. At the same time, I felt I should not care whether the other nuns saw me or not. The Lord said, "Enjoy what I am offering thee." Amidst all this, I recalled that Your Reverence had ordered me to go to Choir, so that these other nuns should not see me in this place, and I dared not let myself be troubled. However, the experience left me utterly exhausted for the rest of the day.

At Compline that night, I experienced those yearnings that come to me frequently, and the words the angel spoke to the

Magdalene came to me, "Woman, whom seekest thou?" (John 20, v. 15.) I responded, "I seek Him Whom my soul loves," nor could I calm myself until after Compline, when I went in to prayers and, to a certain degree, was enraptured during my devotions. Under these circumstances, I began petitioning the Lord in your behalf, urging that you be not forever the water carrier without rations to sustain you at your work the while you add to His store. Afterward, *Doña* María told me of the Mercy Our Lord had granted her by manifesting His Will during the Great Silence and Communion. I encouraged her and we resolved to make every effort to obey His Majesty. Then I went to bed, giving thanks to the Lord because he had one more soul with which to communicate.

I woke at three the following morning, rose and dressed and applied myself to prayer. It occurred to me at once that the Lord had granted *Doña* María that Mercy in order that she be no longer an obstacle in my path. Hitherto, she had wanted to talk when I desired to be silent. His Majesty had at last granted what I had so often begged of Him with tears, since quiet was impossible for me unless she wished for it also. I realized that He had heeded me on Sunday also, when I had entreated Him to bring Your Reverence to me; for, even though you had not come, His Majesty had ordained fulfillment of my plea, which was that *Doña* María and I should receive Communion together. I was further given to understand that if the desire of Your Reverence were granted earlier than the time the Lord named, this Mercy likewise would be given as a favor to me. I was deeply moved by all this and perturbed because I did not know how to respond to such generosity.

Friday morning, after an act of mortification which proved profitless to me and everyone else, I went to prayers. For an hour and a half, I was enraptured, my spirit aflame. As I desired to keep my soul pure for the reception of Our Lord, and could not go to confession, the Lord said to me, "In this fire, thou shalt be purified." I understood also that, ultimately, I should lose myself wholly in order to find myself the more surely in the joy of His tender embrace. The sense of God's Presence remained with me throughout the day and, with it, came a deep yearning to mortify myself. Consequently, I asked permission of the Abbess to perform some public acts of mortification. She replied that she would see to this at the proper time. Saturday, Sunday, Monday and Tuesday, I was completely lost in meditation and unable to go in to prayer.

On Wednesday, after I had come from Confession, I entreated the Lord to deign to converse with me, since He is the life of the soul and without Him, I cannot live. It was made clear to me that the life I desire consists of good works; the Presence for which I pleaded makes this life sweet and may not always be granted while one lives in the flesh; but that if I would find my joy and consolation in fulfillment of the Divine Will, I should always be content and happy, come what might. I was somewhat abstracted later on at Communion and my spirit was kindled. The words of the Spouse came to me, "Let him kiss me with the kiss of his mouth" (Cantic. 1). It seemed to me that nothing except His embrace could satisfy me and I burned with desire. However, the ecstasy was of brief duration. I was left with a great yearning to be scorned, and devised a plan for receiving a reprimand and being given a public penance. While I was at the lectern, yearning for these things, I thought that if the opportunity were offered me then and there, I would comply easily and without regret. Then I heard these words, "Likewise, thou wilt do so later," and I heard further and gave heed, "I have told thee that I will aid thee. How is it that thou canst forget My promise?" This overwhelmed me with shame and confusion. Finally, the Lord did help me to do my part, but this did not bring the result I had desired, since no one wished to reprimand me. Afterward, I was given a note from Father Gaspar Dávila which atoned for this disappointment, since, although it caused me no anxiety, it made me lose time while I kept turning over in my mind what he had said, wondering whether it was good or bad. Then the Lord reminded me of these words, "Thou art Mine and I am thine, so why shouldst thy heart be troubled?" I repeated them to myself over and over, until every care took wing. It seemed to me that, since I belonged to Him, He would care for me; since He was all powerful, He would deliver me from mine enemies; since because of His goodness He loved me, He would likewise defend me, nor would He permit that I be deceived.

At prayer Thursday morning, I had no special feeling except contentment that the Divine Will should be fulfilled in me. It seemed to me that just as the rose is more beautiful because of its surrounding thorns, so the soul forsaken by God and beset by importunate thoughts is a source of great delight to His Majesty if it be steadfast.

In order to afford Him this delight myself, I felt encouraged to remain on my knees, resolved that, for the rest of my life, I would receive gladly whatever the Lord might send; and I rejoiced that His Majesty's sufferings were over and that He would have bliss throughout eternity. Such meditations kept me in a state of abstraction for two hours. All day, I struggled within myself to determine whether or not I were deceived. It did not seem possible to me that I was. That night, at Compline, my heart seemed to melt within me. I turned to the Lord and said, "My God, where are You?" He replied, "I am near." Then, these words came to me: "We will come to him, and will make our abode with him" (John 14, v. 23). Afterward, I went to prayers and the Lord gathered me up, kindling my spirit. He gave me to understand that, little by little, He was granting me what I besought of Him, through the intercession of Our Lady. Since I was resolved to withstand any contumely, and even to seek it in whatever way I could, He told me, "Through My Mother thou shalt have it."

On Friday, after I had accused myself of having committed an error while we were reciting the Office, I was reprimanded in Chapter and given a penance. Then, though I retired, happy because I had performed that slight service for Our Lord, I was unable to lose myself in prayer. All I could do was to humble myself and recognize my unworthiness to receive Communion. Afterward, I felt the immediacy of His Divine Majesty's Presence and offered Him my heart. I bewailed my inner sufferings and entreated Him not to leave me in a state of uncertainty, but to declare whether or not I were deceiving myself. I was made to understand that I should dismiss all care from my mind, leaving everything to His Majesty, and should not feel "up in the air," [85] as Father Gaspar Dávila expresses it, but should depend on Divine Providence, which never fails those who place their trust in Him. I understood further that, when St. Paul was sent to Ananias, he neither elected nor planned the mission but, on the contrary, abandoned himself to the Divine Will, saying, "What shall I do, Lord?" (Acts 22, v. 10.) Then the Lord provided Paul with that teacher, bidding him to go to Ananias. Nor was it something new that His Majesty desired to teach me Himself, since He has done so for many others. With regard to corporal needs, here again it is not contrary to the Gospel to neglect what appertains to them, in order to attend the more to God. Rather, this is in conformity with the Gospel, for such is the meaning of Christ's words: "Seek ye therefore first the kingdom of God, and his justice, and all these things shall be added unto you" (Matt. 6, v. 33). The Lord did not say, "Seek the kingdom of God first and then the rest," but rather told us to seek Him first and the rest would be added. In other words, give heed to the fulfillment of His Will, for He shall take heed that we be provided with all that is needful. He has proceeded in this way with respect to many saints who renounced the world, so that they might give themselves the more freely to contemplation.

On Tuesday, I felt deeply conscious of the fact that I complete nothing, except with a thousand defects, although I serve a Lord of Infinite Majesty, Who merits perfection. It seemed to me that I should be cast out from His Divine Presence. I must have had this thought in mind for an hour, without any suspension whatsoever of my faculties. Finally, I withdrew gradually into myself, as the Lord came nearer and nearer to my soul. It made me realize ever more clearly the great differences in forms of prayer, and how powerless one is in this regard. I believe that by such absences as I have endured lately, along with what He has said, the Lord has desired me to understand this truth completely. It became clear to me that those utterances were not my own, even though at times I wondered—since there were so many—if I myself had not spoken them all. Because of Your Reverence's absence and because I have suffered so much on account of what that other servant of God has written me, I would certainly have been consoled if I had spoken these words myself, but, except at the beginning, I have heard nothing. I understood it to be the Lord's Will for me to keep silent and listen whenever I was with anyone who could teach me or whose office is such that he could. I understood that, even if I already knew what I were hearing, I was to listen in silence as if it were new to me, unless the speaker should be one to whom I reveal my soul, since, for him, it is well to know everything. I understood, moreover, that in conversation with my equals—for, at times, we talk together—I should not do all the talking; and that, when I speak with inferiors, I should likewise mortify myself by stating things in a simple way, not speaking as one who is experienced and able to teach, but as one who both exhorts and encourages herself to achieve virtue.

On Thursday, at morning prayer, my heart felt hard as a stone. Then, at Hours, it began to soften in the Presence of its Spouse, like wax in the rays of the sun. And I heard the Lord say, "Why dost thou desire aught beyond me?" I replied, "I neither need nor desire aught beyond You, Lord, but where are You and whither shall I seek in order to find You?" (Cant. 1, v. 6.) He then gave me to understand that I should find Him amidst insults and contumely, poverty and sorrow; that He was sustained and refreshed among the flowers of such meadows, though bound to the Cross; and that it was love, rather than nails, that held Him there. I enjoyed God's Presence practically the whole day and, in the afternoon, I reflected, with deep emotion, on all that I had learned. I longed to be despised, to be treated according to my deserts, so that, on this path, I might find Him Whom I love. Therefore, I besought the Lord not to let me go empty-handed to receive His gifts, but to permit that I should offer a gift of suffering in return for His love.

Friday, after Prime, when some of the Community met for prayer, I was told it was impossible that God should not weary of having me so much with Him. I replied that His Majesty might well tire of me personally, although He never tired of our petitions for His Mercies. Then I lost myself in prayer, and His Majesty made my unworthiness very plain to me. I marveled that God had suffered to come into His Presence a creature so offensive, and thought that if my companions knew me as God knows me, all would abhor me and none would tolerate me. Later, at Communion, God showed me the Mercy of gathering me to Himself, and I felt my spirit blazing with ardor. Thus, for a time, I enjoyed the Presence of My Spouse. I cannot recall that I felt anything special, except that I had not come with requisite purity to this Divine Sacrament. It seemed to me that one on whom such a boon is bestowed so frequently should lead a life more angelic than human.

During afternoon and evening prayer, though my mind and imagination were restless and turbulent, I think that my will was steady and in its place.

Saturday morning, all my prayers, or most of them, took the form of a yearning to suffer. In the afternoon, following your departure, I yielded to jealousy when one of the nuns told me what a long while she had been with Your Reverence; I felt fearful that she might be outdistancing me in spiritual benefits and I wished to be the only one so favored. I felt this, even though it seemed to me that the Lord wished to grant her Mercies. In order to ward off temptation, I began commending her to God and decided to prostrate myself at her feet that night. And I was aware how far the Lord had obligated me in the matter, since it was through me that she had attained this state of grace. Then I began to fear that such an idea might be caused by pride, for she had no need of me when God, of Himself, could teach her without help of mine.

Sunday, while preparing for Communion, I began to worry about another nun. In my longing, I petitioned the Lord to give her light; and it was borne in upon me that prayer for her, however devout, is a matter of the senses rather than the spirit; that, though it may be natural to a great extent, it does not achieve that true union with God which is wholly pure and without intermixture of possessiveness. This kind of prayer may, at one and the same time, be both good and evil, as is seen in its results. I was further given to understand that, though the supernatural does not predominate in such prayer, the soul, with God's help, can move the will to desire the virtues of humility and austerity, together with those others by means of which we seek to imitate Christ Our Lord. I understood, too, that careful observance in the exercise of these virtues are the efforts by which true prayer and its meaning are recognized. In the purest prayer, however, benefits do not come through these channels, because the soul does not labor, but finds itself guided. It seemed to me that it was as if one impressed a seal on wax; for, when God approaches a soul, He imprints upon it His Divine Spirit, which becomes evident in all its works thereafter; because all these works are sealed by Our Lord, Who gives them life and, through Him, the soul is moved to imitation of Christ. I, myself, who have experienced all this, say it is not strange that one who does not understand the ways and means of such mysteries should be deceived; for the feeling of love, in so far as it pertains to rapture, seems to be always one and the same. At least, there is only one way in which to express it.

In both types of prayer, the soul experiences delight, rejoices in the Presence of God, attains serenity through its powers and is aware of offering love. But only in the second type of prayer does the soul feel satisfied that it has received love. Once I had understood all this, it seemed to me pride and presumption on my part to attempt judgment of the path followed by other nuns. Who asked me to interfere? Nevertheless, I realized immediately that my only motivation was prompted by the deepest desire that this soul and all others should achieve perfection in serving the Lord. I could see that I had given proof of this desire by offering my life and my salvation to that end. Later, at Hours, when my mind returned to these matters, I understood from the Lord that I should write them down lest they be forgotten. This message came to me insistently several times.

Afterward, at Communion, I yearned to love God immeasurably, so that none should have advantage of me in loving and suffering. It seemed to me that, if in heaven there were not this perfection—I mean this perfect union with the Divine Will—there would be sorrow because of the inability to grow in love, a sorrow that it should have an end, a limit which could not be crossed. Then I was made to understand that the surest sign of true love consists in suffering joyously for the Beloved; and I remembered having read that the best sign of love was the abandonment of all else and withdrawal into one's self, while delighting in the Presence of the Beloved. I longed to know how this could be, for I did not understand it and found it hard to believe; it seems to contradict those words of Christ Our Lord: "Greater love than this no man hath, that a man lay down his life for his friends" (John 15, v. 13). Thereupon, the Lord gave me to see that, although the giving of life or bodily health may be understood by "giving of one's soul," this is also understood as giving the will and the fulfillment of one's own desires. He who gives up his will gives up more than he who gives up his life. The greatest sign of love is the renunciation by the soul of all affections and desires, and forgetfulness of self upon entering into enjoyment of all that which God enjoys Himself. This is the reward God will give those who faithfully serve Him. And this cannot be where love is not supreme; but one may suffer for the Beloved, even though this pinnacle of perfection has not been reached.

Thursday morning, the Lord gave me to understand that sometimes I disobey Him by not permitting myself to be carried away when I realize His Majesty wishes to gather me up and that I thereby lose much I might gain. This grieved me, for I realized it was true; but my reason was that I wished to avoid attracting attention. Then I understood that Your Reverence would have me to do so. I understood also that, when the Lord absented Himself, it was in order that I should experience such a hardship; for, when He is present, one feels no lack, neither cold nor hunger nor weariness, nor does it seem even possible to suffer from such causes. I understood further that to endure them, without inner support, was to drink from the pure chalice of the Lord, as His Majesty quaffed it; and He does us a great favor by permitting us to partake a small portion of it in imitation of Him. Also, seeking to know His Will, concerning a certain important matter entrusted to me, I was given to understand that the Lord did not wish me to bring to Him a preoccupied mind, but to await His visitation free from all care; for often when He desires to visit a soul and finds it busied with temporal affairs, He refrains from coming.

Monday, when I begged the Lord to give guidance in this matter of *Doña María*, so that it might benefit her, I understood from Him that, when the Community meets to read, I should tell my faults and try to persuade others to do likewise, because it will benefit us to humble ourselves. While I was giving thanks to the Lord for having manifested His Will to me in this matter, it did not seem right to me that I should do so without first informing Your Reverence. Again I heard: "I shall inform him." Then I understood that I should not take the matter up with Your Reverence so soon. After this, I felt a great yearning to do much for God: I should not like an hour, or even a moment, to go by without some worthy act in His service. It occurred to me that just as there were two altars in the temple, one for sacrifice and one for incense, the Lord desired me to have twain in my heart. On the one, I should always have the fire of His Divine love, whence would issue ardor and fervent prayer; on the other, the knife of mortification, wherewith sensual appetites would be sacrificed. Thus I would please Him and would always have an offering for Him.

I do not know how it was that light was given me Tuesday at Communion, by means of which I perceived that, howsoever widely God may distribute His treasures and impart His gifts, they neither diminish nor decrease. Rather, they grow; not in Him, but in us. Thereupon, with the Spouse, I invited souls to come and delight in their King. And I saw that, however much may be granted them and however greatly they may rejoice, gifts will not be lacking for me if I am prepared to receive them, because He gives Himself wholly to everyone.

This understanding seems to me somewhat in the nature of a remedy for the temptation into which I was led the other day.

Wednesday, as I was feeling rather depressed because some spiritually-minded persons disapproved of my mortifications, I besought Our Lord to manifest His Will and was given to understand that I should not desist so long as I had permission to continue. These words of Christ Our Lord came into my mind: "Every one therefore that shall confess me before men, I will also confess him before my Father who is in heaven" (Matt. 10, v. 32). I was given to see that this should be understood as applying not only to the Confession of the Faith which must be made in the presence of infidels; but, also, to those who confessed Christ Our Lord by their works, welcoming contumely and confusion with all the other virtues resplendent in His Most Holy life; since this is to confess we are His disciples, as must be done before men and not in secret only. Whoever might become vainglorious because of so doing would also become vainglorious over hearing a Mass or giving trifling alms. Neither the one thing nor the other is meritorious without the grace of God; and since these are graces, the glory is not ours. "What hast thou that thou hast not received?" (1 Cor. 4, v. 7.) I also understood from the Lord that I should perfect myself in matters pertaining to the Order, especially with regard to silence when the Rule is that it be observed; and that, at other times, I should speak in a low voice and without laughter. I resolved to do all this, with the most fervent desire to carry out my resolution; but I cannot count on myself.

On Thursday afternoon, when I had given my pupil her lesson in the choir, I became enraptured for an hour, seated there as I was. It seemed to me that everything was reanimated by the Presence of My Spouse. Although, to my sorrow, the great impediment of the senses prevented me from enjoying freely what the Lord offered, He gave me to understand that

He had shown me this Mercy so that I might approach the Communion table confidently, even though I did not go to confession. This was an answer to my doubt as to whether or not I should partake, since I feared the Lord might be angry because I had not prepared myself by confession for other Communions.

On Friday, at Communion, the Lord granted me the Mercy of quietude. I remained in this state of devotion to His Majesty for a long while, and inquired how He had permitted a certain person,[86] of whom you know, to deceive Your Reverence. It was made clear to me this was in order that Your Reverence should learn not to give credence so readily to any one, unless there has been thorough previous examination.

At morning prayer, on Saturday, I was much dismayed, since I thought I detected in myself some signs of pride, which might give rise to suspicion that these things were not of God. One evidence of pride is that, whenever I hear it said that I am far from being a saint, I do not believe it, but feel that God, for His part, has already done much and will soon do more, if, on my part, I offer no obstacle. Other evidence consists in the fact that sometimes I consult God about unnecessary matters, and expect an answer, as happened in the instance mentioned above. It seems that, in such cases, it may be feared that the answer comes from the devil, or from my own mind. Again, when I am with some of the nuns who are closest to me, I keep thinking that, if only the Lord would gather me to Him irresistibly, in their presence, it needs must be of great service and benefit to them, by demonstrating unmistakably that God views these mortifications with favor and, thereby, encourages similar practices on their part. The result is that I long to have Him show me this Mercy, always subject to His Will; but I do not know if my longing is entirely pure. Still another evidence of pride lies in the fact that I hold it as certain I am the cause of reform on the part of some religious; that the Lord has been pleased to hear my supplications and tears and that, though others, worthier than myself, sought this favor of Him, His Majesty deigned to oblige me in this. Moreover, I feel convinced the matter will not stop here, but that there will be greater reforms among these young nuns. When I asked the Lord what I should do to check such thoughts, He replied, "Believe!"

I also examined carefully my own motives in these mortifications, to ascertain if some particle of vainglory adheres to me because all the Community is more edified by what I do than by what the others do. Here, I find it is true that I feel satisfaction in their edification, but that I take no pleasure in having the nuns think the better of me on account of these things. I should be glad to undeceive them, but do not make much of an effort to do so, because that would be worse: to tell them the truth seems a demonstration of humility, also. I think that I am not moved to practice these mortifications by any consideration, except that they are acts of virtue, by which God is pleased, and through which some others are encouraged to do likewise. In so far as regards mortification, I do not feel that I am mortifying myself, because I encounter no difficulties. I am well aware that this is due to God's mercy. Only a short while ago, I would rather have died than prostrate myself before *Doña* María. I had to consider it a thousand times before I could bring myself to do so. But now it seems to me that the place I deserve is at the feet of them all. The benefit I feel is that charity seems to increase; or, better said, one feels that charity is an actual practice. When I conferred on these matters with the Lord, and desired to know how to free myself from pride, I heard, "Trust in God and distrust thyself." Thus it is that, while believing I can do nothing of myself, I may believe that, in God, I can do all things. All this moved me so greatly that I shed many tears. I was shaken, fearful lest I find myself deserted, like one fleeing from an enemy; and it seemed to me as if I had taken refuge in Christ Our Lord, saying, "My Spouse!" and He had responded, "My daughter, thou hast no reason for pride, since all the good of heaven and earth is Mine." I understood this, also, through the words, "Every best gift, and every perfect gift, is from above" (James 1, v. 17).

On Monday morning, it was impossible for me to enter into prayer, either before or after Matins. On the contrary, my mind kept wandering. Afterward, Alarcón preached us a short sermon on mortification. He was quite obviously referring to me as a fool and a child, and said when I believed I was pleasing God, actually I was offending Him greatly. This distressed me somewhat, but the Lord provided for me by gathering me to Himself and reminding me of the affront offered to His Majesty when they called Him a Samaritan and said He was possessed of a devil (John 8, v. 48). Consequently, I attached no importance to what was said of me. Nevertheless, I was disturbed all day because I had been told I offended the Lord. I thought that if this, indeed, were so, everything was the devil's invention: he had deceived me and I had deceived Your Reverence. I wondered, too, whether I had acted hastily in leaving Gaspar Dávila; these thoughts and others gave me great distress. Later on, I came to see that if God Our Lord were not pleased with these mortifications, He would not have granted me special Mercies the first days that I practiced them. It seems that by these means He gave me to understand that the mortifications were pleasing in His sight. Also, on this same day, while at Collation, I was in a state of abstraction, during which time I was given to understand that, since I had done none of these things without the advice and order of my Superior and of Your Reverence, there was no reason why I should be perturbed.

There was opportunity for only one hour of prayer Thursday morning, and it was a period of great distraction. Afterward, during Mass, at the time of the Elevation, while I was wondering whether the Lord was pleased, rather than offended that prayer be abandoned for the office of obedience, these words of the Spouse came to my mind, "How beautiful are thy steps in shoes, O prince's daughter!" (Cant. 7, v. 1.) And it was given me to know that these words were meant for me because the Lord was pleased with me on account of that exercise. Thereupon, I began withdrawing into myself, but there was really no time to do so, since I had to officiate. That night, my prayer took the form of an entreaty to the Lord that He might give *Doña* María courage to prepare herself for leaving the service, because that is best. I found her very timid, unable to make up her mind to take such a step, since she would regret it keenly. I understood that she would discuss the matter with the Lady Abbess.

Saturday, I visited the sick among us, because they told me that they took note of this; it seems to them a foremost act of virtue. In this manner, I lost two hours of the time I customarily spend in prayer. I was worried and wondered if I had done wrong. Was it better to have them criticize me than to fail in my exercise? It seemed to me that I was being told, "It is necessary to yield to the frailties of the frail." All morning, I had gone about fully aware of God's Presence, and carrying in my mind the words, "And passing will minister unto them" (Luke 12, v. 37), for, while I was offering to serve in whatever office might please the Lord, I recalled with enlightenment and appreciation the great mercy God grants His Own by administering that morsel of glory to them in the banquet of eternity: as if the Lord in passing ministers because he satisfies us with the radiance of His lights. Since I had gone about with this thought in mind, my soul was enraptured and regaled and filled with spiritual joy. After I had paid the visits to the sick, I went to prayer so completely exhausted that I was inattentive and unresponsive. Later, at prayer, in spite of my great yearning for God, I could not succeed in losing myself.

Sunday, for about an hour after Communion, I was unable to confer with the Lord. It was as if He were not present. He might as well have been over there in the Indies.[87] Nevertheless, I forced myself to be with Him until the bell rang for Terce. Not long before that, I found myself very tranquil and was given to understand that, because I had persevered, He again assured me of His desire that I should feel no uneasiness, but should take care to carry out His Divine Will in every way. I learned further that it was pleasing to Him for me to attend His Presence reverently; this was what He had shown St. Martha to be the one thing necessary and that which should be held in higher esteem than other exercises. For, if a king should desire that a knight be always beside him, to serve him personally in every needful way, that knight would not exchange office with the cook nor any other who would remove him from the presence of his king, a post which he deemed of greatest prestige and merit. It seemed to me also that to leave off prayer in order to practice some mortification was likewise pleasing to the Lord, since they are very few who embrace the humility and the contumely of the Cross. As for visiting the sick, there is always someone to do that.

Wednesday night, my heart was so elated and filled with light that it was as if no storm had ever raged therein. I perceived clearly, as I had never done before, the suggestion of pride revealed in that feeling; for, though I had believed Your Reverence in this regard, it was blindly.

At three o'clock on Thursday morning, the Lord awakened me and I told Him ardently, "My Lord, Your love keeps me sleepless and apprehensive." Thereupon, I rose and entered into prayer, though for a short time only, because the bell rang soon. I had four hours of prayer after Matins—two before Communion, two afterward, and all on my knees. I was most rapt and kindled in that Divine fire and was told, "I will shew thee all good" (Exodus 33, v. 19), by which I understood that it was Christ Our Lord in Whom are deposited all the treasures of God's knowledge and wisdom, Who addressed me thus. And I responded, "Draw me: we will run after thee to the odour of thy ointments" (Cant. 1, v. 3). The words of St. Francis stayed with me: "My God and my all," with great sweetness and savor for a long while.

Sunday, when I besought the Lord at Communion for light to determine His Will, I was made to understand that not in vain did He command me with such insistence that my soul should be untroubled, since so it must be if it is to accomplish what His Majesty intended. I was told that it would be a hindrance now for me to be concerned, either about myself or about *Doña* María; that, as I knew from experience, any vexation of spirit made me lose sight of essentials. Once the Lord had begun to communicate with my soul, it was the more incumbent upon me to cast aside whatever I deemed an impediment to His Divine visitation. I was made to realize what His Majesty desired was that I should be as much as possible in the Community, without binding myself to anything which might hinder this. For there was hardly anyone in the Community who freely followed her profession. All were as if subject to husbands and under obligations to friends and relatives or to their own creature comforts; and these preoccupations came before the obligations of their profession. I was reminded that His Majesty, Who had given me this desire years before, now wished me to put it into effect. It was for that reason He had ordered me to practice mortification, so that, by these means, I should cease to be withdrawn and mingle more freely with the Community. All this gave me deep sorrow and caused me to shed tears. It seemed to me as if an inner force were compelling me to follow this path, not knowing what I did and with consuming anguish, so that the mandate laid upon me could be executed. In any event, I offered the Lord my submission to His Will in all things. I told Him that contrary orders were being given me, and besought His Majesty to enlighten Your Reverence as to what would be most pleasing in His sight. I told Him that I would do nothing save what I was instructed to do, since it was His Majesty's wish that I obey you.

It was also made manifest to me that the Lord had shown me the Mercy of assuring me that he would not take Mary's role from me now that I wished to change it for Martha's. It is not possible to prevent losing much time from periods of devotion if we perform domestic duties. In the afternoon, during another period of prayer, I again had the same feeling in regard to these matters and I entreated the Lord to declare His Will. I cannot persuade myself that it is aught else, because for years I have experienced these yearnings, which at times have been such as to do great injury to my health, or so I believe. On the other hand, when I perceive that Your Reverence holds a different opinion, this makes me feel that it may not be God's Will, but my own.

Monday night, I was again under such obligation to serve the Lord because He had fulfilled my wishes, and was so grateful to Him that I could not leave off giving thanks. I felt as if my heart had been released from a great affliction which had been an enormous obstacle in my way toward God. My joy was profound.

On Tuesday, at morning prayer, I was helpless from lack of sleep. I entreated the Lord to rouse me. He gave me unexpected joy through a firm conviction that He loves me and delights to dwell in my heart; that I may be sure His mercy will never fail me; and that, trusting all to Him, I need have no care, since He will order everything for my soul's greatest good. I felt immediately an ardent desire for Communion, and wondered why Your Reverence had not ordered me to receive it on the Eve of Easter, as you did not wish me to perform any act of penance. I heard the Voices say, "If thou shouldst ask him for it? . . ." Because, though I had felt this longing, I had not dared speak of it to Your Reverence. Then I said, "My Lord, what You desire is already done by participation in another Communion."

This happened while I was in a state of rapture; and I felt as one does when a window is opened on a room filled with precious jewels, so that, as the light enters, each may be seen, stone by stone. Thus it seemed to me that, though God had previously been with me, I had not perceived Him fully until He sent a ray of light to illuminate my understanding of His real Presence by showing me all the different aspects of His Infinite perfection. Such thoughts so elated my heart that my body seemed incapable of containing it and I trembled from head to foot. This happens frequently now and is an embarrassment, since no one near me can fail to observe it. I do not think there is any help for it, though, possibly, I have not tried hard enough to find one.

Then I besought the Lord's permission to suffer His Passion and these words came to me, "The chastisement of our peace *was* upon him, and by his bruises we are healed" (Isaias 53, v. 5). And these others, "Making peace through the blood of his cross, both as to the things that are on earth, and the things that are in heaven" (Coloss. 1, v. 20). I understood the peace had been extended not only to the blessed in heaven and the just on earth, but to the angels, also. By virtue of this Precious Blood and death through which Christ Our Lord was given power and dominion over men and angels, the good angels vanquished the bad with that act of humility, saying, "Who is like unto God?" After about an hour at prayer, I went to Communion. I must have remained about two hours longer, delighting in the Presence of My Spouse. As I gave Him thanks, I recalled the words of St. Paul: "Jesus . . . having joy set before him, endured the cross, despising the shame, and now sitteth on the right hand of the throne of God" (Hebr. 12, v. 2). This joy was the one to come from the peace that He would make between God and men by means of His Cross. "Justice and peace have kissed" (Psalm 84, v. 11). And, since this Lord, to Whom we owe so much, delights in our good to such an extent that He embraces the Cross, we should strive to satisfy Him, doing all things with perfection, so that they may please Him the more.

At prayer that afternoon, the Lord enlightened me greatly concerning the statement: "And I, if I be lifted up from the earth, will draw all things to myself" (John 12, v. 32). As I saw that many were lost without the light of faith, and others even with it, I desired to know how this could be. The Lord gave me to understand that He uttered those words for all who had been predestined to Himself before the world was created. According to St. John, He did not primarily die for mankind, but for the purpose of uniting in one body, of which He the Lord is head, all the scattered children of God (John 11, v. 52). These were His sheep of whom He said, "And no man shall pluck them out of my hand" (John 10, v. 28). I understood also that He draws them to Himself, not only by the light of faith, but by the bond of charity and that, when He was raised on the Cross, He steadfastly concealed His Own Name and fame by having Himself placed between two thieves, as the greatest sinner of the three. Such were the means God chose for His exaltation, according to St. Paul's saying: "For which cause God also hath exalted him" (Philip. 2, v. 9).

Wednesday, while High Mass was being said, I felt that my heart was overflowing with faith in the goodness of God. It seemed to me as if I could ask with certainty that my prayer would be granted, and I felt I had little to fear, with the Lord on my side. Again, as I prayed for Your Reverence, it seemed that the time had still not come. It was very clear to me, however, that the petition would eventually be granted, so I rejoiced and praised the Lord. At afternoon prayer, I was remorseful because I had spoken more often than had been my intention, and I hoped that Your Reverence would order me not to receive Communion on Thursday, since this seemed to me a just punishment. But the Lord placed me under even greater obligation to Himself by refusing to become angry. He gave me leave to be with Him, in order to take notes of His words and works while He was in the world, especially of His condescension in talking to the Magdalene and to the Samaritan, even though they were women and sinful. I perceived that He condescended similarly in my case, though I know not how to thank Him nor how to serve Him as they did.

As I was about to go to prayers on Thursday, I heard bad news: it was that Your Reverence might be sent away from here. I was somewhat upset as I went in to pray with this on my mind; and I entreated Our Lord not to permit such a thing. However, I was unable to plead fervently or strongly. It was made clear to me that the matter had best be left in the Lord's hands, since He would resolve it to His greater glory and my own advantage. I recalled Job's words, "The Lord gave, and the Lord hath taken away: as it hath pleased the Lord so is it done: blessed be the name of the Lord" (Job 1, v. 21). After this, I was unable to pray for anything more.

Later, I would have liked to postpone Communion until another day, because my thoughts wandered. Finally I communicated, although I do not know how I made up my mind to do so. The Lord first enlightened me by showing me how negligent I had been in failing to carry out what I knew to be His Will, and thus plunged me in the depths of despair. Then He raised me up and held me with my senses suspended, in such a state of harmony and bliss as I had not been granted for many days, I think, even for months. The faculties of my soul were so overpowered that I could ask for nothing in particular. Rather, I presented to Him, in its entirety, everything for which I had asked His favor. I felt that He kindled me, lifted me, united me with Himself so forcibly that my body lacked little of being lifted up with my spirit. As I was saying, "My Lord, I am unworthy of this Mercy," he responded, "And of what Mercy art thou worthy?" This was the second or third time I had been humbled by hearing these words, although I cannot recall just what were the other occasions. I remained for a long while in this rapt state and was given to understand that the Lord desired to transform my soul by this shower of Mercies, just as a rainfall softens and permeates the soil. And I said to the Lord, "My Beloved, bring it to pass that I may no longer be what I have been until now; that, beginning today, I shall be so different You can give me another name." Then I seemed to hear: "Thou shalt no more be called Forsaken: and thy land shall no more be called Desolate: but thou shalt be called My pleasure in her, and thy land inhabited" (Isaias 62, v. 4). This was the name that the Lord wished me to merit with my deeds, not diverging a jot from His Will. All this, I heard with other expressions of endearment and refreshment. Blessed be the Lord. Amen.

During morning prayer on Friday, I was unable to withdraw into myself, but was content to have His Divine Will work within me. Later on, as I was leaving the refectory, where I had eaten only what was provided and was thinking that this had been sufficient, the Lord showed His approval, for He gathered me to Himself. I felt that sensation of loving warmth that I always experience in His Presence, and stopped where I was to give thanks, under pretense of reading a book I held in my hand, until the visitation was over. Afterward, as I made a visit to the Station of the Most Blessed Sacrament, by which great indulgences are gained, wondering whether these would be granted, I heard the Lord say, "To thee, yes."

Likewise, at Mass, these words of the Gospel came to me:

"All power is given to me in heaven and in earth" (Matt. 28, v. 18). This moved me very much. I welcomed the Lord and was overjoyed that He should remain with us in the Blessed Sacrament. I felt a deep desire to receive Him and, since this could not be, besought Him to grant me the copious fruit of Holy Communion. After Hours, there was a brief interval before it was time to go to the refectory. I thought of visiting a sick nun and took up the matter with the Lord to ascertain if this would be right. I understood Him to reply, "Thou hast already left Me once." This was because I had gone from morning prayer a quarter of an hour earlier than usual, in order to visit another sick nun. As the Lord seemed to disapprove my departure this time, I remained until the bell rang.

Monday night, I stayed in the choir. I spent four hours in prayer. When I entreated Our Lord not to forsake the many souls, dependent upon the doctrine of Your Reverence, I could not hear an answer, except in so far as I myself was concerned: I was never more ready than now to be placed wholly in God's hands without human protection. I found great freedom and satisfaction in this thought. Later, at morning prayer, the assurance was repeated: the Lord would not fail me; of that I could be confident. Thereupon, I resigned myself to His Will, resolved not to make the slightest effort, if Your Reverence should leave here, to seek another director, but to trust in the Lord and await His pleasure. In taking this course, I felt that the Lord was gratified to have me beseech Him that Your Reverence might remain here, so long as I did this in a spirit of resignation. I remembered Mother Teresa of Jesus, and thought how deeply she would have felt it and how earnestly she would have sought the Lord's mercy, if she found herself in a situation such as mine. Then I began speaking to her, asking her, since she knew how it felt to be in this plight, if she would not beseech the Lord in my behalf as she would in her own. I was given to understand that I, too, could ask with confidence, as she did, and that what I sought would be granted. I humbled myself in recognition of my unworthiness and gave thanks to the Lord because He deigned to hear me. And, with all my strength, I supplicated His Majesty not to permit them to send Your Reverence away from here and was enabled to plead more fervently than before. However, no response came to me. Later, during Hours, I was abstracted to such a degree that I had to omit the recitation in order to attend the inner Voice. Since I felt the Lord's nearness, I asked Him once more not to take Your Reverence from us and He replied, "I shall not take him from thee." This assurance left me wholly confident. How it is to be managed, His Majesty knows. But now I cannot feel alarmed, even though your departure should appear certain. I was also made to remember that, though I do not deserve such mercy, He has fulfilled His every promise to me. Whenever it has seemed that He was not keeping His word, it was my understanding that was at fault. Rightly understood, all His promises have been fulfilled.

After Vespers on Thursday, I was in a vicious mood and said, "Lord, well I know what would calm me. It would do me much good if You would show me a Mercy as is Your wont." Then I forced myself to go to the shrine, though I did so in a laggard and indifferent way, because my spirits were very low. I set on the floor some candles I was carrying and lifted my eyes to a crucifix I have there and these seemed fixed on His hands together with my heart. He gave me to understand that I should have no fear of being forgotten, since He had my name written upon His hands by dint of His Blood and terrible suffering. Then I had a great longing to respond to this Mercy by inscribing My Beloved's name on my heart, even at an equal cost of blood and suffering. I spent about an hour enraptured by His mercy, all my senses suspended; but I had left the door open and when *Doña* María came in, I had to force myself to speak to her.

On Friday, at Communion, the most I could understand was that I should trust in God. The words, "Trust in God," were repeated many times. I was told that I could do this easily, and that I should not be so diffident, since in having Him, I had everything.

Saturday, at afternoon prayer, it occurred to me that, in order to trust in God, as He wishes me to do, my will must conform absolutely to His, not deviating a jot from what I know to be His desire. It came to my mind that when a child has been naughty, he does not lose his father's aid and protection, because he has not lost the love a father feels for his child. Likewise, Our Lord does not cease to love us because we are guilty of errors in His Divine service, so long as we turn to Him in love, confidence and humility. However, the confidence of those eagerly alert to His Will is very different from this. I recalled the words of Christ: "And he that sent me, is with me, and he hath not left me alone; for I do always the things that please him" (John 8, v. 29). Then I felt a great longing to please God in all my works, and asked, "Lord, what might I do to please Your Eternal Father?" And I heard, "Follow Me." The Lord reminded me of St. Paul's words: "For whom he foreknew, he also predestinated to be made conformable to the image of his Son" (Rom. 8, v. 29). Since I desired to know in what particular I was to follow Him and conform to His Majesty's wishes, He gave me to understand that I should continually take care to do the Divine Will, as had been His Own wont; that His sustenance was as He had told the Apostles, "I have meat to eat, which you know not" (John 4, v. 32). He was sustained by carrying out the mission which His Father had entrusted to Him, and for which He had come into the world; namely, the salvation of souls. He said that

He was greatly gratified to have those who loved Him aid Him in His work, and that I, who had neither the ability nor the office of teacher, should help Him by prayer and the example of my life. He told me that I should prefer the Divine Will, however insignificant in its aspects, to any profit which I might derive from following my own wishes, even if these were to enjoy Him forever, were this possible.

He also made me see the errors I commit in all my works, how sullied they are and how unworthy in His Divine sight. Later on, while I was acting as crucifer in the procession on Saturday, I lifted my eyes to the Lord, entreating Him, since He is the Sun of Justice, to enlighten my heart with a ray of His Divine radiance, and I heard, "Thou hast given enough."

On Sunday, at both Communion and evening prayer, I was unable to do aught but resign myself to the Divine Will. Afterward, as I was preparing for bed, *Doña* María came in to ask that I permit her to kiss my feet. I was unwilling to let her do so, but was left with a desire that I should kiss hers. Consequently, I went alone into one of the corridors, beseeching Our Lord to indicate what it would please Him to have me do under such circumstances. I felt deeply embarrassed that anyone should express a desire of this kind regarding me. The Lord did not enlighten me at all. So I went away. Then, as I was undressing, St. Paul's words came to me: "That in the name of Jesus every knee should bow, of those that are in heaven, on earth, and under the earth" (Philip. 2, v. 10). Thereupon, seated as I was on the bed, I became lost in abstraction and spent about half an hour delighting in the glory of His Holy Name. I felt ashamed that there should be anyone who would kneel at my feet. Then I went to bed, begging the Lord to grant the favor He sometimes shows of waking me to be with Him before Matins. He roused me at two o'clock and kindled me with ardent yearning for Him. I remained for a while at prayer, beseeching Him with respect to the intentions of Your Reverence and myself. I was given to understand that I should tell you to have faith, since this Mercy would be granted you. Later, at Matins, my inner hope and joy were such as to enrapture me when I recalled, "It is to us." A most spacious field was opened to my view, such as is described in that verse of David's, "And I walked at large: because I have sought after thy commandments" (Psalm 118, v. 45). Afterward, as I passed through part of the cloisters, and bowed before one of the steps of the Passion, I gave thanks to God and heard the words, "Without me you can do nothing." [88] And I clearly perceived the truth of this while realizing, nevertheless, that in Him I could do all. Throughout the day, I continued to experience this deep inner peace and joy.

While I was reflecting that the Lord's mercy had granted me some of the things sought in prayer, and that during a year He has given me reason for hope in regard to Your Reverence, I was made to see that everything of worth has a high price. Thereupon, I said, "My Lord, then that which is of greatest value must be done for friends. In this, You show what You are, while giving as God gives." Then I felt a great urge to offer on my own part something special which would induce His Majesty to grant us this favor.

After this, on Tuesday afternoon, a storm rose in my soul that has given me much to think about. I was obsessed by the idea that the liberty and security I feel cannot possibly be good. Since I have offended God in many ways and failed to do His Will as He desires, it seemed presumptuous madness on my part, rather than freedom of spirit, to talk to God with the same confidence as that felt by the saints. Security lies in the fear of God and I fear nothing, neither Hell, nor judgment, nor sin; but I act as though I had served as well as all the saints together. This is why I felt no doubt respecting my salvation. Therefore, I prayed to God and believed that He heard me. It seemed to me that, even though Your Reverence had given me assurance, being human, you might err, and God might permit your error because of my sins. It is quite clear that His Majesty neither reveals His secrets nor communicates except with the humble. Since I am a Lucifer, He would not stoop to grant me so many Mercies. "For the Lord is high, and looketh on the low: and the high he knoweth afar off" (Psalm 137, v. 6), says David. It may be inferred from this that all the Voices I have heard have been lies of the devil, who makes me believe a thousand such so as to have me fall into a vain complacency. Thus I might displease God, and lose merit in whatever I do. As regards my supernatural experiences, which sometimes take place in public, and the fact that I give accounts of them so that all in the Community may see my progress, I remembered amidst my doubts that charity casts out fear. Yet I was not comforted in so remembering, because I perceived that assurance had been meant for those who possessed charity in perfection, which I was far from attaining.

Friday night, for a short time while I was at prayer, the Lord mercifully permitted me to speak to Him and beseech His favors as before. The clouds began to disperse, and my understanding and memory became tranquil. Then my will confidently performed its office.

Afterward, as I reflected that Your Reverence did not want me to vow obedience to you, and resolved that I would obey you in all things, just as if I had taken a vow, I heard Him say, "If thou wouldst only be silent!" It seemed as if the Lord were giving me to understand that, by keeping silent, I would obtain the more quickly from His Majesty what you desired. Then I said, "Lord, You must work a transformation in me." I was given to understand that even my manner of petitioning Him was not as He had ordained; and I resolved to be more careful henceforward in this respect. As I recalled also that Your Reverence would be praying for me at Mass, I said to the Lord, "Mark that prayers are being said for me. Repay him for this service. If You loved me, You would for that reason receive him. Note that the time is ripe, and let light dawn in that heart." [89]

At afternoon prayer, I meditated that a soul bereft of the light of God's mercy is so weak and languid that any breath of temptation could demolish it. It is so discouraged and in such darkness, so dispirited without knowledge of God or of itself, that it becomes permeated with utter misery. I understood the desolation of a soul separated from God by sin, and the havoc wrought within it. After a time, I know not how, St. John's assurance came to me in his relation of what he saw in the celestial Jerusalem: "And the Lamb is the lamp thereof" (Apocal. 21, v. 23). It was made clear to me that my soul, which is God's dwelling-place, must have no other light than that of the Lamb; nor should anything outside itself dazzle the eyes. By this light must I be enlightened, and I must follow it to go aright. Then I saw Christ Our Beloved forsaken on the Cross by the Eternal Father. I remembered that, after asking "Why hast thou forsaken me?" (Matt. 27, v. 46) He had said immediately, "Into thy hands I commend my spirit." [90] That was what I must do in following this light. Even if it should seem God had forsaken me, I must place myself in His hands with perfect trust, for He loves me as a father. I prayed then to God for my intention, and asked that He should not measure time for us in conformity with His periods, which are for all eternity, according to David's saying, "For a thousand years in thy sight *are* as yesterday, which is past" (Psalm 89, v. 4). I besought Him rather to bear in mind how deeply felt is a delay in the fulfillment of one's desire. Thus had His Majesty been restricted and grieved by the delay of His Passion, which was what He most desired in this world, that He might thereby fulfill His obedience to

His Father. Then, even as I wondered if it were scant resignation on my part to plead for this, I was given to understand that first should be the desire for what Christ Our Lord sought in us by His Advent, and by the coming of the Holy Ghost. According to the Gospel, the reason was, "That they may have life, and may have it more abundantly" (John 10, v. 10). This life, with abundance and profit, is what He desires to give.

As I left Prime on Sunday to go to Chapter, I yearned ardently for God. I considered going immediately to the shrine, so as to be better able to comprehend His Will. But this was not what He sought. When the Chapter was over, since in the *calenda* St. Robert[91] was not named, I decided to look up the reason for the omission and found that his feast is not until Thursday. I was so embarrassed to find myself unable to leave Communion that I did not know what to do. I went to prayer, and the Lord began kindling my spirit with ardent longing. I was made to see the Lord desired that I should receive as I had been ordered to do. I could hear the words, "Come, Spouse of Christ, and receive the crown." I knew that this crown was My Spouse, for He is the reward of our victories and the repose from our labors. It seemed to me that I could approach confidently to receive Him, since He received Himself in me, and that the fire I felt purified me and disposed me to approach Him as I should. In the afternoon, while I was in the shrine reading over this manuscript, I became abstracted.

On the Eve of the Feast of St. Catherine of Siena, when I was at Vespers thinking about a servant of God who had begged the Lord for health to be a discalced nun and whose prayer had been heard, I was given to understand, "So shall it be with thee." Later on, at prayer, as I thought about how greatly God loved St. Catherine and how much He did for her, I heard the Voices say, "I will do it for thee likewise." Then I replied, "If I might serve You, Lord, as she did!" Again, I heard Him speak: "That would not be much. It is much that, undeserving as thou art, I deal with thee as if thou wert deserving."

Later on, I wished to fast, as I had not yet eaten meat, but could not make up my mind to do so because I lacked special permission. I begged the Lord to let me know His Will. However, the only thing I was given to understand was that I had always been addicted to fasting. Later, in the refectory, I felt undecided and again asked the Lord to let me know His Will. Then the words of Christ Our Lord came to me: "Man liveth not by bread alone" (Luke 4, v. 4). So I said, "This is a very great truth, Lord," for I saw that one word sufficed to strengthen body and soul. Again I heard: "I will do for thee what I did for her," as if that promise were of itself enough to heal and comfort me. Thereupon, I decided, believing this to be the Lord's Will, to take a light meal and give the rest of my portion as alms. It seemed that this in itself was sufficient to restore me; and I was no longer conscious of the hunger I had felt.

Furthermore, while I was at the shrine and somewhat rapt, a strong breeze came in through the door and I was afraid it might do me harm, since I was not feeling well. However, I decided to remain there quietly and trust in God; and I felt as if His Majesty enfolded me so protectively that nothing could do me harm.

Since I was not to receive Communion Sunday morning, I spent two hours in prayer at the shrine. David's verse came to mind: "I have chosen to be an abject in the house of my God, rather than to dwell in the tabernacles of sinners" (Psalm 83, v. 11). I deemed but vain all the world offers in honors and pleasures and riches, and held it a greater privilege to be a serving maid in the house of God. Afterward, at Mass, I had a tender recollection of the words, "But that the world may know, that I love the Father: and as the Father hath given me commandment, so do I" (John 14, v. 31).

Friday afternoon after I had pondered on the usefulness of your services and had wondered whether or not it was God's Will that Your Reverence should be Rector—which I believed would happen since the Superiors desired it—I heard the Voices say, "Not always is My Will done." These words impressed themselves unforgettably on my mind.

I went to the shrine Saturday afternoon, where the Lord granted me the Mercy of gathering me to Himself. And, reminding me of those words once again, He said, "This is something for thee to weep over: there are still those who resist Me, those of My Own household who learn at My school." I said, "They may not understand, Lord, that this is Your Will." Again, I heard the Voices, "That is clear." It seemed to me that this petition accorded with the Lord's Will and would be granted. All these Mercies kindled my heart with Divine love on the one hand, and consumed and annihilated me on the other. The Lord humbled my pride by reminding me that Balaam's ass had once talked (Numbers 22, v. 28) and that the more inadequate the instrument which God utilizes, the greater the proof of His wisdom, power and goodness. I humbled myself before the Lord and acknowledged that I no more deserved His favor than had Balaam's beast of burden. And I said, "My Lord, since I am so unworthy, do not permit me to remain in such a state. Give me understanding that I may know, appreciate, and render gratitude and service for so many Mercies."

Monday night, I spent an hour and a half prostrate in prayer; and for an additional half hour, I prayed with arms outstretched in the form of the Cross. Love burned within me so that I could hardly contain myself. I begged the Lord to grant me the Mercy of waking me after four hours of sleep;

and I obligated His Majesty by binding my hands with a rope of horsehair. He was so good as to wake me at two o'clock. Before Matins, I spent an hour and a half at prayer, not with any special petition, but praying for everybody with acts of love and praise and resignation. The Lord drew nearer when the bell rang for Matins, and instantly I experienced new light and strength. I know not how, but fleeting as the sensation was, my soul could not doubt it had come from God.

Following Prime, I prayed for an hour before Communion and for an hour and a half afterward, during which time the Lord showed me the Mercy of gathering me to Him. When I besought Him to prepare our hearts for the coming of the Holy Ghost, so that we might receive Him in plenitude and become wholly spiritual, I was given to understand that it would please the Lord for me to remain in the shrine until time for Divine Office, devoting myself to prayer without speaking to anyone. I responded, "You know whether or not it will be done aright, since You have imposed that condition." [92] Then I was given to understand that this was in consideration of the frailty of my heart, which is still timid and does not wholly embolden itself to overcome difficulties.

As I recollected how that person of whom you know had told me she was in doubt as to whether or not she would remain where she was, I was made to see that it is now Our Lord Who guides her. She must believe herself moved by the Holy Ghost when inclined toward any particular act of virtue. It is His Majesty's Will that she let herself be led by Him, in spite of the difficulties of human nature; because, "I can do all things in him who strengtheneth me" (Philip. 4, v. 13).

When Your Reverence wrote me that you were concerned about the efforts to keep you here and said that I should take up the matter with the Lord, I would have liked to do so promptly, and went in to prayer with that purpose in mind. However, since I had to go to confession, a feeling of anxiety and distress came over me. It did not leave me while I prayed the Lord for light by which to examine my conscience, and for words with which to express myself. At a quarter of nine, I went to my cell, exhausted from the labors of the day. I took the discipline, and put on the haircloth, and remained at prayer, but such a dizziness possessed me that I could not prevail against it. In spite of all this, I forced myself to write out my confession, beseeching the Lord to help me and guide my pen, since I did not know how to begin and had not had time for self-examination. Then I read what was written. The Lord, almost without effort on my part, kept recalling to me the whole of my past life, indicating to me how it should be set down in writing. I was at the task from before ten o'clock until one. The dizziness left me. Then I laid my head on my arms and slept about an hour and a half. At Matins, I felt more vigorous and alert than usual, and experienced the same peace as before, despite the fact that I had written down my sins and reread the manuscript several times. I entreated the Lord to make clear what Your Reverence wished to know. I was given to understand that Your Reverence had vowed not to seek preferment in any way, but, on the other hand, not to hinder it, since that would be to go against God's Will; and, in this instance, would be an endeavor to remove the means employed by His Majesty for His purpose. In view of this message and of the fact that five or six days earlier, when praying that the Lord should defend His Own cause and keep Your Reverence here as Rector, I had been told, "I shall do whatever thou askest of Me," I took it for granted that you would remain. I was as sure of this as if I saw it made a reality before my eyes and have been unable to ask anything further in this regard.

On Saturday afternoon, I spent two hours in prayer. It came into my mind that, since I am what I am to God and since He is what He is to me, though I have fully deserved hell, I now have no fear of being damned and God does not cease to show me mercy. I recalled David's words, "So far hath he removed our iniquities from us" (Psalm 102, v. 12). That is why nothing can harm me, and so I need not fear. I saw that God shows His mercy to a soul by communicating with it, because it has been given a new gift of grace. I realized that I am no longer what I once was: then death and sin lived within me, where now is a new gift. And I said to the Lord, "My Lord, since You do not desire me to remember my sins with regard to the damage which they might have wrought in me, because they were offenses against You, I long to have a knife of pain pierce my heart. I would have preferred to suffer all the torments of the martyrs rather than to have committed one single offense against You. If, by years of suffering, I could undo any offense against You, I would consider it a great Mercy to undergo them." These thoughts, and others I do not now recall, came to me in that period of prayer.

Afterward, for a quarter of an hour, I stood with outstretched arms beside the Cross, and told the Lord that another thief sought His mercy. I had stolen from Him that which was His, namely, my own body and soul, and delivered it up to evil. Now I desired to commit another theft, far more profitable to myself, by stealing from Him His Will. I was given to understand that, by loving Him, I should obtain my desire, in accordance with these words, "I love them that love me" (Proverbs 8, v. 17). As I yearned for a single spark of this Divine fire, I came to see that in the heart of Christ Our Lord is fire enough to set the whole world aflame, and in that source I should seek it. So, in the words of the good thief, I entreated Him to remember me: "Lord, remember me" (Luke 23, v. 42). Then I heard Him say, "Let my tongue cleave to my jaws, if I do not remember thee: If I make not Jerusalem the beginning of my joy" (Psalm 136, v. 6). Then the bell rang, and I had to go.

When I received the Lord on Sunday, this thought came to me, "Christ lives and works in me." I kept these words in mind, giving thanks. Then I was seized with such bodily agony that I could not have remained on my knees if it had persisted. I entreated the Lord to alleviate this suffering, since I could not be with Him if it continued. He took away the pain, and I was enabled to kneel two hours longer. Then I became almost overwhelmed by sleep. I begged His Majesty to keep me awake, even if it were by despair, since I would rather suffer than sink into oblivion. Then He brought my sins to my mind, and made me reflect on my effrontery in breaking His Divine law. I shed many remorseful tears even while my heart burned with love for Him to Whom I owe so much. He said, "Mark how I have waked thee."

Friday night, when the message came from Your Reverence to commend a certain invalid to Our Lord, I did so most solicitously, but did not think about him again until late on Sunday, when our Abbess told me that he was either dead or dying. I went into prayer, reproaching myself for my carelessness, and again commended him to God. I asked, "Lord, how is it that I have been so remiss as to obedience in this matter?" Then I seemed to hear Him say, "It is because if thou wert to ask his life of Me, I should have to grant it." I kept wondering why He should have said this, until, finally, I was given to understand that it was because He had promised to grant whatever I might ask. Consequently, it was not possible for me to commend the stricken man to His Majesty except as dead, even though I did not quite dare believe what I had just been given to understand. Therefore, I entreated Him that, if the man were indeed dead, and I had been somewhat to blame in this matter, He would grant me the Mercy of not letting that soul know my part of the responsibility, but would permit it to enter immediately upon the joys of heaven. All this caused me deep emotion, and I marveled to see myself conferring with God as if it were my right. I remembered how, in explanation of the verse, "I will not now call you servants . . . but . . . friends" (John 15, v. 15), St. Gregory says, "It is because the servant does not know what the Master does." The Lord reveals the secrets of His heart to His friends, and so had He done with me. Then I began doubting whether this were true or false, and dared not write it.

Monday morning, I was so sleepy and indifferent that, although I spent two hours at prayer, I could not really enter into it. Then I asked, "How does this conform, Lord, with so many Mercies?" I understood the answer to be that it was to make me realize His Majesty's favors were conferred on me quite gratuitously, and for no merit of my own. Later that afternoon, I was told they thought the invalid had died. It moved me greatly to see there could be no doubt that I had understood aright what had been revealed to me. I went to Vespers and gave thanks, my heart softened by Divine love. At the same time, I knew myself unworthy of so many Mercies. I entreated the Lord to grant that soul the favor of enjoying His glory, and heard the response, "He does so already." Those words were like a fiery dart, kindling my ardor even more. I asked, "Lord, how is it possible for You to grant me so many favors?" and received the reply, "That and more I do for My friends." It seemed to me that a force outside myself was being exerted to make me write this down. In that frame of mind, I went to the shrine and there, prostrating myself, told the Lord, with many tears, that if such were His Will, I would obey, with His Majesty's help. And so I did. Afterward, I remained there to pray. St. Gregory's words came to me: "How great is human dignity in being the friends of God: we are the servants of God, yet He calls us friends." I realized that, high as this dignity is, there is another bond even closer, that of the Spouse. If there is nothing hidden between friends, how could there be concealment from the Spouse? It seemed to me that by this Mercy every stronghold was captured. Therefore, I said, "Lord, if this is to be, let me not live in myself, for I am oppressed in a house so strait and narrow. When I see my own unworthiness and lack in loving and serving You, fears encompass me. Let me live with You and so lift up my heart." Thereupon, although I cannot explain it, I experienced a glimpse of life in God by a sudden light which, had it lasted, would have left nothing more to desire.

Wednesday afternoon, as I withdrew into myself at prayer, I told the Lord that, though previously I did not have leave to dwell on the past, I had now been ordered to return to His Majesty in the same state as before He had received me for His Own. Then I experienced such quietude as if I had never suffered any perturbation whatsoever; and with it, some memories of the past came before me, not to distress but rather to reassure me. But I did not wish to have my mind dwell on anything. I do not know how it was: almost the entire hour was taken up in this reflection. At the end of that time, as I was recalling my sins, I remembered St. Paul's words: "Where sin abounded, grace did more abound" (Rom. 5, v. 20). I saw that from this abundance was born the yearning for penance felt by us who have fallen and the opportunity of making amends to God. Those who have not fallen do not feel this so keenly. With these words in mind, I went to the refectory quite cheerful. Afterward, I returned to the choir for another half hour. There I recalled that thought of St. Ignatius, "I am the wheat of Jesus Christ and must be ground by the teeth of wild beasts in order to be placed on God's table." I felt that I, too, was wheat and, just as the grain must be threshed and milled in various ways before it becomes well-seasoned bread, so must I suffer until seasoned to God's liking. I found this thought very comforting. Later I remembered that, following the Resurrection, the Apostles invited the Lord to partake of broiled fish and a honeycomb, but the Gospel does not say they offered Him bread. Then it occurred to me that I would give Him bread of finest flour, made of my heart by pure labor. So I said, "Let others give the Lord whatever they wish, but I offer my sweat and toil, and am willing to be ground and broken for His Sake." Afterward, I again considered the first point and reflected that a white streak shows more plainly on a black background than against any other color. In the same way, Mercies glow more brightly in the case of one who has sinned than of one who is sinless. I saw that I had no reason to glorify myself. It destroyed the wheel of vanity in me to look down at my feet, which were the chief pride of my youth.[93] I delighted in the fact that all the good put into my soul by God was gratuitous. While these thoughts were passing through my mind, there was some suspension of my powers and senses, but my spirit was ardent.

Later, I reflected that one not knowing God's goodness and His liberality in communicating with His creatures could not possibly keep from being scandalized if He should reveal this confession, together with the record of the Mercies shown me. Such a one would doubt whether these things were true or false. The thought came to me that, just as it is fitting for fire to burn, so it is fitting for God Our Lord to bear with us and pardon us and be merciful. Since all this is natural in Him, we have no cause for marveling that He does so; nor should we wonder because man is an ingrate, and repays God's benefits with ingratitude, for this is characteristic of our corruptible humanity. What did make me marvel was that God, being purity itself, permits souls which are to be His temple to plunge into the mire of vice, so that the devil can say to God: "This soul was my slave before it was Thine, not only through Adam's fall, but through consenting to sin of its own will." I understood from this, as had been made clear to me on another occasion, that God permitted these things in order to demonstrate the virtue and strength of the Blood of Christ

Our Lord which can rescue the soul from the devil and give it a new life of grace.

After this, at Holy Communion, I asked, "Is it possible, Lord, that You delight to come into my heart?" And I understood His answer to be, "It is very possible: 'If your sins be as scarlet, they shall be made as white as snow: and if they be red as crimson, they shall be white as wool' (Isaias 1, v. 18)." For this, I gave thanks. After I had received His Majesty and rejoiced in His Presence, I felt an overwhelming desire to take the vow of the cloistered nuns. I longed to bind myself to God in a thousand ways, knotting one bond over another. Just as this might constrict some spirits, it would broaden mine. And I would feel safer.

Friday, I left Matins at a quarter to six. It was snowing, and the sky was so overcast that it looked as if the storm would go on for hours. This grieved me, because I had been expecting Your Reverence and feared you might not come. So I entered the choir and begged the Lord that He stop the snow for a while, which He could do so easily, in order that it would not hinder your coming. Later, at Prime, I continued my entreaties, and heard Him say, "I shall bring him to thee." When I left Prime, I saw the sky had cleared, and gave thanks to the Lord. But, as Your Reverence did come, I did not think of the matter again, nor give special heed to this Mercy. Afterward, when I was at prayer, the Lord reminded me of it, as though reprimanding me for my heedlessness, and told me that any one of His Mercies was deserving of perpetual gratitude.

I spent three hours in prayer Saturday night, from nine to twelve. For an hour and a half, I was afire with love divine, entreating the Holy Spirit to delay His coming no longer, lest our hope should weaken. In the morning, while praying that Doña María have perseverance, I was given to understand that the Mercies the Lord granted her were credited to me, so that I should not have any hindrance, but rather help from her.

This dismayed me. I said, "My Lord, rather it is through her that You grant mercy to me." Then, once again, I received the same message as before; so I said, "Lord, I give You thanks for this; but I shall not be satisfied until You grant Your servant what he desires. With that Mercy, I should be content, even if You gave me nothing else." Immediately after Communion, these words came to mind: "We will come to him, and will make our abode with him" (John 14, v. 23). I rejoiced that I had felt the Presence, not only of Our Redeemer's Divinity, but also of His Most Holy Body.

While I was at afternoon prayer on Wednesday, a sick nun called for me. She was suffering greatly, her arms spasmodically outflung to form a cross. She wished me to succor her with a relic of Mother Teresa of Jesus in which she had great faith. I replied that I would go to her and, as I entreated the Lord to be merciful to that religious for His servant's sake, I seemed to feel something like a bolt of lightning in my soul. It made me tremble, and I thought I understood that He would grant me this Mercy, too. I paid no heed to this, but, as if overlooking it, continued to pray for the sick nun. Finally, I went to her, comforted by the certainty that God Our Lord was to grant my prayer through the intercession of Mother Teresa of Jesus. The patient likewise was soothed, although she always feels temporarily worse when any relic is brought to her sickbed. At last, I laid it upon her breast and, in a little while, she worsened. One of her eyes closed, her mouth was twisted from the terrible pain in her head and shoulders, and she felt as if she were impaled. When she realized what a condition she was in, she motioned to me to take away the relic. After removing it, I prayed the Lord more fervently than ever to make her better, and made the Sign of the Cross over her eyes and mouth. Her mouth untwisted, but the torment in her head was unabated. Withal, I felt my heart enkindled. Though once more I was given to understand that the Lord would grant His mercy to her through me, I did not believe it, but humbled myself and said this message could not be meant for me, unworthy as I am. This uncertain situation continued. I dared not reach any conclusion regarding it, because I feared it might all be due to the spirit of pride.

Since I was unable to enter into prayer Thursday morning, I heard the news of victory[94] while in the choir. As I gave thanks to the Lord, I recalled the victory of the Hebrews brought about by the petition of Moses when he prayed with arms extended like a cross. So should we pray in order to be heard, crucified by exercises of mortification; for God permits Himself to be conquered by such prayer. With this small ray of light, I remained for two hours withdrawn into myself, my spirit ardent. During that time, I received Holy Communion, and rejoiced in the Presence of the Lord.

While I was at Vespers Friday, the Blessed Sacrament was taken to an ailing nun, and exposed so that it might be returned to the Tabernacle. I said, adoring Him, "My Spouse, how marvelous it is that You are where You are!" I was so moved by these words, recognizing their truth, that the Lord enraptured me and I began withdrawing into myself. However, since I was at Office, I had to resist. The wound remained in my soul. It seemed to me that thenceforward I could not address Him except by the name of Spouse. I prayed fervently for two hours afterward, in accordance with the orders of Your Reverence. I asked My Spouse whether or not I should continue to be active when fatigued from lack of sleep, and was given to understand that if He were to deal with me as He had dealt with St. Catherine, I should be always ready and willing, as she was. She was as frail as I, and as ailing. I acquiesced most willingly in all this, and yearned to do in all things as St. Catherine did, to be pleasing in the sight of Him to Whom I owe so much. Merely for Him to receive my service would be Mercy enough.

I have been fighting against one thought during these last days: it is that the sick religious would now progress in virtue and Our Lord would grant her many Mercies. I strove against this thought by praying Our Lord to grant her the Mercies so long as I surpassed her in loving and suffering. The thought went so far as to suggest that everything I had would prove to be illusion, while what came to her would be spiritually sound, because it entered a purer and more simple soul. To this, I responded that, if such were the Will of God, I sought nothing but its fulfillment, and that He should use me according to His Will, so long as He did not take away His love. Thus beset, twice I thought I heard Him say, "I love thee more," but I dared not receive Him. While I was looking for something else, I found the note.[95] As Your Reverence had said you would like to talk to me about it, I felt that I could read it without scruple. I read it and grew calm. That troublesome thought has not returned to vex me. In consequence, I have been enabled to treat her reverently, as a temple wherein God delights to dwell.

On Sunday, Feast of the Holy Trinity, I was abstracted during Communion, because the day and night preceding I had been unable to enter into prayer. That morning, at Office, one of the nuns kept disturbing me so much that I could not bear it; she did not know what she was doing and, when I called her attention to this, she was annoyed. Finally, I withdrew into myself as best I could and approached the altar rail to receive the Lord. I asked Him why His Majesty so often concealed Himself, since He knew that, without Him, I could do nothing aright; everything seemed crooked and tortured. My heart softened, and I began to savor the aroma of that Divine Bread which nourishes my hopes. It seemed to me that Christ Our Lord's Most Holy Body was like a flower of the field which all may pluck and which all tread upon. So have they done with this Our Lord. Yet, the more He is trampled underfoot, the more fragrance emanates from Him by which to draw all things to Himself. I recalled the words, "And I, if I be lifted up from the earth, will draw all things to myself" (John 12, v. 32). I meditated a while on these and other matters. Then, as I found admission to prayer which, until then, I had not had since Your Reverence had asked me to pray regarding a certain subject, I told the Lord He had before Him a beast of burden, laden with petitions from His servants. He knew their only desire was to ascertain His Will. Therefore, I besought Him to make it clear to the one who would carry it out. Though I begged this insistently, no answer came. I went to Choir, and at Terce was given to understand that I should abstract myself in prayer during the sermon, as is my wont. I heard this verse, "I will lead her into the wilderness: and I will speak to her heart" (Osee 2, v. 14). I began to feel abashed, and inquired of the Lord what He had found in me that He should fix His eyes upon me, without regard to many other souls far abler to serve Him with gratitude. Then St. Paul's words came to me, that God chooses the lowest, weakest and most unworthy channel to reveal the extent of His wisdom, power and virtue (1 Cor. 1, v. 27).

Afterward, during the sermon, I obeyed the Lord and approached the altar in the choir, where I became absorbed in reflections. I told Him that, although obedience required me to bring this problem to His Majesty, I did so very hesitantly. Nevertheless, it was my understanding that as His spouse had permission to treat of whatever matter she wished, there was no real reason for my timidity. I gave Him thanks, and besought Him once more to enlighten a certain person with knowledge of His Divine Will. I was informed that she would remain more humble if the knowledge came to her through other means. When it was made clear that I was to be this chosen medium, I asked, "But Lord, how am I to make my advice credible?" Then I was made to see that His

Majesty would give strength to my words so that they would be believed. This assurance brought light to my soul by which to recognize its own unworthiness, and left it shattered and overcome in the presence of such majesty and grandeur. I perceived that He before Whom the powers of heaven tremble stooped to the lowest on earth and was pleased to communicate with her.

On Friday, after I had been fully aware of God's Presence all day, I felt invigorated, without need of food, at the hour for collation, and went with *Doña* María, who was on her way to supper, to drink a little water. The Lord in His kindness and mercy did not wish me to go unfed, and therefore sent me leavings from His table. I began to withdraw into myself. Since we two were alone, and since Your Reverence has told me that when I am with *Doña* María I need not resist abstraction, I permitted myself to be carried away. I remained for a time in that condition, my spirit kindled, yearning ardently to see myself united with God. It seemed to me as if He were drawing me toward Himself and as if my desire were about to be fulfilled. Then suddenly I was deprived of that rapture. Most sorrowfully I came to myself, trembling all over as I tried to unfold my arms. I do not know what *Doña* María thought of this, for we have not spoken of it.

On Saturday, when I commended a lady (*Doña* María Hervás)[86] of this city to God, and was wondering how He could permit passion to take such hold on a heart so filled with love of His Majesty, I was given to understand, "There is no reason for surprise, since her heart belongs only partially to God." I meditated on this and prayed over it, grieving that there are so few, even among those choosing virtue for their part, who give all their heart to God and love Him purely. It was clear to me that, for souls not wholly detached and freed from all human and sensual love of friends and relatives, and from consideration of their own comfort, ease and pleasure, even in quite normal ways, it is impossible to progress in divine spiritual love, no matter how much these souls seem to strive toward virtue. This is "Denial of one's self," which Christ Our Lord set in first place for those who wish to achieve perfection in following Him (Matt. 16, v. 24).

Afterward, I felt deeply hurt as I went to the Lord with a note from a certain priest (Father Juan Herrera)[86] I said, "My Lord, I would rather be deemed mad and vainglorious than to have it said I am especially favored by You." And He replied, "Why doth it disturb thee?" I responded, "Lord, it has importance, for we human creatures know not how to give glory to You alone for Your works. Hence it is that there are those who believe me somewhat deserving in Your sight, not realizing that all I receive from You is wholly gratuitous." Then I entreated Him to let me die, since there would be time enough thereafter to manifest His glory. These and other matters of like tenor passed through my sorrowful mind and I shed tears, the while I shuddered at my own weakness. St. Paul's words came to me: "We have this treasure in earthen vessels" (2 Cor. 4, v. 7). However, I perceived that though the vessel was fragile, God held it in His hand.

On Wednesday, after Communion, I told the Lord that I did not wish to be burdened with these memoirs and asked that He should put an end to their writing. But His Majesty reminded me, "Be it thy care to do My Will, and give no thought to what may befall thee." Then he added, "I shall look after thy affairs and not let them turn out badly." Later on, at Mass, the Lord drew me close, with deep recognition and appreciation of His Majesty's guidance, so that my heart was alight with gratitude and I said, "Lord, I entrust my all to You." Then I heard Him reply, "Well mayest thou do so." Thereupon, I besought Him to let me go, since I had to read at Refectory; but He replied, "There is still time," as if giving me to understand that He did not wish me to leave until the last possible moment. All this stirred my heart the more. I should have preferred not to bring such bliss to an end; but in order to avoid giving rise to talk, I forced myself to go. After dinner, during prayer, I was somewhat abstracted. This abstraction continued throughout the other hours of prayer and I said, at last, my heart aflame with yearning, "Lord, I would like to be a saint!" Then I seemed to understand that this desire would be granted. It occurred to me that the saints are the stones in the celestial edifice of the heavenly Jerusalem, hewn by blows from the quarry of this world. And in my heart I welcomed this thought and did not shrink from the suffering entailed. All that day, I enjoyed the Presence of Christ Our Lord, while the words of my mouth and the meditations of my heart alike seemed kindled by Divine fire.

It had been in my mind not to take Communion on the Feast Day of Our Father, St. Bernard,[96] since my weakness had been so great that I feared lest it might return and make it impossible for me to carry out my duties; and there was much work to do. When I saw what His Majesty had done for me, I felt somewhat ashamed of my schemes, founded on little faith, and abandoned them, casting myself into the hands of Our Lord. I knew then that, since He is all powerful, He would give me strength if it were good for me to have it. Sweeping left me tired and perspiring, and these words came to mind, "In the sweat of thy face shalt thou eat bread" (Genes. 3, v. 19)—words which may have been a curse to Adam, but for me were a great blessing and mercy, as I understood this to mean the Living Bread, Christ Our Lord in the Blessed Sacrament. Since it had cost His Majesty the sweat of His brow to leave His children this Divine sustenance, it would not be just for me to enjoy it without work and sweat. Whatever I might be called on to suffer seemed to me little enough in exchange for receiving Him.

But later, the Lord certainly made me laugh, for He asked

me whether or not I would cease to fast if some day He deprived me of Communion altogether. "That is much to ask, Lord," I replied. "Everything is possible with Your help; but without it, I know not what I can do." Then I was given to understand that He would not leave me to rely on my own strength, but would succor me; and that He wished it to be as He had said. I became confused and agreed to this and to whatever else He might command. All was so fleeting, without formulation into words, but only an impression on the mind, that it required fixed attention to apprehend it. However, it gave me very special pleasure, faith and confidence.

Tuesday and Wednesday, the Feast of Our Father St. Bernard, were Communion days. Since it seemed to me it would show little faith if I left off fasting because I had to work, I continued to fast without difficulty until Wednesday night, when I became very weak. Nevertheless, I persisted in my determination not to breakfast until after High Mass.

This resolution cost me a good deal Thursday. It is my chief regret that when I am so weakened I am unable to pray or even to kneel, and all is lost in sleeping. As prayer is much better than fasting, I wondered how it could be God's Will for so rigorous a fast to be observed, since there could not be both fasting and prayer. It bewilders me at times to see that the greater the love one carries, the more God seems to leave the burden to one's own strength. During the dreadfully hot days we have been having, I dragged about, exhausted, unable to take thought for praying, or for talking with the Lord or, indeed, for anything. Even what I can usually do best, which is to pray for Your Reverence, I cannot now do effectively at all, but only with such remissness and so limply that my petitions could not even reach the ear of God. I have communicated several times in such a way that I am sure I could have given His Majesty no pleasure.

Last Friday, before Communion, I was falling asleep and,

in order to stay awake, I stretched out my arms in the shape of a cross. Then, tearfully, I began repeating the words of the Spouse: "I sought him whom my soul loveth: I sought him, and found him not." [97] I saw that I could not find Him in the accustomed way, namely, by trial of the flesh through penance, by lowliness, by silence, by denial of my own will and by its resignation to His. Then I came to understand that Our Lord wished me to be a martyr of love, that Divine love itself was to be my executioner, and that in deigning Himself to torment me He was showing me a mark of great favor. All this I felt deeply, intimately, and proudly aware of dying, at the hands of Life Itself.

Since Wednesday until today—Saturday—I have been unable to enter into prayer. What preys upon me is an anxiety, leaving me no peace, since I seem to myself to be upon a road most perilous and uncertain, in danger of colliding with the Will of God and doubtful lest I be mistaking darkness for light and light for darkness. I have been so hard pressed as to beseech the Lord not to take me along this way, for He knows my weakness is such that I stumble and fall, even on level ground. While afflicted with these perplexities, I heard a Voice say fleetingly, "Thou hast not yet learned to know Me and therefore art perturbed." Then, when I said, "Lord, I cannot put all of this out of my mind; what shall I do?" the answer came, "Leave it in My hands."

Sunday, after Refectory, I went to the shrine and besought the Lord to forgive me and be friends with me once more, since I could not bear His prolonged absence. I was given to understand the fault was mine, because I had not cast off my doubts, but had allowed them to overwhelm me. Then I took up the discipline and applied the small chain; and I went to the choir and prayed there from nine to ten. Immediately thereafter, I knelt on the floor at the foot of my bed until about twelve. Through the Lord's mercy, I was enabled to enter into prayer and His love and the joy of His Presence were as a flame within me. Thereupon, recalling again the dangers in these things that I am given to understand about other persons, I now feel confident as far as that is concerned. It seemed to me that, though the vessel was of fragile clay, as St. Thomas says, God held it in His hands, so that it was as firm as a rock in the midst of the sea, which can never be moved by contrary winds or squalls or tempests. I felt sure that everything would come out right in the end.

Later on, at Prime, the Lady Abbess sent me to talk to Lady ———,[98] asking that she stop importuning the Superior about a certain matter. I had been told that a lady, well known to us, was very eager to become a religious in this house; yet, on the other hand, the Community seemed to be dissuading her from the idea. I wished to inquire the Lord's Will in this regard, but I felt it would be audacious for me to do so on my own responsibility and, hence, did not dare. During the sermon that day, however, I thought, what if Father Rector knows something about all this and comes to me and berates me before everyone? And not only he, but the others who may preach to us? What should I do if this matter proved as upsetting here among the Sisters as often happens with things of less moment? Then it seemed to me that, so long as the light I was then enjoying continued to shine for me, I could not be distressed, but could bear anything without anxiety or perturbation. So I offered my will to the Lord, saying that if it should be His desire for me to suffer ignominy, then let it come and welcome. I do not much doubt this will happen, if Our Lord proceeds as He has begun. Throughout the day I was enthralled with His Majesty's Presence; then, when night came, He let me suffer some three hours at prayer. Several times during the day, I laid my problems before Him, as Your Reverence had ordered; but He did not deign to enlighten me.

Tuesday, following Chapter, I went to the shrine. After reading a little in the thesis on love, I became abstracted, suspended, and ardent for a while. Then, when I went to receive Communion, I was again suspended, although not to the same degree. Once more I took up the matter with His Majesty, but was not enlightened. However, with respect to these fears I have, Our Lord gave me to understand that He would like me to leave off worrying about dangers I might encounter on the road along which He leads me; all this should be left in His hands. While I was being given to understand this, my heart seemed full and I was left with no more anxiety in this regard than I would have felt had it concerned someone other than myself.

Later, at Terce, it was made particularly clear to me that I had no part in any of this, no more than a tongue that does not move of its own accord; and my plea that the Lord would not lead me along that way had been resistance to His Holy Will. Then I reflected that His Divine Majesty takes no offense when we humble ourselves; and I realized that though humility had been my intention, I had not achieved it, but rather had offered God advice, although His Majesty already knew full well that, without His aid, I cannot stand on my feet, much less walk. I was made to understand that humility is recognition, almost certainly, of the fact that I can do nothing good of myself, nor do I deserve His favor. Therefore, I should be resigned to the Divine Will, and let myself be borne whithersoever it may be His Majesty's pleasure, even though, in my own sight, I should seem about to fall headlong down a precipice. I felt, too, that together with the instruction itself, resignation sufficient for anything and everything the Lord might send was given me, also. All the foregoing occurred while my soul was rapt and attentive to its God.

On another day, I was given to understand that I should not eat meat and that some affront must be offered me on that account, so that I might suffer in imitation of St. Catherine. I understood further that the Lord would help me at Communion, just as He had helped her, and that I should lose consciousness during excessive prayer. All these gave me such delight and solace that I begged those who were praying on either side of me to help me give thanks to His Majesty for a Mercy he had granted a soul. I asked one to say, "We praise thee, Lord," and the other, "Praise the Lord, O my soul." For a time, I was so enraptured that my whole body trembled. I do not know how all this can be believed.

Thursday, at Communion, I recalled the words the angel said to St. John, showing him the fountain of living waters, "Adore God" (Apocal. 22). And I remembered also the words, "This is the true God and life eternal" (1 John 5, v. 20). That most holy body was the body of God, and any of its members, any drop of blood, any tear, was member, blood or tear of God. I recalled, too, "No man cometh to the Father, but by me" (John 14, v. 6). None can please His Eternal Father if not incorporated in Him through faith and love. Then it seemed as if He were inviting me to enter through His Divine Heart, urging, "Come in! Come in!" over and over again, until my heart was afire with love and longing; but I knew not the how nor the where. My emotion was so vehement that my faculties were suspended and my head and my hands benumbed. Then I asked, "Lord, what is this conflict into which You plunge me?" The answer came, "Enter into the dark and secret place." Next it seemed to me that I was lifted up and set in a place wherein I was given the utmost appreciation of that Incomprehensible Being. Nevertheless, my soul could see nothing, but was as one who warms himself at a great fire behind a curtain, so that, although he can see neither its size nor its flame, he perceives it to be a fire with a mighty blaze, for he feels its scorching heat. Thus the soul, though it sees nothing, needs must believe this is God, by virtue of the awe and reverence inspired by that Majesty with Whom he seems to be in contact, even though in darkness and beyond a curtain. It also came to me that divinity is a mirror in which all creatures see themselves; and that it is like the sea whence all rivers flow and whither all return. These things were not pictured to me distinctly, but rather in a confused mass, together with more which I do not recall. While preoccupied with these reflections, I was summoned to sing the lesson at Terce. It cost me an effort to go, and my arms ached and trembled until they returned to normal. Blessed be the Lord. Amen.

Friday night, when I had three hours of prayer, I observed very clearly, during that period of devotion, how different is the way of prayer by means of which God has shown me the present Mercies, and the ordinary method through which He has favored me these many years past. It seemed to me that something of this difference might be perceived in the negative method, which St. Dionysius offers us for knowing God. The saint avers that God is neither good nor true nor wise in the sense that other beings are; the goodness, truth and wisdom which are in Him are such that no created understanding can comprehend them; they can be comprehended only by another understanding infinitely great; in other words, only by the Lord Himself. So it is that in this other way of prayer, neither the love's ardor nor the Beloved's embrace, nor the delight and sweetness, nor the desire, are like those experienced in ordinary prayer. The difference is so vast it cannot be expressed nor even understood.

It was time for Refectory and, since I had received Communion and now felt the Lord's Presence, I besought Him to declare His Will as to whether I should remain with Him or go. And I was given to understand, "It is quite clear, since I have come to thee, that I wish thee to remain here." Therefore, I most thankfully remained and began to be absorbed. *Doña* María came in, but I told her I would dine at the second table. During the entire refectory period, which must have lasted about an hour, I burned with an ardent desire to be united with My Spouse. I was still in this state when the time came for the second table, and did not know what to do, since the Lord did not wish me to leave, nor did I wish to go. I asked, "Lord, what shall I do, since I have been ordered not to omit dinner?" I understood the answer to be that the order did not apply to this occasion and that, even though I ate nothing, the Blessed Sacrament would sustain me. I was further given to understand that such had been His way with St. Catherine: "Not in bread alone doth man live, but in every word that proceedeth from the mouth of God" (Matt. 4, v. 4). That was enough to make me resolve that I would stay as long as Our Lord wished. I asked *Doña* María to conceal my absence from table, if she could, since I was then in no condition for food, but would eat something later if I felt the need. Although, in my own mind, I pictured how each of the Sisters would express herself on the subject, if they noticed I was not there, in order to submit to the Divine Will, I resigned myself to whatever might come. So I remained for another hour, burning in that Divine fire. It seemed to me that I would be wholly purified after so long a time in the kiln of love. Altogether, I was there for five hours and a half, uninterruptedly. I stood for one hour, and spent the rest of the time on my knees. While in the end I was left with no strength whatever, I do not believe this weakness came from lack of food so much as from the force of my absorption and the long period spent in kneeling. At three o'clock, I took some raisins and a little water, and felt better.

On various occasions, the Lord has indicated that He does not desire me to eat on the days I take Communion. During more than eight years, on every day I took Communion, I no sooner sat at table with bread and meat before me than I visualized the body of Our Lord so vividly that it became unbearable: my eyes were fountains of tears, and to open my mouth for food was torture. Since I was, nevertheless, forced to eat by my aunt—may she rest in peace!—many times I was in such a state that I had to rise and leave the table, weeping. Everybody who witnessed such an occurrence was scandalized, and all expressed themselves in ways which required patience to bear.

Then there were three additional years during which I felt the Presence of Our Redeemer's body. It seemed as if the Species was not consumed for many hours. I also suffered considerably when I ate during the time I felt this Presence. However, obedience smooths out everything.

Now it seems as if Our Lord has undertaken another approach. If He continues in this new way, I think we needs must obey Him, for He leaves us no freedom, since He has bound the soul to Himself by withdrawal of the senses. I do not mean I could not exert sufficient force to go wherever I wished; but, if I did so, I should lose much of what the Lord offers me.

Wednesday, the hours of prayer, both morning and afternoon, brought me nothing but complete aridity. Then, as Compline was ending, I felt the need to withdraw into myself, and remained, absorbed, in the choir stall. *Doña* María came to call me to supper. I delayed a little, but it was not long enough. By forcing myself, I managed to go in, though I could hardly walk a step. I took two mouthfuls of salad, then retired to my cell and gave myself up to prayer until, gradually, I felt restored to normal. After I had given myself the discipline, I was so tired and lightheaded that I went to bed at eleven. I slept until Matins, and rose as exhausted as if I had never gone to bed at all. After Lauds, I resolved to give myself the discipline. Then I began to feel a drowsiness which I finally overcame with Divine help. When Prime ended at seven o'clock, I went to prayer, and again felt very drowsy until eight. Then I began to rouse myself, ashamed of my luke-warmness and my sloth. When the bell rang for Mass, I went to receive, begging the Lord to forgive me and prepare my heart. After receiving, I delighted in His Presence for more than half an hour; then, since my sister-nuns needed me to help them sing the Mass, I asked the Lord to permit me to go, if such were His Will. The impression I received was that His Majesty wished me to withdraw into myself after Mass if I went to my cell. I told His Majesty to do His Will, assuring Him I would not resist even though the Community gossiped about me. All this made me feel that the Lord wishes our own consent, even when He does a favor. I have several times seen evidence of this. Finally, I made a great effort and went to help at Mass. It seems that such was the Lord's Will, because though, as a rule, I cannot let out my voice, on this occasion I could; so much so, that it was as if I were leading the singing. When Mass ended, I felt as if I were withdrawing into myself, and wondered for a moment what to do. I determined to leave, and went to my cell. It was about ten o'clock. I stayed there until three in the afternoon, after having been at prayer until two o'clock. Then I said the Hours, and wrote a little. I missed Sext, None and Refectory because the Lord kept me so fully occupied and so absorbed that I felt it would be folly to lose this opportunity of being with Him.

I besought the Lord insistently to grant me this Mercy with-out delay: that we should be in accord and that, if it so pleased Him, He should declare to you His Will with regard to receiving the Discalced Franciscan Friars in this house, so that you could make up your mind as to what you were to answer. I was given to understand it had been prophesied that the lion and the lamb would eat from one manger at the coming of the Lord and, furthermore, that they would remain together in peace and unity if they were moved by the same spirit. I begged the Lord to explain this more clearly, but He would not do so.

After this, I went to Vespers. When they were over, our Abbess called me and asked why I was absent from Refectory these days. I replied that I had been unable to go. She understood me, but said that, according to a memorandum she had received, I should not miss it. I told her that I would not miss Refectory whenever able to go, but that sometimes it was impossible. This she conceded. I took the matter to Our Lord, and said, "My Lord, see what is now raised against us." The answer was: "Let not thy heart be troubled. Follow My Divine inspiration and attend not to what they may say." I asked Him also if He would give me permission to take a morsel of food immediately. I understood Him to say, "In two hours," and I replied, "It is well, for my only wish is to do Your Will." Then I heard Him say, "Thou canst do all things through Me. Nature was miraculously sustained in the saints by what they ate. Who can prevent Me from doing the same now with whomsoever I choose?"

Sunday, after having been with Your Reverence, I felt in my soul an extraordinary joy, impossible to conceal, because I was convinced that certainly these Mercies come from the hand of God. My heart was bursting with the desire to do and to endure whatever the Lord wills; I deemed everything I have done hitherto of little worth. After Vespers, I went to prayer. The hour was spent in bringing to mind all these special Mercies and in giving thanks for them to the Lord. Meanwhile, two or three times, I experienced the desire to receive the Blessed Sacrament on Monday. Each time I lifted my eyes to a crucifix, saying, "O My Lord, would that I were worthy to receive You!" This said, I would return to my thanksgiving and, without effort, would again repeat the same words fervently. Then I seemed to hear, "He is more lenient with thee than I would be." As I was pondering what this might mean, the Lord gave me to understand that if His Majesty alone were my guide, He would command me to receive Him oftener, but that He left this matter in the hands of Your Reverence. I asked, "If such be Your Will, My Lord, why do You not have him carry it out?" Then I understood Him to reply, "I give him the desire to do so, but other considerations prevail with him." While at Vespers, I had apprehended something with regard to this, but so fleetingly that I did not understand what nor wherefore; I realized only that it had to do with Communion. I longed for the Lord to make it clear to me and, feeling Him near, turned to Him. "My Lord, what did that mean?" I asked. He repeated to me this verse: "He raiseth up the needy from the dust, and lifteth up the poor from the dunghill" (1 Kings 2, v. 8). He gave me to understand that this, together with another verse, was what He wished to tell me: "That he may place him with princes, with the princes of his people." [99] All these barbs pierced my heart. However, during the night prayer and again during the morning, I was greatly troubled by drowsiness.

This occurred also on Monday, although I resisted as much as I could. I do not believe that anything was lost, for I came out of the struggle ready to challenge all hell if necessary, and as absorbed as if I had been so during prayer. Thus I spent the entire day, most attentive to the Lord. Toward afternoon, it occurred to me that it would be well for me only to sit on my bed and seek support by leaning against the wall when I sleep while in His Presence. I can sleep in that position. I recalled that His Majesty never laid Himself down to sleep, nor did His Blessed Mother;[100] and I thought He would like me to imitate Him in this. Immediately, I offered to do so, saying to the Lord I would serve Him in this way if He would enable me to get along with so little sleep, and to have no need of it during the day; and I promised that, while my senses slept, my heart would keep watch.

That night, I felt very listless, and was hardly able to eat. When Compline ended, at eight o'clock, I went to my cell and was closeted there until after eleven. At first, I was so sluggish and remiss that I sat idle until nine. After that, I remained on my knees, or standing, but meantime experiencing great aridity. While in that condition, desiring to fall asleep, I heard a noise in my cell and was somewhat frightened, but my fear soon passed, as I reflected that nothing can harm me if it be not the Lord's Will; and that, if it were His Will, and He desired devils to ill-treat and wound me, then I would offer myself up for this suffering. The fright roused me, so that I laughed to think how little the devil had profited. I took the discipline, and then went to bed, sitting as I had resolved to do. After twelve, I fell asleep, but woke again at half-past three. I was able to pray for an hour, forcing myself not to fall asleep meanwhile; and, half-dreaming, yearned for Communion. I went to Terce when the bell rang. There and at Mass, I had to be attentive to the Office. The Lord inclined my heart to withdraw; yet it seemed that His indications were less forceful than usual, for I could dissimulate, and spent the whole of Terce in this struggle.

When I felt the impulse growing stronger, I went to my cell and lay prostrate in the Lord's Presence, offering myself for whatever He might desire of me. Though wounded, I did not know the cause of the pain that made me grieve and moan from the depths of my soul. Soon the Lord enlightened me by sending such a hunger to receive Him that my soul yearned with tearful anxiety and I cried, "I desire to receive the Body of My Lord Jesus Christ!" Then I realized those were the words St. Catherine used to say, and that God was granting me one of the Mercies He had granted her. It also came to me that, through the Blessed Sacrament, the Lord imparts to all not only the virtue of His blood, but its sweetness, and that to those who receive it with fervent prayer its sweetness is such that they feel transported to the Biblical land of milk and honey.[101] The Lord filled my heart with these and other thoughts until the anguish I felt began to abate. If all this had occurred before Mass, I do not think I could have waited another day to receive. Since I was an hour and a half at this prayer, and the nuns began coming from the refectory, I ate at the second table.

During this time, I was consumed by Divine love and recalled the words of the Spouse, "My beloved to me, and I to him" (Cant. 2, v. 16). It seemed to me I neither desired nor could desire any other good, and that the Lord, too, was pleased that I should be His. I felt as if He embraced me, fleetingly; but however fleetingly, my heart was filled with bliss and I trembled with love and longing. While I was enjoying this Mercy, impertinent and profitless thoughts did not fail to mingle with it and to fatigue my soul by hampering its delectation. I was absorbed until half-past two; then the Lord departed and I felt tired and sleepy. What I am saying is that it was as if the King should visit a prisoner and have him unshackled throughout the visit. Then, at His Majesty's departure, the chains would be fastened on again. So it is when God Our Lord favors a soul by visiting it. It seems as if the chains and shackles of the passions were removed because the soul is granted freedom and dominion as regards them, neither suffering from lack of sleep nor experiencing hunger, thirst, or weariness. But the moment the Divine visit ends, the poor creature is enchained and imprisoned as before.

At early Mass on Sunday, when ready to receive, I felt the Presence of the Lord and was touched that He wished to come to me when I was in such an unsatisfactory state. I besought Him to take my heart in His hands and give it angelic purity, kindling His Divine love within me. I desired ardently to receive Him, yet, at the same time, shrank from doing so, because I was so unworthy. After having received Him, I was wholly absorbed for more than two hours. I reflected on how little understood is this Divine union wrought by the Holy Sacrament. Then the Lord was pleased to enlighten me somewhat in that regard by those words God spoke to Abraham: "Go forth out of thy country, and from thy kindred, and out of thy father's house, and come into the land which I shall shew thee" (Genes. 12, v. 1). I understand that for the soul to leave its country is to give up its own will and inordinate desires by uprooting them wholly, so that it may pass over to God for Whom it renounces all else. Then His Majesty shows the soul the land of the living, which I understood to be the Kingdom of God, founded on charity and unity. And I understood further that this is not only the dwelling-place of the living, but that the blessed also are to enjoy it forever, because the virtue of charity does not end, like the other virtues, with this life, but continues with even greater perfection into the next. Since God is charity, it follows that this land and portion God promises are likewise charity. "Thou art my portion in the land of the living" (Psalm 141, v. 6). But this portion will be granted us only if we renounce everything of our own. Then Christ's words came into my mind, "As the living Father hath sent me, and I live by the Father; so he that eateth me, the same also shall live by me" (John 6, v. 58). I understood this to mean that, just as the Father lives of Himself that life of God infinitely blessed, so Christ Our Lord lives through the Father the life of God, shared not only by grace and by love, but also by union with the Divine Being. I understood further that the soul, receiving Christ by emerging from itself through renunciation of its own to the Divine Will, shall not only live a life of grace such as is granted by the Blessed Sacrament to those who receive it in a state of grace, but, united to

Christ Our Lord, also shall live the life of God. Thus, by means of this union, it may be Christ Who lives and works in the soul which may have the Lord Himself as its portion, ever attentive to the Yes or No of His Divine lips.

This reflection occurred while I was consumed with Divine love, and it seemed as if I were one of those souls which had wholly surrendered to God, with no will of its own. It was also revealed to me that from the heart of Christ Our Lord, burning with the fire of love, sparks leap into the hearts of the elect, and enkindle those hearts in accordance with the disposition found therein; those that are the least dulled by worldly affections catch fire immediately.

Later, at Terce, I envisioned a nun very cleanly dressed; and entering into my own heart, reflected that the Lord had not only purified me by Communion, but had revived me with those words, "Thy youth shall be renewed like the eagle's" (Psalm 102, v. 5). That state of mind lasted a long time, with those words echoing in my soul. I was also conscious, with unutterable joy, of the Presence of Christ Our Lord Whom I seemed to have in my heart. And I said to Him, "With such company, My Beloved, how fully do I live a new life. Confirm this in me, Lord, for Your glory."

Thursday, before Communion, I spent an hour and a half praying, but without warmth, unable to enter into the devotional spirit. Later, for the time it takes to say a *Credo*,[102] I felt a longing to receive, and did so. For another hour, I rejoiced in His Presence. That afternoon, I had two more hours of prayer in calm and silence, so that it seemed as if I did nothing but enjoy the Lord's Presence and do Him reverence inwardly and outwardly. I felt much withdrawn into myself, with a great desire to keep silent forever.

All day long I felt comforted to see how the Lord was keeping His promise to give me strength for whatever He ordained. So it was that, after spending the entire night on my knees, I was able to fulfill my accustomed duties at the usual hours throughout the day. In spite of attending solemn Vespers, which are so wearying, and of eating nothing since six o'clock, I went without supper. Thereupon, I told the Lord He nourished me so well that I had no need of other food.

During Terce on Friday, the Lord did not leave off the promptings in my heart that invited me to Him and I did not cease excusing myself. I said Doña María de Castro would be scandalized if she should see me. I was given to understand, "Some other day she will be, without My having willed it." Then I said I would importune Your Reverence with these problems and understood the answer to be, "May he have the courage to refuse thee!" In spite of all this, I did not give in, because I did not know whether or not I was imagining a conversation, and to approach Communion on my own initiative seemed to me too great an impertinence. Though finally I did ask that a Host be provided for me, at the last moment I felt so hesitant and doubtful that I dared not receive.

All day my heart felt oppressed and I could not pray; I was confused and ashamed because I had not permitted myself to be led by God. Then I heard Him say, "I know not wherefore thou dost not allow Me to have My Will." He said further that, though He had ordered me to follow the Divine inspiration, I had dared resist it and that, "Whatsoever the Lord pleased he hath done, in heaven, in earth, in the sea, and in all the deeps" (Psalm 134, v. 6). Only I, who am under greater obligation than all these other creatures, have refused to obey Him. Then, when I besought the Lord with tears not to despise the works of His hands, I was told that previously He had offered to guide me and wished to raise me from the dust, but I had not wished it.

Saturday, there arose another cloud of doubts and fears, when I heard the news concerning a Franciscan novice, a

Friar Minor, who was moved by the devil to do excessive penance and to pray day and night. Consequently, he came to hold in low esteem the precepts of his Superiors, believing that, in his own case, it was sufficient to follow the precepts God gave him. He said, therefore, that he had a greater Teacher Whom he must obey. I have pondered this deeply. It seems to me very possible that I am like the novice in question and that the Lord permits such a situation because my sins are so numerous. It also seems to me that my penance, which increases daily, will end by depriving me of my strength; and that if it does not do so, then this may be because the devil, too, can strengthen me for his own purposes. At the very least, when the Community knows about all this, my behavior would be deemed a singularity and all the nuns will be scandalized if I continue in this same way. Yet I shall not fail to carry out scrupulously what I believe to be God's Will, even though my Superior commands me to desist; for failure to observe His Will seems wrong to me, and it also seems wrong to act contrary to her wishes. In saying this, I am referring to penance, but from my viewpoint the same considerations must hold good with respect to Communion; namely, that it is not God Who inspires me with yearning to receive, but the devil, with the purpose of making me demonstrate singularity and thereby scandalizing some of the nuns and causing others to esteem me as better than the rest. I find no loophole by which to escape. If I seek comfort in the fact that I trust nothing to myself alone, this answer comes: it is possible for Your Reverence to be deceived as well as I, and if all these Mercies really come from God, as I believe, my soul would be far advanced in virtue since such would be God's purpose in granting His favor. Souls do grow in strength through Mercies when these come from Him. Yet, in me, no such improvement can be seen. I remembered that I have not obeyed implicitly even regarding what God has most enjoined upon me, which is silence; and I reflected that it is temerity for me to receive so frequently; that if Your Reverence orders me to do so, it is because you think there is improvement in me and this must be due to the fact that I have misinformed you, telling you all about the Mercies I am granted, but nothing about the errors I commit, which I do not even recognize as such.

All this conflict lasted until Sunday. I dared not receive because I did not know God's Will. I thought of writing to Your Reverence, but it seemed to me that, busy as you are, you would be unable to reply and that it must molest you to have so many notes from me. Later, it occurred to me that the Lord was permitting me to suffer this present perturbation, which was preventing me from receiving Him, as a punishment for my refusal to receive Him Friday. Thereupon, I fully made up my mind not to receive, since I felt so uncertain. Perhaps the whole conflict is a temptation, but in any event I have neither the light to comprehend it nor the strength to withstand it.

Sunday, I spent two hours in prayer after being with Your Reverence. The fresh Mercy I had received made my heart rejoice and the darkness began to disappear, because the Lord gave me faith in your word. I felt under great obligation, and perceived that with so much help, everything that the Lord commands me to do is little. The period of prayer was devoted to giving thanks. When, later on, I was about to depart, I knelt before an image of Our Lady and was given to understand that this additional Communion which has been granted me is due to Her intercession. Throughout the entire Octave of the Visitation, I had besought Our Lady insistently for three Divine favors: for me, silence; for Your Reverence the Mercy we expect; and for each of us the acceptance of four hours as a sufficiency of sleep. While giving thanks for this Communion, I was made to understand that, through Her intercession, these requests would be granted.

It occurred to me one day that whoever deals so much with God should leave off all empty formalities and should never descend to wrangling with anybody. Afterward, I also thought that the Lord wants us to be grateful; and when I took up the matter with His Majesty, asking Him whether or not it be true that He wants me to show gratitude in the small ways I can, I was given to understand that He did, so long as my demonstration attracted no attention.

Wednesday, after having slept on my knees, I was very tired when I awoke, and dozed during Matins. I could hardly bear up, and was heartened only by the grace of God. When Matins ended, I took the discipline, then spent one hour in prayer before Communion, and two hours afterward, again on my knees. The whole period was one of devotion and rejoicing, so that it should have been no drain on my strength; nevertheless, I felt exhausted all day. After Vespers, I spent three arid hours in prayer, though these brought me inner peace and quietude. I knelt for one hour, lay prostrate another, and remained seated during the third. About two o'clock I ate, then spent two hours more in prayer, during which time I did nothing except experience the pleasure of the Lord's Presence.

On Friday, while serving at Refectory, I felt the Presence of the Blessed Sacrament and also felt my heart expand. The thought came to me that with such a morsel, I could well do without food for the entire day. Later on, I was in prayer three hours, and once more reflected that the Lord remained with me in order to nourish both body and soul. I felt that He would have done as much throughout all these years that He has shown me this Mercy, if I had been permitted to fast as I desired. Now I offered to do whatever the Lord might command, though I felt a certain fear lest my strength be insufficient for carrying out my promise. Then I heard Him ask, "If thou confessest Me to be all powerful, why dost thou fear?" I replied, "My Lord, I fear because of my sins." Then I understood Him to say, "They are already washed away with My blood." That night I remained in the choir, though I was able to spend only one hour in prayer because I felt very languid and my hands and my heart trembled. Therefore, I asked the Lord's permission to lean against the choir stall and go to sleep. I must have slept about two hours, and woke feeling rested and energetic enough for Matins. Afterward, I swept the choir and waited on table at Refectory. I felt strong enough to forego food until night, if necessary.

Saturday morning, I resolved to go to sleep at nine because I felt that was what Your Reverence wished me to do, even though I could not recall a special order to that effect. However, what with one thing and another, ten o'clock struck before I retired. Kneeling, I begged the Lord that I might fall asleep immediately and wake in four hours; but that if he desired me to spend the accustomed hour in prayer, He should take away my drowsiness. This is what His Majesty did and I did not fall asleep until half-past eleven. At half-past three I woke again, unwearied, after having spent all that time on my knees. Blessed be the Lord!

Sunday, after Communion, I spent two hours in prayer. At first, I was somewhat abstracted, and the Lord gave me to understand how He was gradually fulfilling His promise that Communion would transfer me into Himself. He told me to observe that it was His Majesty Who worked within me, since the things He had me do were beyond my unaided strength. It seemed to me that He held in His hand and directed all my senses, both physical and spiritual. Only my tongue failed to obey Him. As I gave Him thanks for these Mercies and offered to serve Him in even more difficult ways, if He should so command, I entreated Him to keep all this secret; else there would be a thousand obstacles blocking my way. The Lord reminded me of what He had said before, "If I desire it, who can withstand Me?" And I understood from this that should it be to

His glory for my fast to become public knowledge, it should not be concealed. Later on, it seemed to me that I slept, and in my dream saw a prisoner to whom the accusation of his crimes was being read. He admitted his errors and recognized his guilt, offering to bear whatever penalty was imposed. Then, in my dream, I saw his accusers stab him many times with a dagger. I seemed to wake, and reflected I was that prisoner in the shackles of my sins and could but confess my guilt, acknowledging that I deserved severe punishment, and offering to suffer it in whatever way the Lord might be pleased to send it. Then I was made to understand that, so far, I had not even begun to suffer; many affronts and great contumely were to be my lot. Several times over I was told this, and offered my will to the Lord.

Afterward, I was very abstracted at Mass and during the Elevation felt excited and wounded. I understood that the Lord wished me to go to my cell. I went and prostrated myself before His Majesty, entreating Him to make clear what He wanted me to do. He told me, "Thou shouldst remain with Me, for there are few who stay in My Presence and answer when I call." These words grieved my soul and kindled Divine love the more in my heart, when I considered how Our Lord left many of His servants to whom He might reveal His secrets, and deigned to enter this most unworthy soul, therein to rest and converse. Then I remembered Your Reverence and dared to say, "If, My Lord, I am the favored one and have found grace in Your sight, show me the Mercy of granting Your servant the desire of his heart." I importuned Him further, confident of being heard. I remained with the Lord from half-past ten until half-past one: I committed a grave error in my Office, upon which the other nuns commented. I wrote until three o'clock, then I went to Vespers. Afterward, I leaned against one of the choir stalls for two hours more.

Tuesday, I spent two hours on my knees. I was very abstracted at Communion, lost in the love of My Spouse and in the joy of His Presence. Throughout the day, I maintained a special inner abstraction without being able to accomplish anything. It gave me great peace and satisfaction to drop off to sleep from time to time while I knelt. Once, when I woke chilled to the marrow, I sat down a little while to get warm. The pain left me and did not return all day. I dragged myself to Matins and afterward felt stronger. Then I received, and prayed for two hours, most aridly and half asleep. Nevertheless, I redoubled my efforts.

That day, as I was commending a sick person to God, these words came to my mind, "Heaven and earth shall pass away, but my word shall not pass away" (Mark 13, v. 31). Thereupon, my faith increased and I continued to commend that invalid to God in the belief that he would live.

After two arid hours of prayer Monday morning, I was deeply absorbed throughout Mass and very desirous of keeping silent. This I proposed to do, so that the Lord would remain with me, and I could take up with Him a certain subject which He was revealing to me in a special light. While I was in the midst of these thoughts, Doña María began talking nonsense, as she often does. In order to check her, I became very grave, pretending to be angry; but to no avail since, when she wishes to talk, only God can stop her. She distracted me to such a degree that I lost sight of the Mercy the Lord was beginning to grant me. I was so disappointed that, during the two hours of prayer that afternoon, I could do nothing but weep. I reflected that, though I wished Him to remove all obstacles, this one alone He could not remove. I realized that Doña María often hindered me and made me indulge in untimely talk and laughter. I reflected furthermore that, though with additional Communion, I was under greater obligation than ever to keep my heart for God alone, ever awaiting His coming in solitude and silence, I could not achieve this state.

The reflection grieved me and I begged the Lord to set matters right, since there was nothing I could do by myself.

As I was wondering whether the Lord would approve some questions I had discussed with Father Domingo Bañez, I understood Him to say, "I am thy Teacher and thou hast no need of another; I show thee the way and enable thee to walk therein. I command thee in accordance with My Will and make it possible for thee to obey My commands." Thereupon, I became even more deeply absorbed, and felt as if Christ Our Lord was as near me as if we were speaking face to face. Then He assured me, "I am remaining with thee," and I asked, "Even when I do not feel Your Presence, My Beloved?" I understood the answer to be, "Even then, for when thou art unaware of My Presence, it is to give scope to thy faith and trust." All these Mercies increased my love, though I deemed myself unworthy of any favor. I remained all day in His Presence, with my strength redoubled.

After Vespers, it had been my intention to engage in prayer; but I was told to practice a *Magnificat* on the organ. While awaiting the arrival of the singers, I knelt at the door of the choir, somewhat worried on the one hand because I did not wish to waste time and, on the other, because I did not wish to annoy the choristers by withdrawing. In this perplexity, I was given to understand that if the Lord so desired, He could command me to remain where I was with His Majesty. Immediately, I felt abstracted to such a degree that I could not move from the place. The singers were entering the choir by this time, and were quite aware of my state. Half-kneeling, I continued in that condition. Just then, one of the nuns came in, and I felt greatly agitated as she approached me. I entreated the Lord to let me be seated, the better to dissimulate my absorption. At the cost of great effort, I was enabled to sit down and covered my face with my hand. For about an hour and a half I continued in this state of suspension, rejoicing in the Presence of the Lord Who lifted me up with such force that I was exhausted. All that I achieved by this was the opportunity to love and rejoice. I thought how generously the Lord repays, even in this life, the little that is done for Him and I recalled the verse, "For thou considerest labour and sorrow," [103] and "Come to me, all you that labour, and are burdened, and I will refresh you" (Matt. 11, v. 28).

As Your Reverence said in your note that it indicated little resistance and humility on my part for me to express such regret at not knowing the Divine Will, I tried on Sunday to place myself in the Lord's hands and embrace darkness, since His Majesty so desired, until light should come. The Lord permitted me to do this in quietude. Afterward, I received Him, but in such obscurity that I remained as before.

That day, I visited a sick nun. Those with her were talking about my penances and my long hours of prayer. They thought it all excessive and did not envy me. Then I went to my devotions, thinking that if I could give even one soul some slight appreciation of what God is—His Incomprehensible Being, His Infinite Goodness, the fulfillment of His Divine Will—I would embrace any suffering unrestrainedly, nor could there be aught I would not endure for the pleasure and service of God. I felt that the greater the suffering, the greater would be the joy in the realization that this was the soul's offering to its God and that however much is done for God is all too little. I thought also of all that worldly people suffer for the sake of material gains and sometimes only for vain hopes. It grieved me exceedingly to think that though God is Who He is, and has bestowed so many benefits upon us; and that though we have such certainty of enjoying Him if only we do our part, we continually haggle over whatever service we render Him; to such an extent we think that any trifle we offer Him places God under an obligation to us. I feel like shouting from the housetops to set men right and get them on the road they should follow. It is a pity that the only good works which are appreciated and valued are the ones clearly apparent, while more important works, the ones most worthy to be garnered, are often overlooked or disregarded. I reflected that we should give profound consideration to God's Will, placing it above our own pleasure and satisfaction even in small things; or better said, our own pleasure should be contingent upon fulfillment of the Divine Will and on that alone. These thoughts left in me a great desire always to ascertain the right way of pleasing the Lord; and I deemed as nothing whatever good I can achieve, since I cannot do for God even so much as those who love the world do for it.

Tuesday, I took Communion timorously, trusting in obedience. I told the Lord of my great need and begged Him to enlighten Your Reverence. The words of Father Baltasar Alvarez kept recurring to me: "This question of hit or miss, with respect to God's Will, is highly important, since in this matter there can be no insignificant hit and no insignificant miss." That is just what I felt about the problem of my fasting. These reflections caused me many tears and I besought the Lord for light; yet my heart remained unsoftened and in the same darkness as before.

After I had been with Your Reverence Wednesday, I went to prayer, and continued praying until three o'clock that afternoon. During some of those hours, I felt a high excitement, with my heart elated and confident that I was pleasing His Majesty. This brought peace and quietude to my soul. Since Your Reverence had sent me no message, about twelve o'clock I asked the Lord to remind Your Reverence that I was awaiting you. I was given to understand that it was His Majesty who was detaining *me*, because He desired me to be with Him. I seemed to hear the Lord say, "Thou dost Me honor by praying to Me; thou pleasest Me by loving Me; and the nuns who see thee are edified and glorify Me. Why desirest thou then to depart?"

Friday, after Communion, I still felt hard of heart. I could neither pray nor meditate on the Communion just celebrated. I went to Terce dejectedly, begging pardon of the Lord for having lodged Him so poorly. During Mass, I thought of the fasts and penances the Lord had ordained for me and how difficult they could be amidst such darkness and aridity. Job's words came to me as a consolation, "Although he should kill me, I will trust in him" (Job 13, v. 15). Thereupon, I felt courage to do and to endure even unto the Day of Judgment whatever might be the Lord's Will, trusting that His Majesty would aid me in accordance with His promise, "No one hath hoped in the Lord, and hath been confounded" (Eccles. 2, v. 11).

Later on, at Hours, when it seemed as if He wished to draw me to Himself, I strove not to let myself be carried away. Then I heard the words: "Who can resist God?" I replied, "If God so wills, He can easily deprive me of power to resist; but I shall resist in so far as I can because that is the Divine Will and is what I have been commanded to do."

As I reflected that Mother Teresa of Jesus was not perturbed when people spoke praisefully of her, it was borne in on me that it is not humility, but lack of it, for us to hide God's gifts. Such a concealment is, in a way, an effort to make the Divine favors our own, and its source the soul's failure to comprehend that all which is good comes from God.

After this, I suffered greatly because the Lady Abbess urged me to eat. I felt that if I had received the favor proffered by the Lord, I could better have borne this affliction; but the one without the other was intolerable. In this state of turmoil, I besought the Lord's mercy before an image of Christ at the Column. He reminded me that He had once asked me, "What will He not do for thee still, Who has already suffered so much for thee?" And, as I gazed on His most holy hands, I heard, "Thou didst not place thy heart in My hands. The blood of wounded hands must leave its stain and thou hast heretofore known that it was good therein to lay thy heart." When I responded that this was true, He asked, "Of what dost thou complain?" I replied, "My Lord, not that I suffer, but that I am ignorant of Your Will." Then I begged Him that for my greater certainty He would bring Your Reverence and the Lady Abbess into accord as to what would be most pleasing in His sight, since my sole desire was to carry out His Divine Will. His Majesty heard me, and so arranged that I was left free to do without scruple whatever Your Reverence might command.

As I thought about that servant of God whom, according to what Your Reverence told me, Our Lord was leading by way of love without insisting that she do penance, I complained that such was not His Majesty's method with me, and that though I wished none to excel me in love and suffering, yet in love many had a great advantage. Then I was made to see that the Lord with His Own hand was placing me on the Cross because He desired me to accompany Him there, and that this was all because He loved me well; and that if I willingly acceded, and suffered with good grace, it was because I was moved by the same love. Without love, this anguish could not be borne. At that, my heart was exalted and I felt such a flame of love as seemed to consume and purify my soul, transporting it from its own actions and operations and suspending the physical senses without effort. Thus it was that, there in the refectory, without so much as lifting my eyes or doing anything to bring it about, I heard these words, "Why desirest thou to see My creatures when thou canst place thine eyes on Me?"

After dinner, one of the religious came to me, and she and

Doña María began saying that I held such lofty ideas that nothing less than sainthood would content me. I replied that this was true, and that I believed everything possible should be done to this end, cost what it might; also, that I had courage enough for the undertaking, even though, so far, I had accomplished nothing and there was so much yet to do. These words of encouragement to them so enkindled my own heart with a desire for sainthood that, throughout the day, I did not leave off beseeching God to show me this Mercy. I felt a great determination, an invincible courage, for achieving whatever I believed to be the Lord's Will, however difficult; and it seemed to me that this resolution made the devils quake and fear to attack us. I reflected that, in order to carve a saint from stone, it is necessary to cut the stone here and there with the aid of compasses and gauges; it is by dint of hard blows that the eyes and other features come into being. I remembered what efforts a master workman puts forth, and how often the stone resists, almost as if it had feeling. It is the same in the life of the spirit. In order to transform stones into the children of Abraham, all excesses must be cut away and the hammer of mortification is needful to bring forth the eyes and other features of a saint, humble, simple and chaste, with a saint's characteristic composure and modesty. Consequently, even as the stone, we must submit to the artisan's hands, though he seem to rend us into fragments and destroy us, for if we fend off the blows and flee from them, the image will never come to light.

Thereupon, I began praying with increased fervor. It came into my mind how little we do for God, how clumsy we are in His holy service. Since we are unmoved by what He is in Himself, we should at least be tirelessly and continually alert because of what He is for us and because of our hope to enjoy Him.

At present, Communion sometimes seems to take away my

strength and the faintness remains. I used to feel the Presence of Christ Our Lord in the Sacrament: I had the sense of being companioned by Him all day, so that it seemed, and I believed it to be, a special grace He showed me by remaining with me bodily during those hours. Now I no longer feel this. In consequence, I have been deprived of immense benefits, because those experiences always enkindled my heart with gratitude and brought me reverence, peace, security, joy and courage, both inwardly and outwardly, which enabled me to vanquish difficulties. Now I feel the lack of all this, since Your Reverence has told me these things are delusions, although Our Lord made it seem they were true. Just as there is a great difference between one Mercy and another, there are differences in gratitude; and since it is lacking somewhat in gratefulness to disbelieve that the Lord is really the companion of the soul, it may be this is the reason I have not now the faith I felt before. The Lord delights in receiving for His gifts gratitude and appreciation which there is no way of showing if the gifts are not recognized as such.

When I took up with the Lord the problem of a certain person whose fear lest her penance might result in loss of health kept her from doing those things that would give the Lord greater glory, I understood the answer to be, "If she had faith, she could do all things."

Thursday evening, I remained absorbed at table in the refectory a good while after the others left. My whole being was given over more and more to devotion and desire.

Saturday I received Communion and spent two hours in prayer. After refectory, while giving thanks, I felt as if wounded, with the yearnings and anguish which foretell absorption. I went to the shrine and there, prostrate at the feet of the Lord, I offered myself to the Divine Will. It seemed as though He put His arms about me and asked if I were ready to carry on the fast for a week. I said I was prepared to do so at any time His Majesty might wish. Although this occurred so subtly and delicately as to be hardly noticeable, it has left me deeply conscious of the tender love He showed me. After two more hours of ardent prayer, I wished to take the discipline. I recalled that Father Alvarez was accustomed to take discipline for a quarter of an hour and I desired to prolong mine similarly. Since Your Reverence had not set a fixed period for it, I decided I could do this without disobedience. Meanwhile, I reflected how well I deserved any pain I might be called on to endure for my sins, and how, by the present means, the devil was avenging in me offenses against His Majesty, as if the Lord had given him permission to do so. This thought sustained my courage, which was strengthened still more when I lifted my eyes to the image of that Most Innocent Lamb, Who suffered so cruelly for my sins.

I felt content to have done this small thing for the Lord. Afterward, I knelt at prayer for two hours more; yet though I spent the day in this manner, I experienced no weakness.

After Communion on Sunday, I prayed for two hours. God enlightened me as to the meaning of St. Paul's words, "The law is not made for the just man" (1 Timothy 1, v. 9), for the very things that the laws command him are written in his heart. The just man would act in the same way, with or without precept, because his will is in unison with the Will of God. His Majesty gave me to understand that I might converse with Him and ask for whatever I desired, since such communication could not be denied the spouse.

That evening, after Vespers, I went to the shrine, where the Lord gathered me to Himself for an hour and a half, which I spent ardently, while He made many things clear to me. One of these was Our Lord's pleasure in having us suffer, since in doing so we imitate Him. It seemed to me that such suffering for His sake is a characteristic or sign that love imprints upon its own, by which means they are recognized. It is like an iron branding His chosen ones as His slaves. Though, in the eyes of the world, it would seem madness to embrace the Cross and despise for its sake worldly pleasures, honors and riches, in God's sight there can be no straighter course. I asked myself whether or not I should wish the Lord to communicate with me by some more special vision. My decision was that I desired to know neither more nor less than His Majesty willed.

In this regard, I have been given two signs. The first was on the Sunday of the Jubilee. As I went into the choir with the procession, there was so extraordinary a light that it seemed to me as if all our Community were entering the gate of heaven, the while God Our Lord gave us His blessing. Such was my inmost bliss that I felt, if I had the opportunity of withdrawing into myself, I could keep on going straight into heaven. On the second occasion, while I was at Office, I envisioned on the abbatial chair a throne of Majesty whereon was seated the Holy Trinity, seemingly fenced about by a ring of fire. This vision, fleeting as it was, remained in my mind for hours.

With respect to the order of Your Reverence that I should burn certain papers, this is what I was given to understand: "Why shouldst thou wish to burn them? Thou keepest the words of men; why not keep Mine? My doctrine is worthy of being written in letters of gold on the hearts of men, and the Mercies I grant thee will serve to inspire confidence in those who know of them; since, doing so much for thee who deservest it not, what will I do for one who is ready to receive My words and merit them?"

After Communion, I spent half an hour giving thanks before going into the choir. Although I was completely aware of those who were with me during High Mass, my heart was ardent with desire for its God, and I heard these words, "I have given thee My Mother to be thine."

Later on, at Hours, I envisioned myself between My Mother and My Spouse. It was as a spouse that the Lord treated me, drawing me to Himself; and the Virgin Our Lady likewise treated me as Her daughter. She took from Her neck a precious jewel and hung it on mine, that I might delight the eyes of My Spouse therewith. This jewel is composed of the words She had taught me: "Behold the handmaid of the Lord." My bliss at receiving this favor brought on complete abstraction, as I leaned there against a choir stall. I did not go to Refectory until second table. If these things are verities, it is needful that the Lord cast a veil over them. They should not be shown by the dazzling light they have of themselves, which may be more than the heart can endure.

While I was at table in the refectory, it seemed as if Our Lady put Her arms about me and thanked me for my fast. I cannot comprehend how I, who receive so many Mercies, deserve to be thanked for fasting or even for exhausting myself in His Majesty's service.

All day Wednesday I enjoyed Our Lady's Presence. She granted me the favor of allowing me to become enraptured while at prayer. During these days, every time I am absorbed, a lock seems set upon my heart and another upon my eyes and lips and I desire to be alone all the time.

As I was entering into prayer Thursday morning, the Lord drew me to Himself and kindled my heart with His love. I entreated Him prayerfully to permit Himself to be seen and loved, and had recourse to the intercession of Our Lady. I called Her "Mother," for such She is, and petitioned Her to obtain this blessing from Her Divine Son. Then I heard the Lord's voice saying, "No living man sees Me." I replied, "My Lord, reveal Yourself as You were wont to do with Your friends." Then, taking thought, all in a moment, I said, "Forgive, Lord, my audacity; love is to blame." And it came to my mind that in the Canticle of Solomon, the spouse entered into the heart with the same saying, "Let him kiss me with the kiss of his mouth" (Cant. 1), and that her petition had been granted immediately, for she went on to say, "For thy breasts are better than wine." He nourished me not only with the milk of His breasts, but with all of Himself. I recalled Job's words, "What is a man that thou shouldst magnify him? or why dost thou set thy heart upon him? Thou visitest him early in the morning, and thou provest him suddenly" (Job 7, v. 17 & 18). As my heart became calmer, I again invoked the aid of My Mother and My Lady, and was given to understand that I should not fatigue myself. Thereupon, I became absorbed once more and, remembering my jewel, presented it to the Lord as I said, "Be it done to me according to thy word." Thereupon, I envisioned that the Lord values this precious gem so greatly that He always bears it on His heart, "And thy law in the midst of my heart" (Psalm 39, v. 9). He obeyed always, even to the point of giving His life on the Cross. These and similar reflections increased my ardor. When summoned to Communion, I asked the blessing of the Lord and His Mother in approaching to receive Him. I heard the words, "Come My chosen one and I shall place thee on My Throne." I felt deeply moved as I received Communion and, since it was then time for Terce, begged the Lord to let me go to Choir if such were His pleasure; for He was holding me close to Himself. Then I heard Him say, " 'I held her: and I will not let her go'[104] and I shall hide her in the secret places of My Being. I shall regale her and make her lose affection for everything created because of her delight in Me." Amidst all these Mercies, I kept remembering, "Thou visitest him early in the morning, and thou provest him suddenly" (Job 7, v. 18). So it came about that I was still enraptured in the Lord's embrace when some of the nuns came to tell me I was to play the organ at Mass. I made a great effort and went immediately to the choir. But it was the Lord Who played the organ, just as He did everything else, for I myself did not know what I was doing, although I never lost sight of the favor shown me. Consequently, as soon as the music was over, I once more became enraptured and so remained until the bell rang for Refectory. The Lord again made me aware, as heretofore, of His Presence in the Blessed Sacrament, to my intense delight and gratification. Yet I perceive the more the Lord heaps up in the measure of His Mercies, the slower I am in knowing how to render due service to Him and how to demonstrate my consciousness of their value and of my gratitude.

Before this occurred, I had gone to the shrine after seeing a priest. I was completely in the dark as to what was in store for me. I do not know whether or not it was while I commended this priest to God, as he had asked me to do, that I was given to understand I should remain calm and should realize I had pleased His Majesty at Office. What grandeur can there be in a secret place for one who has not God's love? What baseness it would be to desist from striving and working if such is His desire! I try to keep Him always present. Foremost in my thoughts is the remembrance that He said, "What importeth it to thee if I declare through thee My Will toward others?"

Thursday, after I had received and had besought the Lord to purify my every intent, so that I should do only those things pleasing in His eyes, it came to me as a special enlightenment that, while I desired to excel, it was not for the sake of doing more than another did, but because of my greater indebtedness. She who was foremost in sin should be foremost in suffering and she who was the greatest offender should give the greatest service. It is likewise certain that even though there were no one, past or present, with whom to compete, neither in the eyes of angels nor in those of men, nor any reward what-

soever for my efforts, I still would not fail to persist in what
I am now doing, because those are not the considerations
which move me. I consider only that the Lord desires me
to serve Him in this fashion: that my way of life be pleasing
in His sight for He has declared such to be His Will. Thus,
bound hand and foot, I am prohibited from doing anything
else, because He deserves to be infinitely loved, obeyed, and
served for Himself. It may be I am deceived; but this is the
end I seek in all I do.

I pondered whether or not it would be well to ask that
Your Reverence write to the Father Rector of Salamanca and
request him to come here some day, so that we might understand each other better, since leave for this had not been
granted another priest. Then I heard these words, "Leave thou
that problem to Me." I entreated the Lord with prayers and
many tears not to desert me, because it seemed as if He had
forgotten me. The response was, "The mother forgetteth not
the babe in her arms, nor will I be forgetful of thee whose
name I have inscribed upon my hands" (Isaias 49, v. 15 & 16).

I felt sure the Bishop was coming Saturday. Consequently,
I thought it would be well to receive that day's Communion
on Friday. Afterward, it occurred to me that, by doing so, I
might cause comment. Then I heard these words: "When
able to receive Me, thou foregoest it?" Despite all this, since
I doubted whether or not it was God Who had spoken, I
did not reach a decision.

On All Saints' Eve, at Vespers, I felt the Lord's Presence
and was filled with a great yearning to be a saint. As I reflected
on the reasons for this, I found it to be a desire to come closer
to God. The more nearly a soul approaches perfection, the
more largely it participates in the Divine Nature; and the
more the soul is transformed in the Lord, the more pleasing
it is in His eyes.

In the midst of my prayers, it seemed to me that St.

Catherine and St. Agnes, to whom I already owed so much, rose from their places on the left hand of God, amid the rest of the saints, and prostrated themselves before the Throne of Divine Majesty, entreating Him to grant me this Mercy. Then it seemed to me that Our Lady came forward from the right and prostrated Herself likewise, voicing the same prayer. Afterward, that antiphon which I do not recall having dwelt upon heretofore came to my mind: "Before the Throne of the Trinity, Dear Mother of Mercy, merciful to those needing mercy, Be our Advocate." I felt an extraordinary joy and the greatest confidence that those petitions would be granted. Somewhat abstracted, I was consumed with the love of God.

After I had received Communion Saturday, the Lord gathered me up and for a while I was filled with desire. When I besought His Majesty to reveal His Will, He said, "Wait thou a while." I remembered that when St. John heard the voices of the saints, crying for the Lord to avenge their blood, they had been answered, "That they should rest for a little time, till . . . their brethren . . . should be filled up" (Apocal. 6, v. 11). And it amused me that He should call the time until Judgment Day "a little while." If my own bit of time is to be as long as that, patience is really needed. Besides all this, when I entreated Our Lord to number me among His saints, I was given to understand that Our Lady had already made this plea for me.

That day I felt my fever abating. When I recalled that Our Lady had promised me health for carrying out my obligations, I was made to see that the promise would hold good only if I did, indeed, carry them out. Later on, when the bell rang for None, I felt well and strong.

On All Souls' Day, following Terce, penitential psalms were said for a young nun because of a remark she made when finishing breakfast, just after she had been to Matins. What she had said was that she hoped God, Who had brought us together here, would keep us together in heaven at the eternal table. It seemed to me that this table must be circular in form, since God's Being has neither beginning nor end; and that the sustenance upon it must consist of His Divine perfections. I began entreating the Lord to permit a certain soul, from this day forward, to enjoy such bliss. I said that, if I possessed anything of value in His eyes, and His Majesty would be pleased to bestow it upon her for her greater satisfaction, I should deem it well given. Since it was not necessary for me to play at Mass, I continued praying for her until the psalms were completed. During the Preface, I went to the lectern, and importuned the Lord once more. There I was given to understand that I should pray for some other religious, since this one no longer had need. (She had died two years and a half before at the age of seventy.) I observed that she was not yet in heaven and was given to understand that, because of her rather flighty disposition, she had been required to suffer somewhat. As I wondered that the Lord should remember her and move me to pray for her, I was told she deserved this Mercy because of her great charity toward the poor. This favor left me shamed and abashed, yet at the same time grateful because I had been treated as if my services had deserved it.

At Hours, I felt extremely faint and decided, since this was not a Communion day, I would remedy my need by eating more freely. I was possessed of an inner impatience, almost a desperation, at finding myself forced to do so many things. Just as a madman with bound hands may become so enraged he can break his bonds, so I felt I should like to break the laws of God. This anger persisted every day, even on Communion days, because they are so numerous. Then I began to fear lest thus I had offended God. It seemed to me I had. I could go for an entire day without lifting my heart to His Majesty or withdrawing into myself. As I took collation that evening, my faintness increased and, to make matters worse,

I was conscious of inner turmoil at table. When I called on the Lord for help, the thought came to me that He was neither My Lord nor My God. Many who call Him Lord do not obey Him. He is Lord only of those who do His Will and give Him their hearts. Since I failed in this, I had no claim to call Him so. Ideas similar to this crowded into my mind until I seemed to be out of my senses. With it came such inward and outward restlessness that I could not calm myself. A fury was rending me apart. These things all seemed like so many signs of the hell that awaited me. Meantime, I urged the Lord that, if it were so, He condemn me immediately before I offend Him again. The preceding day, I had asked *Doña* María to pray to God for me, lest I be lost. In order to bring me some consolation, she told me what the Lord had said to her: namely, that all this was for my good, lest the Mercies He has granted me incite my vanity and pride. It seemed to me that these words did not come from God, but from *Doña* María's imagination. It was just as if she said, "As I do." It occurred to me later that there was no reason for me to value revelations so highly since *Doña* María also had them. I resisted this thought and humbled myself by saying it was I who deserved no such Mercies, but they were most rightly granted her.

Thursday, I did not hear the bell for Matins and went in late, much embarrassed at having overslept. My conviction is that the Lord did not wake me because He is indifferent to my services. I asked myself why this thought should so grieve me, since these acts are not for my own benefit nor are they acceptable to God. My conclusion was to continue them nevertheless, because He is worthy of being worshiped. He grants a Mercy when He permits Himself to be served by one who should by this time be burning in hell.

Saturday morning, the Lord began to enlighten the darkness of my understanding, and to banish all temptation. I came back to my senses like one awakening from a deep sleep. As I gave thanks to God, it occurred to me that I fully deserved hell and could count myself among the damned, and that the Lord desired me to recognize this fact; because everything else is owing to His grace.

While at High Mass on Sunday, I felt bathed in light and joy. In this state, I was given to understand that, ordinarily, I should conform to St. Catherine's custom and take food— which I believe was fruit and vegetables—before breakfast, as she did.[105] I was thinking this over, and asking the Lord whether or not He had taken me out of hell in order to eat herbs, when our Lady Abbess sent word for me to receive Holy Communion. The Host had been consecrated for a religious who had later decided not to receive. I bowed my head and obeyed, well aware that this was a device of the Lord's. When I asked what had caused Him to single me out from all the rest for this Mercy, He gave me to understand that it was because He wished me to be chosen during my lifetime. Our Lord had prepared the way for this Communion the preceding night, without my knowledge, by sending the customary faintness and insisting I should not eat, and by making me sleep on my knees with my head cushioned on an overshoe. I had heard the account of a saint who slept with a stone for a pillow, and it occurred to me that I could use my overshoe, since its presence could be better concealed.

At Hours on Tuesday, I entreated the Lord to remove all obstacles from my path, so that I might hasten to Him. The thought came to mind that I had been wearing too many wimples. The fewer I possessed, the better I would be keeping the vow of poverty; but I told myself they were necessary to keep my head from getting cold. Then I was given to understand that my real reason lay in lack of faith and trust in the Lord. Then I said that if such were the Lord's Will, I would take the wimples off.

On the Feast of Our Lady, I made up my mind to eat at noon, so that *Doña* María, who ate at the second table, would not notice my abstinence. I do not think this pleased Our Lady. From that day until Sunday, I was to have no dealings with the Lord, neither through prayer nor otherwise.

It occurred to me Sunday at Communion that it would be well for me to dress less warmly than usual this winter. The saints were satisfied with one tunic and a coat. I was told, "Fear not the cold: I am the true warmth." As I remembered that the Lord had spoken these same words to Mother Teresa, He said, "I speak them also to thee." Then the question came, "Desirest thou not to be a saint?" I answered, "Yes, Lord," and was given to understand, "Then this is the way. 'The Lord conducted the just . . . through the right ways' " (Wisdom 10, v. 10). These straight paths which lead to life constitute the imitation of Christ Our Lord.

On St. Catherine's Day, I began to feel gravely preoccupied as to whether Father Alarcón had been right when he said the reason I spent so much time on my knees was to demonstrate signs of sainthood. I entreated the Lord that my intention should not be warped, but directed toward His glory. I could not calm myself enough to take Communion. The doubt beset me that what he had said might be true without my realizing it. I resolved to seek peace by telling our Lady Abbess what I felt. She heartened me greatly, and ordered me to receive, which I did, somewhat more calmly. I asked Our Lord whether or not I should inform her I am not eating meat; because I knew that, after all, this would greatly displease her. I understood His reply to be, "It is already time." While I earnestly besought His Majesty to clarify His wishes about my eating, I thought that there would really be nothing extraordinary, much less anything miraculous, about it even if we did eat less variety of food. The poor sustain themselves with bread and onions. When they have a sardine, they think it is a feast.

With such nourishment as this, they work all day long. If poverty forces that privation upon them, because they have no alternative, why should not the love of God enable me to bear as much? In my case, performance of such penances are a special obligation placed upon me by the Lord, Who grants me the great Mercy of His help in carrying them out; and they are pleasing in His Majesty's sight. The most perfect thing, and the most agreeable in the Eternal Father's eyes, is for us to conform our lives to that of Christ Our Lord, Who Himself never indulged in delicate foods, as is evident in the miracle of the barley loaves which the Apostles had to share with Our Lord (John 6).

On the preceding Sunday at the shrine, I had been informed my letter had been taken to the Bishop and I should commend the matter to God. This I did, with wonted fervor and constancy; so that for a full hour my eyes flowed with tears while the Lord permitted me to say a thousand persuasive things to Him in the hope of this favor. At the conclusion of my prayer, these words came into my mind: "Thou shalt have what thou hast asked" (4 Kings 2, v. 10). I was comforted by this. The further hope stayed with me that the Bishop's answer to my letter would be one of approval. Afterward, when no answer came, I reflected on what I had been given to understand. It seemed to me I had been deceived. Remembering that, two or three days previously, I had assured the Lord three Communions would content me, I now entreated Him not to permit there should be fewer than three. His response was that such had been His promise: it would be as I had asked. So it has been. In no week have I communicated less than thrice, in one way or another. Though all my companions here have left off Communion, I have never missed it. May the Lord be blessed forever.

While I was commending the affairs of a certain person to the Lord, it occurred to me that I should write to her. I reflected on what to say so that the Lord might enlighten her. Nevertheless, it seemed to me an uphill task. Shedding bitter tears, I begged the Lord not to command me to do this, but to find some other means of giving counsel, since I am unfit to do so. When I prayed for that soul's welfare, He asked, "Desirest thou not to help Me?" My reply was, "Most willingly, My Lord, with anguish and whatever else You deem fit for me to suffer, but this letter would be a proclamation and a show of sanctity on my part; and I have no such desire." Then I understood Him to say, "I would be glorified in thee." However, I did not leave off beseeching Him not to command this, yet not to be angry because of my resistance to His Will. At last I said, "My Lord, I am not a saint. You can entrust anything to some saints; but as for me, what can I do except cause ruin to others and to myself?" Then it occurred to me that His reason for placing her in such a position was that Your Reverence no longer knew what to do with her; my letter might calm her, and could cause no comment, since her husband is a relative of mine.

Then it came to my mind that St. Catherine had done likewise. So I asked, "Lord, is it needful for me to imitate her in this also?" I was given to understand that, "Her best service was to help Me save souls." Finally I said, "Then, Lord, I shall do likewise with prayer and suffering, but charge me not to do so with words and writing." He replied, "And if such be My Desire?" And then He asked further, "What wilt thou have left save shame and confusion, seeing thou art what thou art?" Afterward, while I wondered whether or not Our Lord would grant me the Mercy of permitting me to receive on the Day of the Incarnation, I heard these words: "If thou dost what else I command thee to do."

While I pondered the words of Maestro Avila and others, who said that these inner Voices come from God, though rarely and only in cases of great need, it seemed to me that the very fact they often dealt with matters of little importance, in my case, made them suspect. Yet, while this is true in general, I thought that when God takes the soul in charge, to direct it in everything, and employs these inner Voices as means for declaring His Will, they needs must speak frequently. How else could they set forth the rules for eating and drinking, speaking and observing silence, sleeping and waking; for prayer during periods of work and periods of rest; for inner and outer deportment; and in this latter respect for reminder, correction, reprimand and encouragement, such as a teacher gives a pupil and a tutor a child? This reasoning appeals to me greatly and seems to me convincing.

Again on Saturday, I felt certain I could receive the Lord. I went to the shrine for a brief period of prayer and entreated His Majesty to delay no longer permission to receive Him, since Your Reverence had agreed to all He asked. It was made clear to me that I must first prepare myself by commencing the daily ration of bread and herbs; and since I had dedicated this fast to Our Lady, I must begin it on Her Feast Day. It seemed to me as if She were there beside me and were saying She wished to initiate me, with Her Own hand in this method of fasting, and assuring me I would carry it out with Her blessing. She asked that when I seated myself to partake of the herbs, I should do so in Her name and in that of My Spouse. She further assured me that, with faith, I could live on herbs alone for the two or three days of Communion. I was moved to tears as I was given to understand all this and implored Her help lest the devil mislead me. I besought Her to remove my impediment so I might receive the Lord. I understood Her answer to be, "Tomorrow." My prayer left me abashed and humbled. It was very clear to me that all these Mercies are pure grace and that I respond very ill to the obligations they impose upon me.

I was very eager to learn what this food was to be, and

whether I might eat every sort of herb. It was given me to understand that I could have two kinds of herbs at every meal and even bread, though this I must take as it was served me, without saying how I wished to have it prepared. The reason for that injunction was that I had been having the bread toasted so as to eat it warm.

Today I received the Lord, and besought Him not to let this fast become generally known, but to mitigate its rigors. This petition I made at Father Alarcón's bidding. I understood the answer to be, "If they give thee Communion every day, thou wilt be enabled to eat a little every day in the manner I have instructed thee: when it is not My Will for thee to eat, I shall inform thee." Then I replied, "Well, Lord, what shall I do meanwhile?" And I understood that I had already been told that if Communions were on three successive days, I might eat on the afternoon of the third.

After I received Communion Sunday, the words, "I am thy sustenance," brought great joy and satisfaction to my soul. I felt the Lord's Presence, and begged Him to care for me and not permit me to be deceived. He told me, "Rest assured"; and thereby confirmed me in the peace and security I felt.

When I asked the Lord why He pressed me so hard with these fasts, and prohibited me from eating anything except herbs, His reply was that very few persons possess the virtue of temperance, and He desired to show me the Mercy of being one of these. I besought Him to prepare my heart and teach me what I should do to deserve the favor He intended to grant of having me receive Him more frequently. I understood his answer to be that I should keep continually alert so that I might know the Divine Will in all things, execute it perfectly, and avoid worldly communications.

Thursday, when I besought the Lord to permit me to approach and receive Him, I understood the answer to be, "Let

My blood suffice thee"; I was further given to understand that He had ordered me to confess so that, though denied Communion, I should not be left without the grace of the Sacrament. These words also came to me: "It is so that they may see thee surrender, for on the day when I give Myself to all others, but deny Myself to thee, thou sufferest, but endurest well." I responded, "Lord, all is Yours; and well I know myself unworthy even to savor the Bread, much less to receive it."

Again on Friday, I was taut during the reading of the Passion. As I strove to overcome this impediment, I heard the words, "Who can prevail against His strength?" The tautness continued until seven o'clock that evening.

Saturday, at the blessing of the Paschal candle, it seemed to me that I was being reprimanded for having asked that if He so willed I be permitted to eat at the same hour as the rest of the Community. Therefore, I besought His Majesty to pay no heed to that request, but to use me as His Own. If He wished me to fast all day, with my teeth and my hands alike clamped, it was well with me. They were clamped, throughout the Mass and Vespers of Our Lady. Then the Lord was pleased to make me well again, and I went to officiate, and ate in the refectory.

Easter Sunday, during Matins, while I was wondering whether or not I should be able to receive Communion, I was told I could not do so until my Spiritual Advisers conformed to the Divine Will. With the Host already prepared, at the very moment of the Offertory, I was impeded.

On the Feast of the Incarnation, I received Communion. Soon thereafter, I became taut. When I asked the Lord His intention, the answer came, "That thou stay with Me." So it was I could not take part in the singing with the organ, but remained rapt, speaking to no one. Our Lord also gave me to understand, with respect to Father Alarcón's remark, that my impediment and abstraction came from the devil, that the devil could have no power over a soul which had resigned itself to the Divine Will. When a soul lacks detachment, the devil takes advantage of this fact for the soul's deception.

Saturday morning, I went to the shrine to await the Lord's indication whether or not He would permit me to receive Him. On the way, I kept thinking of how the other nuns awaited Mass, serenely sure that they would receive the Lord and be comforted by Him. This thought was uppermost as I entered the shrine and presented myself to the Lord in prayer. He asked, "What desirest thou?" and I replied, "That You look upon me." He answered, "I am already looking upon thee." Then I recalled the miracle of the five loaves, remembering how first He lifted His Divine eyes and then, moved to pity, said, "I will not send them away fasting, lest they faint on the way." [106] As I yearned for Him to regard me with the same compassion, I understood Him to say, "I shall sustain thee by My virtue: I have assured thee that I shall not deprive thee of the benefit of the Sacrament." These words filled my heart with joy and gratitude. In the procession, I helped a nun, who was not strong enough to do so alone, carry the cross. I forced some of the silver prongs of the cross into my palm and the pain they gave me brought to mind His Majesty's promise to show me a special Mercy. I was bathed in joy and beatitude, and felt courageous enough to suffer death itself. Later, during the sermon, it seemed that the Lord approached me. I felt that His arms were about me, and the fire of His Divine love was enkindled in my heart. He left me so enraptured, so lost to every other thought, that I did not hear a word of the sermon.

On Sunday, during the morning Mass, I was taut once more. Afterward, I spent an hour and a half at prayer, striving not to fall asleep and incapable of doing anything more. Nevertheless, I enjoyed the sense of God's Presence throughout the day. I visited the sick nuns, and had occasion to hear and talk more than usual. This was no pleasure.

At Chapter, as I was wondering how I was to receive the Lord, since I felt certain He would allow me to do so, I heard these words: "On the other hand, if they once see that thy impediment is removed and thou canst receive, they will be less rigorous and will give thee Communion daily." Then I asked, "Lord, can You not employ other means for this end?" He replied that these were the means He had already chosen. I was discouraged, and doubted whether or not it had indeed been God Who spoke. "Lord, is it You?" I questioned. The answer was, "Observe the sign that I have given thee." This He said, because yesterday afternoon, while the other nuns were at supper, I went to the wall and embraced a great cross which is standing there, imploring the Lord, as Your Reverence had instructed me, to give me some way of knowing when these words I hear are His Majesty's, and when they are prompted by my own spirit. He had replied that whenever I was left with a feeling of humility and resignation, I should believe it was His Majesty Who spoke. Afterward, I thought that I had done wrong, since Your Reverence had told me to resist such conversations. While I pondered this problem, and discussed it in a give-and-take with God, His Majesty said, "If thou canst refrain from hearing, do so; but once thou hast heard, it is not well to forget, nor to be ungrateful."

Doña Leonor had brought me a message from her brother, asking that I speak with him since he desired to discuss something with me. Two or three times on Friday, I felt a stirring in my soul such as comes when the Lord wishes to draw me to Himself. However, I paid no heed to these indications. Later, I recalled the message that had been brought, and heard His Majesty say, "Talk with him." I felt abashed, and His Majesty spoke again, saying, "He is My servant." I replied, "Lord,

I can do nothing of this kind without consulting my Spiritual Advisers." He said, "Say that it is My desire." I was worried as to whether this was the voice of God, since it seemed to me that by such means I might encounter the greatest and most dangerous temptation possible. Afterward, I fell asleep, and forgot all about the matter. It recurred to my mind at Matins, and brought the same perplexities as before. While I was wondering what to say to *Doña* Leonor's brother, I heard these words: "Trouble not thyself about that." The Lord then reminded me that, once before, on a similar occasion, He had told me, "If anyone seek thy advice as to what he should do, in order to attain the Mercy of My intimacy, tell him to prepare himself by mortification and penance, and I will help him." I had then asked, "Who am I, Lord, that anyone should wish to advise with me?" His Majesty's reply was, "It would be not on thine own account, but out of respect for Me." When I excused myself once again, saying, "I cannot speak, for I am a child" (Jeremias 1, v. 6), His Majesty had replied, "I will teach thee."

While I reflected on the Dialogue of St. Catherine, with a great yearning to imitate those things which the Lord had therein instructed her to do, I withdrew into myself. I was given to understand that the Lord was telling me this very thing, granting what I had entreated of Him so ardently: namely, that I should not only be moved to imitate this saint with regard to penance, but that His Majesty would have me imitate her as well in the solid virtues most pleasing in His sight. He told me that in this respect He desired me to exert myself as she did, watching day and night to carry out His Divine Will. His Majesty said to me, "More greatly blessed will be whoever believes in Me and obeys Me. I am Thy Spouse, and I desire thy good even more than thou dost." He said more which I do not now recall, all with a view to making me trust His Divine Majesty and encourage me in this exercise for the abnegation of myself and my own will.

As I took the discipline, a doubt passed through my mind as to whether or not what one of the religious said about her feelings and revelations were true or false. Then I was assured that, although she had her faults and imperfections, the Lord granted her His Mercies. His goodness is best realized in this. Furthermore, I was made to understand that her nature is vigorous and free, and that, while permitting her much bodily suffering to hold her in check, He had shown her His favor so that she might bear it. The while I adored His judgment, I heard Him say: "I am worthy of praise in all things."

Furthermore, as I thought over what I had said to Your Reverence about not wanting revelations, I felt myself being reprimanded. I was shown that I must resign myself trustfully in the Lord's hands, since He knows what is best. Once again, I besought Him not to lead me by that path because it is beset with doubt and danger. I told Him that in particular I did not wish to know that lady's private affairs. His Majesty said, "If it be My wish that thou shalt, of what avail is thine that thou shalt not?" On another occasion, when I commended her to the Lord, I understood Him to say, "Bear with this for the present."

On St. Agnes' Day, I felt great faintness after having communicated. It occurred to me that I did wrong in softening the rigors of my penance, even though I did experience such weakness. It seemed to me that I should strive not to fail in any respect, and should conceal my infirmity without complaint, since in this way I would obligate the Lord to finish what He had begun in me. I felt that by failing in this regard, I placed an impediment to His grace and rendered ineffectual the promises He had pledged me. These reflections so afflicted me that I besought the Lord to release me from this exercise, these fasts and fainting spells, and permit me to employ myself wholly in His love, in comparison with which all else is of little worth. His answer was, "It is not little, but much, to conform to My Will in this."

I besought the Lord in prayer not to deprive me of His Presence, since whenever I acted in contradiction to what I believed to be His Will, I did so through obedience to my Spiritual Advisers.

Since then, I have been receiving Communion every day. When one of my Spiritual Advisers wished to deprive me of one penance I practice, these words came to me: "Now that thou hast more help and couldst achieve more, they wish to take from thee what thou art already doing."

On the day they brought Our Lady of Sanzoles from Her place, as Her image was entering our church, I was overcome by faintness which prevented me from moving forward to see Her. I began imploring Her to beseech Her Son that the Divine dew of His grace might enter and permeate my soul, and there prevail; that it should not be "As a morning cloud, and as the dew that goeth away in the morning" (Osee 6, v. 4). Then I heard His Majesty reply, "I promise thee this." My heart, which had been heavy, was so uplifted that I felt certain it would be as He said.

One day while I was calling insistently upon the Lord from the darkness of my heart, He asked me, "What desirest thou?" "You, My Lord," I answered: "For what have I in heaven?" [107] I heard Him answer, "Here am I," and these words came to me, "Jesus, through His birth, gave Himself as our companion; on the Holy Table He gave Himself as our sustenance; through His death He gave Himself for our salvation; reigning, He gives Himself as our reward." I felt that for me all this was my fellowship, my delight, my prize, my reward. Then I reflected that what had been given me to strengthen my endurance of suffering, though I knew not what it must be, was also the cause of the fainting spell that day when all the nuns witnessed it and because of which I had to suffer in many different ways.

On another day, I returned to these reflections, saying, "Let this chalice pass from me." [108] I did not mean that I had no wish to quaff from the chalice, but rather that I am unworthy to be singled out in such an extraordinary way. The response I received was that the Lord desired by these means to manifest His omnipotence, sustaining me by His power, and desired also to rouse other souls from their inertia by force of this example. Thus I was given to understand it would be demonstrated that it is He Himself Who worked through His saints, and He Who now continues to work through whomsoever submits and yields to Him. As I pondered the fact that He does not designate on what days we should act, but rather encourages us continually to venture our utmost, it came to me that He proceeds in this manner so as not to weaken our faith.

After this, while at the lectern, I felt a pain in my heart. The thought came to mind that since my heart cleaves to that of Our Lord, and His suffers inwardly, wounded as it is by the lance, mine must suffer likewise.

When my thoughts dwelt on a very saintly discalced nun, I asked His Majesty, "How is it, Lord, that you assured her way, while You permit mine to be so dubious and insecure?" I understood his answer to be: "Why shouldst thou deem it dubious? I do not withdraw thee from the Rules for the Saints. From common rules, yes. It is My Will to show this particularity toward thee. Thou mightst have reason to doubt if thine acts were contrary to theirs." I replied, "Lord, what gives rise to anxiety is Your nonconformity with obedience to my Superiors, because through these means You are wont to indicate Your Will." When this occurred, I did not understand at all what it meant. That night, as I said the Rosary, I was made to see that Superiors do not always issue their orders in accordance with God's Will. Nevertheless, it is His Will for them to be obeyed and He desired me to do this. I was given to understand also that when He seemed to be inflicting punishment on me by depriving me of Communion, or by having food make me ill when my Superiors order me to discontinue fasting, I am not receiving punishment for guilt, since I am not obligated to obey. Rather, the Lord has pleasure in this because it demonstrates to them that these orders they give me are not in accordance with His Will.

On another occasion a Host had been prepared for me. I was trying to envision the Lord, present and crowned with thorns, and granting me the Mercy of seeing Him when His most holy hands were shackled. As I yearned to receive Him, and implored His permission to approach the altar, I heard Him say: "Art thou not to suffer something in consequence of having Me present here, wounded and afflicted?" I replied that there must be some other way of contumely and mortification to make me suffer more. Then these words came to me: "Will it not suffice that the attention of all those congregated here be fixed on thee if thou art not permitted to reach the Communion rail in order to receive Me?" Then His Majesty told me that, though He desired to come to my soul even more than I desired to receive Him, it was better this once that He should not come. He said that since He had granted me the Mercy of permitting me to see His Divine hands, I should yield to the Divine Will with my own hands tied. Then I offered myself for whatever it was His Will to do with me. This all happened during Mass. After the Elevation, my hands and jaws became locked. I assured His Majesty that all was well with me, since I had no other pleasure than His Own. Then He told me, "Now thou wilt see My face"; and little by little, as in shadow, with the words, "Behold the Man," He showed me His countenance, most piteous and blackened and covered with blood from the thorns. Throughout that day whenever I found myself alone, I could see Him at my side, the Spouse of my soul.

One Friday when I desired to evoke the Presence of the Lord on the Cross, these words came into my mind, "I sat down under his shadow, whom I desired" (Cant. 2, v. 3). Yet I could not picture Him forth. The most I could do was to envision the foot of the Cross. I entreated Him that, since He permitted Himself to be neither seen nor received, I might gather fruit of this tree of life. Therefore, He sent me more than the usual pain, accompanied by inner discouragement and depression.

On another occasion, when I intended to leave off Communion because of some other occupation and had asked permission to do so, I felt, toward the close of Mass in the high choir, an intense desire to receive. It seemed to me that I was being pushed onward, and was being told not to forego Communion for anything else that might be offered. At last the force impelling me onward became so strong that I went down to the lower choir and, bathed in tears, found a Host prepared for me there. As I communicated and gave thanks for this Mercy, I understood His Majesty to say, "Thou hast given Me more delight than if thou hadst anointed all My wounds."

When, while conversing with the Lord, I expressed the wish that all men might be freely conscious of Him, this doctrine was manifested to me: the reason that we are less conscious than we should be of God and His Infinite goodness is because of the exalted value we set on any trifling service we render Him. We consider that in return for such things He should grant us His Mercies. Often God does grant a Mercy to a soul not yet fully prepared, in order to show that His favor has been gratuitous since no service has preceded it. Though disposition is required, the Lord's purpose, seemingly, is to obligate that soul; not to pay anything owing to it, since the disposition likewise is gratuitous. Hence we should not look on aught we do for Him as reason for His favor. Just as a slave's service and earnings belong to his master and the slave himself receives no payment, and whatever the master gives him is gratuitous and should be thankfully accepted, so we should be eager to give God whatever He may ask. Nor should we deem that therefore His mercy is due us. We must realize that when He grants His mercy, He does so gratuitously. Our Lord does not await our service before He shows us His favor.

One day at Vespers, the Lord said, "They do not let me do as I wish with thee." I answered regretfully, "Lord, if it be Your Will, who can resist?" Then I was made to see that He left matters as they were in order to deal with them gently. His Majesty's words were fixed in my mind for the next two days. I was doubtful and distressed lest God's purpose was being thwarted in some way. I wondered if it had been an impediment to my spiritual growth to have been bound as I had been for twenty years, denied any opportunity to plunge into those things the Lord inspired me to do.

Later, at afternoon prayer, I was made to see that, since the Lord is omnipotent and can do with me unhindered whatever He will, He had desired to surrender His omnipotence by placing it in the hands of His ministers, upholding them in whatever they might ordain; all for the purpose of teaching me obedience. I was given to understand that He was not content with having interpreted this lesson Himself during the thirty-three years of His life on earth, but now from heaven wished to interpret it to us by way of ordaining obedience to men. It was manifested to me that I was further indebted to Him because He humbles Himself in order to teach me. Thereupon, I gave thanks to His Majesty, and felt greatly comforted. I could not doubt that it was God Who had been speaking, since the doctrine set forth conformed so exactly to what He had declared to all men is most pleasing in His sight. Therefore, I said, "Lord, I have no will of my own: my will is to carry out Yours." His answer was, "It is My Will that thou obey and follow Me in this, for your Superiors will yield eventually when they behold other marvels." He had told me that it was not His desire to force wills, because they are free. When I wondered what the future marvels to which He had referred might be, I was given to understand, "They are those marvels which I shall work in thee." All this has relieved me of my anxiety, and left me desirous of obeying in everything.

Afterward, although I know not how, it seemed to me that my heart was like a shrine enclosing the Divine *Agnus Dei*[109] which I should adorn with the flowers of those virtues which the Lord deemed most fragrant and most pleasing to His sight. I petitioned Our Lady the Virgin to tell me how I should deck that shrine, and understood that She would have me place upon it the jewel consisting of those two precious stones She had given me. Those words engraved thereon, "Behold the handmaid of the Lord" and "humility and resignation" made the jewel resplendent in the eyes of the Most High.

I besought the Lord urgently not to permit deception as to what seemed to be His Will with regard to removing me from the jurisdiction of my confessor. I told Him how greatly I esteemed the Mercy He showed me by wishing to direct me Himself, but asked Him to make His Will clear to others, as He had to me. I implored Him to inspire them to give me the necessary orders, since such was the rule He had established for His Church, and such the path His saints had followed. His Majesty responded, "Formerly all were directed by My Spirit." He gave me to understand that a saint should always place his trust in God, and that when trust was so placed, His Majesty assumed the direction. He showed me that I should have no fear of losing the merit of obedience, since the Lord did not wish me to place my trust anywhere whatsoever without first consulting Him. Furthermore, He said I should obey the orders laid on me even when they were contrary to what I understood to be His wishes.

During afternoon prayer, it came into my mind that, by obeying in this manner, I was exercising humility to a great degree, since, though aware of God's Will, I submitted to man's opinion as His Majesty desired me to do. Therefore, when He set up an impediment so that I could not carry out the orders given me, I should accept it as a spiritual exercise. Thereby the consequent fears and doubts make the soul recur to prayer and all the more fervently seek the light, while exercising faith, confidence, resignation and humility. I was given to understand that not only I myself but all persons who were associated with me would benefit therefrom. I was grateful for these consoling assurances.

No less did I importune the Lord to authorize me to take a midday meal. In view of His objections to granting this, I proposed eating only a dish of herbs daily during the month of May, with a bit of bread at night. I asked His Majesty to concede me this for the time being. I did not understand Him to say anything that specifically granted or denied my request, and consequently resolved to eat. Throughout the entire day of peace and quietude, I felt the Lord's Presence, and that seemed to me a sure sign His Majesty had not taken my decision amiss.

I returned to my petition on another day, recollecting I had been told I should have no need of a teacher. This made me feel very regretful since I feared there might be some deception in that regard. With this thought in mind, I asked the Lord to watch over me. His response was, "Canst thou not forget thyself?" Then I remembered how often He had told me to do His Will without anxiety as to what might befall me. I said, "But, Lord, how can I be calm when assailed by so many doubts and fears?" He replied, "Through Me." I recalled also that many days before this He had said, "Thou needest no teacher, since I am thine. I show thee the way it should be thine to follow. I teach thee My Will and give thee the means for carrying it out." Then I understood that I had been told these things because of what is happening now and of what is to happen. At the time, I had not understood this; nor did that which was told me seem then to lead anywhere, even though the words when spoken had given me so extraordinary a sensation that I never doubted it was the Lord's voice. Afterward, I went to receive Communion, but while Mass was being said, my jaws began to lock. In spite of my every effort to open my mouth, it was clamped. I took out the relic of Father Baltasar Alvarez and applied it to my mouth, imploring the Lord that if it were the devil who afflicted me, His Majesty would put him to flight through the merits of His saint. The moment the relic touched my jaws they relaxed, but were locked again immediately and the relic did not loosen them a second time. I was given to understand that His Majesty did not wish me to receive, the more to enkindle my desire for Him. I responded that I was equally ready to receive or to refrain: His Will be done. At the same time, I felt an inexpressible joy that remained with me all day. I was given to understand also that other reasons for my not being permitted to communicate were my confessor's wishes and the scandal afforded some weak souls that cannot bear too much light. I besought His Majesty to allow me to act in accordance with these considerations when I desired to honor His priests. His answer was, "What greater honor for them than that when the case was in My hands, I placed it in theirs?"

When I asked the Lord whether or not I could discuss

some of these Mercies with a person for whom I feel close friendship, He answered, "My daughter, My secret is to be a secret." Because I felt worn out with physical faintness and spiritual desolation, I implored the Lord not to leave me. He perceived I could do nothing without Him, and I understood Him to say, "Take courage, for thou shalt have much to endure." He said further, "Daughter, have courage, for I am with thee." It went to my heart to have Him call me "Daughter" and I was deeply moved because He employed so loving a word. He gave me to understand, "The more hard pressed, the more beloved."

While receiving Communion, I had been distraught, unable to think clearly. Immediately thereafter, I asked His Majesty, "My Lord, does this offend You?" He responded, "No, for it is involuntary." When I asked, "Why do You permit it, Lord?" I understood Him to say, "For thy spiritual exercise." Reflecting upon these answers two or three days later, I told the Lord, "Your words, My Beloved, cannot be forgotten," and heard Him reply, "Why do thy Superiors order thee not to write them down?" I responded, "Probably they do not believe them to be Yours, Lord."

Another day, beset by a certain anxiety, I lifted my eyes to the crucifix and said, "Behold, O Lord, my affliction" (Lament. 1, v. 9). His Majesty answered me, "Thou beholdest My affliction and My innocence." Once when my faintness left me with Communion, He took note of how well I felt, and said, 'Thou seest it is I Who kill and Who give life. 'The Lord killeth and maketh alive, he bringeth down to hell and bringeth back again' " (1 Kings 2, v. 6).

While writing about these Mercies, I was filled with compunction and bathed in tears. It seemed to me as if I were being vouchsafed a special glimpse of that Incomprehensible Being. I perceived that the more this light was communicated to the soul, the more worthless and useless the soul seemed in its own eyes. I asked His Majesty, "When, My Lord, will I feel living, fervent charity lodged in my soul?" His answer was, "When thou bearest some suffering."

After Communion on Saturday, I asked the Lord why He employed my impediment as a means for granting the Mercy of receiving Him so frequently. It would be a natural consequence for the Community to deem it all an invention and deception of my own. His Majesty gave me to understand that I should reflect upon that impediment which He Himself had used for His exaltation; namely, His death upon the Cross, which is folly in the eyes of the world and is virtue and wisdom in His Eternal Father's eyes, and the eyes of all men who have faith with love. I was made to see that, likewise, some persons would deem His Majesty's way with me evil, but all to whom light had been given would see clearly. I was shown that His Majesty's purpose was to direct me to Himself. He asked, "What greater honor couldst thou have than for Me to lead thee?" He gave me to understand that my sufferings now were in the likeness of the Cross of Christ Our Lord. It seemed to me that I saw myself crucified near His Majesty and that the light emanating from His Cross illuminated and glorified mine; I seemed to hear the angels, who were gazing thereon, say in joy and wonder, "Who is this that ascends the palm tree and eats of its fruit?" And I heard the answer, "She is one who is not, and yet is, and lives in Christ." Then I was given to understand that these things were wrought by virtue of the Divine Sacrament in accordance with the words of Christ Our Lord: "He that eateth me, the same also shall live by me" (John 6, v. 58). I understood further that the radiance of the Cross was the luster Christ gave to all suffering which, by suffering Himself, He consecrated and authorized in His Divine Person. His Majesty said to me, "Fear not, for I am with thee and will help thee."

At Chapter on Sunday, I was moved to pray for a priest to

whom I am under obligation. I had been told he was ill. I said to the Lord, among other things, "My Lord, remember that I am indebted to this priest for his good will and his care and watchfulness in my behalf." Then I was given to understand that the Lord felt impelled to show Mercies to all persons who helped me and watched for my soul's welfare. After Communion, I remembered it had been a long time since the Lord had granted me the Mercy of a suspension such as had been His wont. These had meant much to me, and I began yearning fervently that He would resume that Mercy. I told Him I was well aware of my own unworthiness, but, since I knew from experience what benefits my soul derived therefrom, it should not surprise His Majesty that I desired it. This longing remained with me all morning. I did not feel afflicted, but kindled and exhilarated. I kept importuning the Lord to lift up my heart and to show me His countenance. I repeated the verse of rejoicing in one of the Masses that says, "A little while, and now you shall not see me" (John 16, v. 16). I was given to understand that what I asked for could not be enjoyed in this life, except in small measure. Thereupon the desire in my heart seemed to flame the higher for that small measure. The morning went by at last without my having been granted anything. That afternoon, caught unawares in the midst of a sermon, I was enraptured for a considerable time, while my heart became a burning coal. When I returned to myself, I had to go to that priest of whom I have spoken and who was calling for me. Afterward, I was distressed by what he told me about the publicity these things received. Then I recollected that the Lord had given me to understand this was the reason for the consolation of His Presence lasting so short a time.

On Monday, I shed many tears, remembering that the knowledge of what takes place between God and my soul—a knowledge which even the angels do not obtain, unless God reveals it to them—was in the possession of many persons who had no right to know about it. I could not control my distress, even in the Presence of God. I remembered the priest had told that when an artist paints a picture, he does not wish it to be seen before it is completed, lest it be stained and marred; and I feared the same thing might happen to me if the Lord let go my hand. His Majesty reminded me of His promise that the fire of charity would never be extinguished in my heart and soul. He repeated to me what he had said to St. Thomas, "Be not faithless, but believing" (John 20, v. 27). With this, the clouds encompassing me dispersed a little. Later on, I received Communion. Before going to give thanks, I was made to understand that the Lord would have His Will, that there was no need to feel distress. I do not know what the exact words were, but I know the distress left me and I felt as if it had never been. Blessed be the Lord.

Tuesday morning, I was half asleep during prayer. I made an effort, and implored the Lord to wake me. I understood Him to say: "Exert thyself, and conquer, for thus did My saints." Afterward, I received Communion and spent first three, then two hours, or five in all, at prayer. I experienced nothing in particular, but resigned my will to God's pleasure, not my own. When Vespers ended, without warning, I was enraptured for a while by Divine love there in the choir stall. I petitioned the Lord to let me receive a letter from Father Luis de la Puente, and heard Him reply, "Since thou hast Me, thou canst scarcely need the help of man."

Wednesday, I prayed for two hours before Communion. Later, I received during Terce. Since I wished to go to the choir and help in the singing of the Mass, I asked the Lord if I had His permission. I heard Him reply, "Go if thou canst." I did not understand His reason for saying this, since I could go easily enough. Then, when I attempted to stand, I began to be enraptured and my hands and my head became numb. I was in this state for an hour, my heart aflame. It seemed to me the Lord was drawing me up to Himself bodily. I said, "My Beloved Prince!" and thought of the verse, "Whence the rivers come, they return" (Eccles. 1, v. 7). While I was thinking this, and wondering if the devil could cause such a change in the body, I felt my spirit enkindled, and heard the words, "Fear not. It is I." [110] This made me certain it was God. The bell rang for Refectory, where it was my turn to serve. I felt well and rested, though I had spent four hours on my knees, and though such a suspension of the senses usually leaves me stiff-jointed and exhausted.

After None, I remained at prayer. Remembering a certain saintly brother, I implored My Mother, Our Lady, to have St. Joseph pray for me. I was given to understand I would be his companion in glory. While I was reflecting that the Lord was having me imitate St. Catherine, and did not wish us to be companions, it came to me that I had companions already. This Mercy touched me deeply; and I perceived it is necessary to be ever more diligent and careful so as not to relax in the Divine service, wherein we must compete with One Who took such pains.

Before Communion on Friday, I experienced a great yearning. After receiving, this desire uplifted me so that I became enraptured. I felt deeply satisfied and gladdened. Since I found myself under so many obligations to God for which I made no return, I said, "What shall I render to the Lord, for all the things that he hath rendered to me?" (Psalm 115, v. 12.) I was given to understand that although I could do without food by virtue of the Most Blessed Sacrament, the Lord agreed for me to eat in order to avoid scandal if my ration were shortened. I understood this last to be a reference to some bread fried in olive oil, which I ate with the vegetables. Since I was not permitted to fast completely on a single Friday, I felt it was better, if I had to eat something, for it to be bread.

Saturday, when sweeping the choir, I cleaned a picture of Christ Our Lord. It came to my mind, as I did so, that if I wished to heal His wounds and alleviate His pains, I should strive to procure the welfare of souls and their spiritual increase. I remembered how He had been deterred in this by human sinfulness and indifference. I reflected that Our Lord does not deprive me of prayer, although my Superiors do not let me carry out what I understand to be His Will with regard to fasting. Instead, He has once more granted me the Mercy of those suspensions which I used to experience. I was given to understand that His Majesty's reason for this was that my Spiritual Adviser, in ordering me to eat, was not acting through lack of faith, since he truly believed that God would not let my strength fail me because of the fast. His objection is any innovation in the custom of the Community. He was reluctant, therefore, to give me the requested permission.

I reflected also on how much it distresses me to have this manuscript read. "What can they read about thee there except that you didst not merit, nor canst thou merit, the Mercies which have been granted thee? And what can they read of Me except that I deign to show these Mercies only through My grace and generosity? And what remains for thee save shame when thou seest the poor repayment thou makest of thy debt, and the slight gratitude thou showest for My favor?"

Furthermore, I was made to understand that God had granted me these Mercies, so that the person to whom I was to transmit these meditations would understand clearly that many high mysteries are revealed and many admirable concepts developed through the medium of prayer without the labor of study. Truths are thus consumed with a savor unlike that in books. Considering this fact, he should devote more time to prayer, placing his whole trust in God and not in his own work.

While I pondered the differing opinions that are held with regard to my own experiences, and recollected how all those around are ever on the alert to see whether or not my spiritual well-being is impaired or whether or not I have failed in what I have undertaken, I turned to the Lord somewhat sorrowfully and asked Him to come back to me, as I was dependent on His help. He said, "It is well that thou art. It is well to be established on a firm rock. Winds shall rise and cover it, but they will not be able to move it."

I reflected also on the slight benefit that had been derived by speaking with a certain person. Then I was given to understand that God did not hold lightly the consolations of a just person, but is pleased when anyone who serves Him consoles and cheers a soul, even though nothing further is achieved. From this, I deduced that if He is pleased when cheer and consolation are offered, how deeply He must be offended with those persons who bring disturbance and affliction to His servants!

I had undergone a painful illness that brought me to the point of death. The Lord had shut Himself away from me to such an extent that I had no memory of any Mercy of His during the period of my illness. I was still bedridden, fearful of a relapse if I should get up, when I understood His Majesty to say, "Unless thou leavest thy bed, thou wilt never be cured." He told me further that if I did not rise, the fevers would recur. Since I could not clothe myself, I asked the nuns to dress me, trusting meanwhile in the Lord, because I felt very ill that day. Almost at once, I became much better.

One day at prayer, I told the Lord that everybody, both in and out of the convent, felt I should not go on with my penance. I assured Him that if such were His Will, I would yield, even though that would be wholly contrary to the yearnings instilled by Him to suffer for His sake. I understood His response to be, "Why should it be for My greater glory if thou dost what they wish rather than what I wish?" I was further made to understand that if I did leave off my penance, the fault would not be mine, but that of those who, though enlightened, were incapable of realizing that they regarded as a poison what should serve as an antidote. This was revealed to me while I was grieving with bitter tears, fearful that relinquishment of penance might be a punishment for my previous failure to carry out the Lord's Will. I felt this apprehension because I had understood, before my illness, that my fasts would be permitted thenceforward for some time: a permission that was not in conformity with limitation of the fast to a fortnight.

When I told the Lord other persons were noticing that He no longer granted me Mercies as He once did, I understood Him to say that those persons would likewise note that the conversations in which He manifested His Divine Will to me were many and continual.

Before I took to my bed, I had suffered for several days from fainting spells and fever. I asked the Lord why He denied me health which would enable me to go on with what I had begun, especially since things had become calmer and better adjusted. His reply was that, for the time being, He desired my humiliation rather than my fasts. A few days ago, I was given to understand that my illness was sent by the Lord as a means of convincing our Lady Abbess, who had refused to believe my chosen course was in accordance with His Will. Now she would come to see more clearly, because she would miss me in the choir and would grieve for my sufferings; and also, because I had prayed for her enlightenment.

I had withdrawn into myself one day, and was rejoicing so much in the Lord's Presence that I felt as if I were within

His Divine Heart. In the midst of my rapture, I mourned lest I lose this favor because of having to deal with other persons and to attend the needs of the body. Therefore, I asked the Lord why, when I had been on the point of leaving this world, He had permitted my return to it. Then He made me comprehend it was because, as yet, I lacked the merits equal to the degree of glory He has predestined for me.

It was manifested to me that since His truth would serve as my defense, I was not to yield to the darkness and doubts that beset me; nor to vainglory in good works, symbolized in the arrow that flies by day; nor to the noonday devil transfigured as an angel of light (Psalm 90, v. 5 & 6). Against all these, He would defend me and be my shield.

On another occasion, when I was very ill and had been prohibited all penances, I besought the Lord in the names of Mother Teresa of Jesus and the saintly Peter of Alcántara to grant me health. I asked also that my Superiors be made aware of the Mercies which He had shown me. I understood Him to reply that He would do so for the honor of His saints, on condition my Superiors give me permission to do penance and fast. They would not agree to the latter, but permitted the other penances, and my health began to improve.

With some resentment, I called the Lord's attention to the fact that I had been deprived of Communion. He answered, "Suffer it for the present: another time is coming."

Again, when I begged the Lord to preserve the health He had given me and be satisfied with what I could do, He gave me to understand that for the time being He wished me to eat meat every day, though only enough to sustain me. I understood further that if my Superiors would agree to my foregoing eggs and fish, He would exact nothing more for the present. Since the House had never more greatly needed examples of penitence, abstinence, mortifications of the flesh and contempt for all temporal things, the Lord said He wished to make use of me in this regard. I also heard Him ask, "Why do they wish to deprive thee of the merit obtained through abstinence?"

Just as I was about to take Communion at the first Mass on the Feast of our Father St. Benedict, the conviction came to me that I could not receive. I felt that I should become tense again, and that His Majesty had taken this means to indicate His Will with respect to my fasts and Communion. I understood that thus His promise to me would be fulfilled. Nevertheless, it seemed very uphill work to recur to this method once again. Somewhat fearfully, I pled, "Lord, permit me not to be deceived." His answer was, "Trust in Me and fear not."

Another time, while in a state of exaltation, I withdrew somewhat into myself, while I meditated on the meekness of Christ Our Lord amid insults. I remembered especially how the mob had jeered, "He hath Beelzebub, and by the prince of devils he casteth out devils" (Mark 3, v. 22). During these reflections, my senses were to some degree suspended, and the Lord's answer came into my mind: "If a kingdom be divided against itself, that kingdom cannot stand." [111] These words brought a light enabling me to perceive that the penances and fasts I had practiced had not been inspired by the devil. Each such act in itself had humbled me, by proving that it was impossible for me to perform any one of them unless I were given supernatural strength. Therefore, I could feel no vainglory. If I looked on the work from God's standpoint, I saw that it was indeed exalted and felt abashed and confused because such a thing had been wrought through me. That experience left me with the certainty that it had all been an act of God.

The Acts the Lord has taught me in order to move the soul to love are the following:

1. It seems to me the first is for the soul to take pleasure in that Highest Good, in Whom are all the perfections we see in earthly creatures, with the infinite advantage of being in their original state; and this without discourse of the understanding. Only, I know not how, the seeker finds present the good it desires, and embraces it with satisfaction and delight. It seems to me that this is as if we placed an amber bead near a straw and the natural virtue which the amber possesses made the straw cleave to it. So it is that the soul, purified of all care for the things of this life and this world, is inspired and attracted by the Divine virtues into which it is drawn and with which it is united.

2. The soul, from out this captivity in which it has been attracted, is impelled to utter St. Paul's words, "Lord, what wilt thou have me to do?" [112] For it finds itself without wish, will, nor desire of its own. It deems itself to belong to God and as such will be dealt with by the Lord Himself.

3. Here is revealed how the work of love is most pleasing in God's sight and is His Majesty's method for all eternity; and how the soul begins yearning to love infinitely if this be possible.

4. The soul, perceiving that this is not possible, cannot be satisfied with less, because the good it loves is infinite and deserves to be loved infinitely. Therefore, the soul lifts the eyes of its understanding and considers how this Being of Infinite perfections knows and comprehends Itself Infinitely. Because It comprehends Itself, It loves Itself with Infinite love; and, loving Itself, delights Infinitely in Itself. The soul further reflects how this Being, knowing Itself, loving Itself, and delighting in Itself, is exceedingly blessed and glorious; and how no good and no glory can be desired for the Almighty which He does not already have in Himself. The soul continues to delight in and enjoy this utmost Perfection, and is fulfilled by seeing God loved as He wishes to be.

5. It is an attribute of love to desire the good of the beloved. The soul knows that the Infinite Being is an immense sea of every good and glory. Even though all creatures should join together in offering this Lord every perfection that had been bestowed separately upon them, and though all the angels and holy souls which have been or shall be to the end of the world should offer Him their love and service, they could not add one iota to His glory, since this is in Himself and, being already infinite, cannot be increased. His glory consists in His Own Infinitely Perfect Being. Therefore, the soul turns with all its strength to desire and to love His very Being in Whom are enclosed all beauty and all perfection. The soul delights and rejoices perpetually in the fact that this Lord is in Himself so good and so holy, so full of glory and majesty, so wise, so rich, so powerful, so merciful, so tender and so loving that all the universe has need of Him while He has need of none. The Lord gave me to understand that this joy is the prize He promises in the Gospel to the faithful servant when He says, "Enter thou into the joy of thy lord" (Matt. 25, v. 23). For the soul rejoices in what causes the Lord Himself to rejoice, which is in His Being and in His glory.

6. The soul likewise desires with ardent yearning that all men know and love their Creator, as it desires to know and love Him; and that it and they and all creatures never for one moment leave off praising Him.

7. It would delight the soul beyond measure to be chosen as an instrument of the Lord in attaining all this. The soul would gladly suffer to that end any pain, even the pain of hell itself, so long as it did not lack God's friendship and His mercy. All this the soul would undergo not only for mankind as a whole, but even to ensure the progress of one single other soul in the Divine service. For this the soul would suffer whatever the Lord willed, and for this it offers health, honor, and life.

8. The soul desires also, if it were possible, to hold within its

grasp the will of all mankind so that this might be submitted and subjected to the Will of the Lord. For He alone deserves to be obeyed, revered and served by all His creatures for what He alone is.

9. It is also an attribute of love so to join the wills of lovers that there is no freedom to love nor to hate nor to choose except as the beloved loves or hates or chooses. Thus it is that the soul recognizes this Lord as loving mankind immeasurably. The soul remembers that to redeem man and loosen the chains he had forged for himself, Our Lord suffered an ignominious and painful death. This knowledge engenders in the soul likewise a love for all mankind, a desire that all be saved, lest so great a price should have been paid in vain. Often the soul forgets itself and its own needs as it prays insistently and persistently for the salvation and spiritual life of its neighbors. The soul offers its whole fortune, wishing it were greater, to expend thus profitably in delighting God. These things the soul does without respect for persons, desiring the good of all alike, since it views all mankind as the property of Christ Our Lord and desires that treasure to be enriched by the pleasure and satisfaction of the Lord Himself, to Whom the soul wishes to give everything, even at the cost of losing itself.

10. In the same degree that God loves souls, and loves the gifts and rewards of grace which He has bestowed upon them, in order to make them more pleasing in His sight, in that degree He abhors the evil of sin with which souls make themselves odious to their God. This is the principal reason why the soul that is in truth dedicated to love hates sin so much that if it were possible—as it is not—by means of breaking the Divine law to enjoy God forever, the soul would choose rather to forego this good than to incur a single sin. What is most possible, and is to be seen every day, is for God, by His grace, to lift souls out of grievous sin to a very high state of perfection, advancing them in heaven by degrees of glory. I

say that the soul I am describing would choose the lowest degree in heaven—though eagerly desirous of knowing the higher, and thus knowing God more freely and, if possible, loving and enjoying Him boundlessly—rather than to lose one instant of the grace and friendship of God, or to commit a single act displeasing in His Divine eyes. And this is not because of the harmful consequences of the sin, but because the soul is resolved not to see in itself something it abhors, since that thing is also abhorrent to God Himself.

11. Because the soul abhors sin, it abhors and flees from whatever things might occasion falling into sin. These things are principally pleasures, honors and wealth. The soul loves their opposites and cherishes what all the world deems to be unhappiness and misfortune; such as poverty, suffering, and contumely. These things serve the soul as its wall of defense against vices. Moreover, they were chosen by the soul's Beloved Lord for Himself when He came into the world as Man; and, though Lord of all that is in it, took for His portion the world's rejection and what the world considers wretchedness. Thus the soul is impelled to embrace the things chosen by its Lord, which afford it a pleasure it can find in naught else. Nor can the soul be at peace when there is no way for it to experience these things. The soul feels happy and fortunate in being able to conform to Him Whom it loves and to wear His colors. So highly does the soul esteem this privilege that angels well might envy it (were envy possible to them), and might elect for their part, if they could, to suffer for their God as He suffered for Man, choosing of their own free will, for love of Him, even as He chose pain and suffering. For in this lies the power of love: that it joins and unites separate spirits, so that they conform to each other as if they were one.

⚜ Notes

Foreword

1. *Precedentes de un GLORIOSO REINADO 1465-1475 Narración His-
tórica Ilustrada con Siete Documentos Originales é Inéditos Existentes en el
Archivo Municipal de Avila Por el Excmo. Señor* D. MANUEL DE FO-
RONDA Y AGUILERA *Cronista de la Ciudad. Con un Prólogo del Excmo.
Señor* D. CESÁREO FERNÁNDEZ DURO *de las Reales Academias de la
Historia y de Bellas Artes de San Fernando y Presidente de la Real Sociedad
Geográfica de Madrid.* Published by *Imprenta de los Hijos de M. G. Her-
nández.* Madrid, 1901.

2. This gathering, which was held in a field identified by four stone bulls
of prehistoric origin, to which it owes its name, was destined to change the
history, not only of the Kingdom of Castile, but of all Spain and, in time, of
the whole world. The date was September 19, 1468.

3. These children were Isabel the Younger, who was then widowed, following her marriage to Prince Alfonso of Portugal and who later married his cousin,
Manoel; Juan, who married Margaret of Austria and died within a few months
after his marriage; Juana, who married Philip of Austria and who has come
down in history with the tragic title of *Juana la Loca* (Joan the Mad); María,
who eventually married her sister Isabel's widower; and Catalina, better known
as Catherine of Aragon, who married first Arthur, Prince of Wales and, afterward, his brother Henry, the infamous Henry the VIII.

4. Obviously, the life, writings and achievements of St. Catherine of Siena
were subjects of welcome and thorough study at the Convent of Santa Ana
from the very time of its foundation, for I have discovered in its library
numerous volumes relating to these, some of great antiquity. The most interesting and attractive of all is a translation of her *Dialogues* from Italian into
Spanish, made by Gerónimo de Gigli and published in 1797. This is beautifully presented, is embellished with several very fine steel engravings, numerous chapter headings and endings; and the whole is in a state of perfect
preservation. Of course, this copy postdates the period of María Vela, but

similar ones were available to her and, obviously, she profited by their perusal.

5. After careful consideration, it has been decided that these Latin quotations should be translated into English, since, for anyone to whom they were incomprehensible, the flow of the narrative would be interrupted by the constant necessity of consulting notes.

6. The text, which supplements the Biography in the first and some of the later editions of Vaquero's work, is as arresting as the manner of its presentation. This supplementary text takes the form of several prologues and forewords written by various illustrious personages, all of whom express unqualified admiration and enthusiasm for Vaquero's work. Also included in the complementary material are two sonnets, addressed directly to María Vela, one of which contains an ingenious play on words. *Vela* is the Spanish word for candle and the sonneteer makes the most of the symbolic meaning which may be given to the Venerable's name by comparing it to a lovely light.

7. The anonymous parish priest, who was Maria Vela's second biographer, writes: "The same [the general of artillery] was related to *Don* Antonio Vela Carrillo who possessed the title of the noble house of Tabladillo which, to this day, boasts two noble marquéses of the same name." However, the Prior of Santo Tomás has supplied me with the following notation:

"There is not and there never has been any Marqués of Tabladillo or of the *Casa de* Tabladillo.

"The present Marqués of Peñafuente, owner of the *dehesa* (country seat) of Tabladillo, who is over seventy years old, states that his father tried to obtain or legalize the title of Marqués of Tabladillo, but was unable to find any proof or any document attesting the existence of such a title of nobility. He believes that such a designation is explained by the fact that the people around the estate always refer, colloquially, to the owner as 'Marqués of Tabladillo.'

"However, the present owners of Tabladillo also believe that they are related to the Velas of María Vela's time. That place has been in their ancestors' possession from time immemorial and it is certain that the *dehesa* belonged to the Velas. Dr. Vaquero affirms that in his time the *Casa de* Tabladillo belonged to Antonio Vela Carrillo, eldest son of Blasco Núñez Vela, the first Viceroy of Peru and brother of María Vela's grandmother. The mansion of the Velas in Avila has the same characteristics as that of Tabladillo. The coat-of-arms of the Velas' residence in the city (at present the *Audiencia*) may be examined and compared with that of Tabladillo."

Such examination and comparison reveal the fact that the two coats-of-arms are indeed identical; and, incidentally, it may not be amiss to mention that one of the pleasantest interludes in the course of the work on María Vela's Diary was an evening spent at Tabladillo with the Marqués and Marquésa of Peñafuente, their large and delightful family, the Prior of Santo Tomás and the resident chaplain.

8. Father Luis de la Puente writes in his Prologue to the *Life of Baltasar Alvarez:* "This Father (Francisco de Salcedo) joined the Society shortly after the death of his saintly uncle (Baltasar Alvarez). He was a pupil, not only in his studies during the three years I taught Arts at León, but also in his spirit when I was Master of Novices at Villagarcia." (Quoted by Camilo María Abad, *Vida del V. P. Luis de la Puente,* Universidad Pontificia Comillas, Santander, 1957, p. 101.)

Salcedo was the son of Baltasar's sister, Elvira, to whom Puente dedicated a treatise on spiritual life and addressed it to Burgos where she was living. Salcedo died in the "prime of his life" while he was Rector at Soria. (Abad, pp. 338 and 339.)

9. Vaquero, Miguel Gonzalez. *La Mujer Fuerte.* Part II. Chapter 11.

10. Luis de la Puente's best-known work is *Meditations on the Mysteries of Our Holy Faith* (Valladolid, 1605), which has undergone many editions and several translations. It is still widely used for meditations and spiritual reading. He also wrote the *Life of Father Baltasar Alvarez, S. J.,* confessor of St. Teresa. (I am indebted to the Prior of Santo Tomás for this information.)

11. Vaquero, Miguel Gonzalez. *La Mujer Fuerte.* Part II. Chapter 36.

12. This quotation is given as presented by Amarie Dennis in her excellent book, *St. Francis Borgia.* She gives as her source *Monumenta Ignatiana: Epistolae et Instructiones,* Vol. II, page 233.

13. Authorities differ on this point. Father Gonzales, secretary to the Rector of the Diocesan Seminary of Avila, subscribes to the former theory. The Hospital of Mosen Rubi is now the Convent of the Dominican Nuns of Avila. The adjoining chapel, *Capilla de Mosen Rubi de Bracamonte,* is built in Renaissance style and contains some fine statuary, pictures and stained glass windows. It remains one of the principal sights of Avila. Miguel Gonzalez Vaquero always refers to himself and is nearly always referred to by others as Dr. Vaquero, a rather unusual designation at that period. He was probably in possession of a doctorate from Salamanca in both Philosophy and Theology.

14. Vaquero, Miguel Gonzalez. *La Mujer Fuerte.*

15. By special permission, the nuns in the Augustinian Convent—formerly the Royal Palace—of Madrigal de las Altas Torres are allowed to admit visitors to see the room where Isabel was born, though this is in what is now the cloister. The present writer cannot help feeling that a similar permit, which would allow visitors who obviously come with a serious purpose and not out of idle curiosity, to see the room at Santa Ana's Convent so closely connected with Isabel's later history, would be beneficial in many of its results.

16. A *fanega* equals about one and a half bushels and a *celemin* about a peck.

17. *Vna.* is an abbreviation of *vecina,* literally neighbor, but is here used in the sense of native, Muñoyerro being the village of the Martin family's origin.

18. The seven Spaniards were King Fernando III of Castile and León,

Teresa de Avila, Juan de la Cruz, Ignacio Loyola, Francisco Xavier, Francisco Borgia and Luis Beltran. St. Luis Beltran, O. P., was born in Valencia. For a number of years he was a missionary in Colombia. He died in his native city in 1581, one year before the death of St. Teresa, with whom he was in frequent correspondence.

19. Canonization of these martyrs did not take place until 1862.

Chapter 1

20. Literally, *oracion de recogimiento*, which may be translated either as abstraction or concentration. To the average layman, the latter definition is probably clearer, for what María Vela meant to say was that she acquired the power of concentrating on religious subjects and excluding from her mind all those which interfered with her devotions. However, abstraction is the proper technical term and is thus described in A *Catholic Dictionary:* "With modern writers intellectual abstraction primarily signifies ignoring or omission of the attributes *not* attended to; with the schoolmen it was understood primarily to mean the positive side of the operation, the assumption by the mind of the part selected, or the attributes which *are* attended to."

21. "Meditation is the prayer of beginners in the spiritual life and is proper to the purgative way (q.v.). It grows gradually into effective prayer, in which the will requires less assistance from the reflections of the mind, but almost at once begins to make acts of love, humility, etc. Finally, there may come a time when, through no fault of her own, the soul can neither reflect nor make acts. She has fallen into aridity (q.v.). Yet she truly desires union with God. She is ripe for the prayer of simplicity (q.v.), and should be guided into it. St. John-of-the-Cross speaks severely of directors who in such circumstances would still force the soul to meditate." (A *Catholic Dictionary.*)

22. Everyone whom I have consulted has been puzzled as to how best to translate María Vela's statement, which, in Spanish, reads: *haciame enrredar con un hilo los corredores.* The Prior of Santo Tomás translated this passage: "She tried to amuse me and made me play with a thread in the corridors." But he admitted that he was far from satisfied with this rendition and that he preferred the one on which Muna Lee decided, which is the one I have used. Literally, the verb *enredar* (modern spelling) means to entangle, ensnare, knot, etc. The nuns at Santa Ana try to explain the statement by saying that, at the time of María Vela, there was no glass in the windows leading from the cloisters to the patio and that María Vela was encouraged to string cords from one side of the window frames to another. This would seem no more childish than moving stones from one place to another or counting tiles on the roof, but, on the other hand, there does not seem to be any absolute authority for interpreting the passage in this way.

Chapter 2

23. Matins were at three in the morning.

24. The passages beginning after the sentence ending, "with unsatisfied yearnings," are puzzling if literally translated. This is one of the few instances where I have felt it better to try to interpret María Vela's meaning, rather than to give her exact wording.

25. Chapter of Faults, where the religious accuse themselves of their transgressions of the Rule and are given a penance.

26. In the text, here and in many other places, María Vela refers to the Voices simply with the word "they," but her meaning is clear.

27. This is not what we envision by that word—a stopper in a bottle—but a small round block, fashioned from the cork oak that grows so abundantly on the road to Salamanca, and that served as the only seat in her cell.

28. Third Book of Kings 19:8.

29. In this same general connection, it is interesting to note the words of Thomas à Kempis in Book IV—a devout exhortation to Holy Communion —of *The Imitation of Christ*. Here he says:

"The most devout King David danced before the ark of God with all his might, commemorating the benefits bestowed on the fathers in times past.

"He made musical instruments of sundry kinds; he put forth psalms, and appointed them to be sung with joy; he himself likewise often sang to the harp, inspired with the grace of the Holy Ghost.

"He taught the people of Israel to praise God with their whole heart, and to join their voices in blessing and magnifying Him every day.

"If so great devotion was then used, and such remembrance of the praise of God before the ark of the covenant, how great ought to be the reverence and devotion which I and all Christian people should have in the presence of this sacrament, in the receiving of the all-transcending body of Christ!"

30. The verb which María Vela uses is *"levantar,"* which may be translated in many different ways, among them by "impute," which is the translation that other competent persons have given in this passage. However, as it seems to me that she was referring to the fact that her absence would be noticed and that this might again stir up trouble in the convent, as it had before, I feel that "aroused" better interprets her meaning.

Chapter 3

31. Quotations all from Psalm 90.
32. August 6th.
33. November 21st.

Chapter 5

34. She refers here to the Primitive Rule. María Vela had been left a legacy by her uncle, the Bishop of Burgos, with which to found a convent that would adhere to this Primitive Rule, which Santa Ana did not. Probably, because of objections on the part of her Superiors, she was unable to do this. Hence her desire to do the next best thing; namely, to introduce certain reforms, as far as her personal habits were concerned, without leaving Santa Ana.

35. September 14th.

36. October 4th.

37. August 20th.

Chapter 6

38. June 24th.

39. This occurred in June, 1603, when one of the Inquisitors of the Tribunal of Valladolid came to Avila on the customary inspection trip. The edict (announcing the opening of the investigation of heretical doctrines and enjoining the denouncers to appear before the Inquisitor) was first read at the Cathedral. Later, it was read in the convents of nuns. When it came the turn of the Convent of Santa Ana, Doña María, according to her confessor, Dr. Vaquero, listened attentively to the reading, but "she did not think that any of the provisions concerned her nor that anybody would apply them to her." [*La Mujer Fuerte: Doña María Vela y Cueto por el Parroco de Cardeñosa*. Chap. VII, Avila, 1917.]

40. María Vela says seven in her script. Then she goes on to enumerate eight counts. Possibly, she considered the last two as substantially one, though, to this translator, they seem to have no relation to each other.

Chapter 9

41. This is our first intimation that María Vela made a determined effort to deserve the title by which she has, ever since her death, been officially known in Avila: *La Mujer Fuerte de Santa Ana* (the Strong Woman of Santa Ana).

42. María Vela's phrase, "*con un descuydo de mia cuydados*," (with a carelessness of my cares) has a paradoxical twist often employed by the Spanish mystics.

43. May 1st.

44. 2 Corinthians 12:9.

45. Matthew 12:45.

46. By this she means the Feast of Santiago de Compostela (July 25th), the patron saint of Spain. The St. James whose feast is celebrated with that

of St. Philip, to whom she has previously referred, is the one we often speak of as St. James the Less.

47. July 26th.

48. September 21st.

49. It is the custom at most convents to close, bolt and bar the main door fairly early in the evening, not later than eight or eight-thirty, and not to unlock it again until morning. Only a great emergency abrogates this rule.

50. September 29th.

51. October 28th.

52. "Ana de los Angeles, a witness in the process of canonization of Teresa de Jesús, testified that Father Baltasar Alvarez, S. J., 'in order to test her spirit, commanded her, among other trials, to make a general confession with her face uncovered.' At that time, Father Efren explains, women generally confessed with their faces covered by a veil, while the confessor sat in an ordinary armchair." (*Biografía de Santa Teresa*, p. 453.) When women knelt at the confessional, they did not cover their faces.

53. The St. John here mentioned, who is commemorated on May 6th as St. John before the Latin Gate, is also known as St. John the Evangelist, whose feast day is on December 27th. He is often described in English as St. John before the Latin Gate because he was brought to Rome under the Emperor Domitian and thrown into a vat of boiling oil, from which he miraculously came out unharmed. A church dedicated to him was built near the Latin Gate of Rome, the traditional scene of this event.

54. Dr. Vaquero and his contemporaries spelled this Sanzoles, *but the modern spelling is Sonsoles*. It is a shrine a mile south of Avila on the hill across the Valley Ambles. For its history see B. F. Folio 53 or the interpretation thereof in *The Land of Stones and Saints*, p. 119.

55. August 10th.

56. Here follow some jottings, mostly in ejaculatory form, with the diarist speaking sometimes in the first person, sometimes in the third. (To avoid confusion, I have translated them in the first person whenever this was possible.)

57. Matthew 8:7.

58. 1 Corinthians 10:13.

59. Matthew 10:38.

60. Micheas 3:11.

61. Romans 8:35, 36 and 37.

Chapter 10

62. In cathedral cities, the public ceremonies of this feast, especially the Procession of the Blessed Sacrament, are usually held on Corpus Christi Day. In other churches, whether in a cathedral city or elsewhere, and in the religious

communities, the procession is not necessarily held on the day of the feast, but may be on any day within the octave.

63. October 4th.

Addenda to Chapter 10

64. In the first copy of the diary, made immediately after María Vela's death, the figures and letters "39b" appear after this paragraph. They are not in the original script or in the second copy and they do not seem to have any connection with the text, though they are interesting from the viewpoint of format.

65. This reference is probably to an illustration in a large illuminated book, such as were provided at that period for general use in the choir.

66. Adaptation of 2 Peter 1:17.

67. December 18th.

68. Psalm 106:2.

69. John 1:14.

70. Luke 1:51.

71. Here, María Vela is referring to her confessor.

72. Exodus 2:21; Numbers 12:1.

73. It is very important to remember that the word, imaginary, as used in this sense, does not mean fancied—something unreal. It means something that forms an image, that is, a definite impression or picture.

74. Apocalypse 4:4.

75. Vespers. Feast of St. Michael. Breviary.

76. It will be remembered that one of the most famous stories told by St. Teresa of Avila refers to three successive visions, in the first of which she saw Our Lord's hands; in the second, His countenance; and, in the third, His whole Sacred Person. María Vela, who was well acquainted with St. Teresa's *Works,* may well have been unconsciously influenced by this moving account and hoping that she might have the same supernatural experience. If so, her hope was fulfilled. Of course, it is also possible that she was not familiar with the portion of St. Teresa's *Autobiography* in which the account of this triple vision appears and that her experience was wholly one of divine inspiration, uninfluenced by anything she had read.

77. Here, María Vela is referring to her confessor.

78. 3 Kings 19:7.

79. If this were a true vision, she would seem to be entitled to beatification, as her advocates are claiming.

Notes for the Mercies

80. The words, "despite my natural instability," do not appear in the original, but seem necessary to the translator for clarification of the text.

81. The word, *"ermita,"* means not only a hermitage, but a chapel or a very small church. The present Abbess at Santa Ana's was asked whether or not they do have a number of small hermitages, like the one at San José, and she said they have only one chapel or *"ermita"* in the corner of their garden, where nuns may go occasionally to pray; they do not live there.

82. From the Office of St. Agnes.

83. Though Father Salcedo did write a short Life of his uncle, Father Baltasar Alvarez, it seems probable from María Vela's text that, in this instance, it was the life of a saint which her confessor was writing.

84. This is a literal translation of María Vela's text, which it seems impossible to put into idiomatic English because its actual meaning is obscure, not only to myself, but to other translators with whom I have conferred.

85. Surprising as it may seem, this is a literal translation, so *en el ayre*— up in the air—must have been a current colloquialism then, as now.

86. María Vela always gave the names of the persons to whom she referred. These names, however, were carefully crossed out and the words, "a certain person," substituted either by Vaquero or by some subsequent reader.

87. At this period, the entire region which we call Latin America was known in Spain as the Indies and Spaniards who went there and afterward returned to Spain were called *Indianos*. Outstanding among these were brothers of St. Teresa.

88. John 15:5.

89. At this point, it would seem that María Vela is beginning to get bolder; she not only beseeches the Lord, she ventures to admonish Him. Moreover, this happens more than once.

90. Luke 23:46.

91. By *calenda*, she obviously means the Calendar of Saints. St. Robert was the actual founder of the Cistercians; St. Bernard the monk under whom the Order was extended.

92. What María Vela actually says is, *"Vos no sabeis si le a de hazer mal, porque lo mandais con esa condicion."* ("You know not whether it will be done badly, since You have ordered it with this condition.") Both my fellow translators—the Prior of Santo Tomás and Muna Lee—and I believe there was a slip of the pen here, and that the word *"no"* should not appear before the word *"sabeis,"* for otherwise the passage would not seem to make sense, especially considering María Vela's implicit faith in the Lord's omnipotent knowledge. In the other copy of the Diary the word *"no"* has been crossed out.

93. It is recorded by Vaquero and others that María Vela had very beautiful hands. It seems possible from this statement of hers that her feet were also very beautiful and a cause of vanity to her.

94. The victory is not identified, but obviously it refers to the recovery of the nun.

95. María Vela gives no explanation of what note she means. Possibly she

refers to some notation made by her confessor, and the next sentences indicate that it might have been about *Doña* María.

96. August 20th.

97. Canticle 3:1.

98. The original has "the Prioress." See Note 86.

99. Psalm 112:8.

100. María Vela is probably referring to Our Lord's saying that the Son of God has no place to lay His head, a statement which she did not fully understand. There is no authority for making the statement she does about Our Lady.

101. "That he might suck honey out of the rock." Deuteronomy 32:13.

102. This is still a common Spanish expression meaning a short while. It dates from the period when all timepieces were scarce and nuns, of course, had no watches. Therefore, they said, "As long as it takes to say an *Ave*," meaning only a minute; a *Credo* or a *Pater Noster* took a little longer.

103. Psalm 10:14, according to the Hebrews.

104. Canticle 3:4.

105. I am not quite sure that María Vela understood the habits of St. Catherine of Siena correctly. In *The Saints: A Concise Biographical Dictionary*, edited by John Coulson, we are told that for three years after Catherine joined the Third Order of St. Dominic, she never left her room, except to go to Mass and to confession, and spoke to no one except her confessor. The dictionary also states that "during this period, Catherine trained herself to live on a spoonful of herbs a day and to make a couple of hours of sleep every night suffice." Toward the end of her life "for a whole year, she lived corporally on the Blessed Sacrament and took less than an hour's sleep every night." I have found no reference to the fact that she took herbs and fruit before breakfast.

106. Matthew 15:32.

107. Psalm 72:25.

108. Matthew 26:39.

109. María Vela is referring to the wax medallions bearing the mystical figure of the Lamb (*Agnus*) which, since the early middle ages, were blessed by the Pope at the same time as the Paschal Candle on Holy Saturday. At present, they are blessed several times during the year and are given out to the faithful.

110. Luke 24:36.

111. Mark 3:24.

112. Acts 9:6.